GETTING THE COAL

Impressions of a twentieth century mining community.

EUROPEAN RECORD
FOR COAL DRIVAGE
400 YARDS IN 1 WEEK.

D1224876

Compiled and edited by Jeanne Ca~~~~ ~~~ ~~~~ Tracey Roberts.

Typing: Vivien Parry assisted by Colin Hyde, Steve Peace, Alex Patterson, Christopher Gormley, Jane Bowley, Neil Briers.

Typeset by Steve Duckworth at Mantle Community Arts Ltd.

Photographs courtesy British Coal, Leicester Mercury, Coalville Times, Coalville 150 Group and the contributors.

Special thanks to all the interviewers and to Bob York (Snibston Discovery Park) and Chris Matchett.

Published by Mantle Oral History Project 1992.
The Springboard Centre
Mantle Lane
Coalville
Leicestershire. LE67 3DW.
Tel: 0530 839531

Printed by The Alden Press, Oxford.

Copyright: © Mantle Oral History Project. 1992.
Copyright of poems: The authors.

ISBN 0 9515040 1 0
The views expressed in this book are not necessarily those of the editors or publishers.

Introduction

When Bagworth Colliery closed in February 1991, it marked the end of deep mining in the Leicestershire coalfield. The history of coal mining in the area stretches back at least two thousand years. The recent discovery of the remains of a fifteenth century mine at British Coal's opencast site at Coleorton near Ashby de la Zouch indicates that the pillar and stall method of extracting coal was in use over four hundred years ago. In March 1827, the Leicester Chronicle reported that 'Coals are about to be got at a place called Long Lane, Whitwick.' The area around Long Lane eventually grew into a town which became Coalville in 1833. William Stenson and George Stephenson both played an important part in developing the industry which brought work and prosperity to the town and much of the surrounding area.

Getting the Coal is our way of commemorating the lives of the people involved in the mining industry in Leicestershire. The book consists almost entirely of extracts from tape-recorded interviews carried out by the Mantle Oral History Project over a period of six years. The contributors recall their work, home life and leisure, covering the period from the beginning of the twentieth century. All the extracts are in the words of the contributors. We hope that this will help to give a little flavour of the local dialect. Good times and bad times are remembered here but this is definitely not an exercise in nostalgia. It is rather a picture of communities united by a single industry, the traces of which have all but disappeared. We are grateful to the many people who were willing and brave enough to put their memories down on tape.

Jeanne Carswell and Tracey Roberts.

Dates of pit closures:

Ibstock	1929
Coleorton	1934
New Lount	1968
Snibston	1983
Desford and Merry Lees	1984
Whitwick (merged with South Leicester 1984)	1986
Ellistown (merged with Bagworth 1986)	1989
Bagworth (merged with Nailstone 1967)	1991

People used to say: "Give a miner a pigeon, he starts a club. Give him a ferret and he'll catch a rabbit. Give him a greyhound and he'll start a race. And, of course, a couple of pints and he'll start a fight." To some extent it was true but not always. I found some remarkably good men.

Frank Smith.

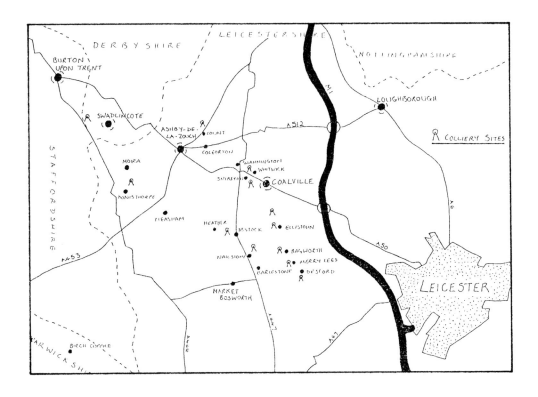

Contents

The Mantle Oral History Project was established in 1986 to create a sound archive in which the people of North West Leicestershire recall, in their own words, their own history.

The tradition of Oral History is as old as the spoken word. Down the ages people have passed on their experiences by word of mouth to succeeding generations. Today, thanks to modern technology, we are able to record these memories and keep them safe. The history of the rich and powerful is already available but ordinary men and women have not, in the past, had the opportunity to leave any permanent record of their lives. Too much has been forgotten about the experiences, attitudes and lifestyles of these neglected history makers. Oral History helps to give a different perspective of the twentieth century so that future generations will have a unique and vivid insight into the working and social life of their forebears.

To obtain more information and catalogue of publications, please send a stamped addressed envelope (9"x 6") to:

Mantle Oral History Project

The Springboard Centre

Mantle Lane

Coalville

Leicestershire

LE67 3DW

At Work

Harry Sheffield: The boys I played with after work all worked down the mine ... they got twice as much money as I did in the factory. Almost as soon as I was fourteen [1915], I told my mother I wanted to go down the mine. My father didn't want me to ... conditions were bad , you see. He knew what I were putting myself in for. He tried to persuade me to stop on at the factory but I weren't having that!

Jack Adcock: I started at Ibstock colliery. I was thirteen on the Wednesday. That was in the First World War, 1915. They wanted an office boy and the headmaster at the school, he said, "Well, you're a good scholar Jack, they want an office boy, will you go and see about having it?" So, of course, I went and had an interview at the colliery with the head man and he said, "Yes, start as soon as possible." I was thirteen on the Wednesday and I went and started in the office on the Thursday, so I didn't lose any time between schooling and working.

It was sitting down and getting all the correspondence and everything off like that, or any office work as a boy could do at that time of day. Of course, there were the senior men in the office who were doing the working, the writing. I had to make the tea, but of course we didn't have so many tea breaks as they do now!

In the morning I used to leave home at quarter past eight because I'd got to go down to the post office at Ibstock and collect the mail. Well of course it took me some time to walk down to the post office and back again up to the colliery, it used to take me to about five minutes to nine. I'd start work at nine o'clock in the office. So, of course, it made quite a longish day. You had a break for dinner and then you knocked off work at five o'clock at night. But, if all the letters and everything wasn't done in all the offices I had to stop 'til all the mail was in and get it down to Ibstock post office, which was about a mile and a half away, so they could send it off with the night postage. And of course some nights I didn't get home 'til seven at night. Now, I got the fantastic wage of five shillings per week. That was for six days' work.

Frank Smith: I think, as a last resort people went to the pit. It was difficult to get into, for example, the Co-op, or be a bus conductor, or to work at the quarry. It was a last resort, pit. "He'll have to go to pit." because there was not a great deal of employment. There were brickworks, of course — that were equally hard ... and quarry. But then you had to have relatives that worked there before you got in. Labour was so plentiful in those days [1925] you had to be grateful for what employment you got.

My dad took me down. I held his coat in this shaft and it was three hundred and sixty-five yards deep. I were equipped in my slippers (they didn't have pit boots then) and some long trousers that my mother had got me, a few studs in the shoes and a cap and a coat that was a bit tight, a bottle of water and my snap in a snap bag round my arm, and I went down the pit. I went down the pit shaft with my dad, hanging onto his coat, and when we got down half way the sensation is that you're coming back and I said, "We're going back Dad." He says, "No, it's alright." That's when you're all cramped up, twelve of you in a little cage affair, you know ... and then you get out in this bottom where there's a modicum of light, candles and things about. Then look around and see, well, is this like pit? Because no-one has any idea what pit is like. You've seen some winding wheels but you don't know what it's like underground, you can't envisage what it's like. I walked behind him holding his coat tail ... every few yards there'd be an obstacle in the way, a piece of coal down or a piece of stone, and they'd shout, "Up!" So you'd pick your feet up. And you also kept your head down because of hitting the roof and low supports — bars we used to

1

Working with picks and shovels

call them, some of them broken and some of them darting down, and pieces of roadway sticking out the side.

On the first day, the pit bottom deputy said to my dad, "Frank, I want the lad to stop here. We're going to show him how to brake tubs." A chap named Jack Burton ... the tubs come off a haulage system; they're released to run down a slight inclination into the pit bottom, in tens and twelves, and then you'd let them run down to the onsetter ... and you'd brake the tubs with a hand brake to steady them down. I let one go by too quickly and it bumped into another, caused a bit of coal to fall off ... I got hit up the backside with a piece of wood by Jack Burton ... I didn't let any more tubs run away.

Len Bramley: A coalface would be probably, say two hundred yards long and that face was partitioned off in twenty yard lengths and a gang of blokes, they'd have twenty yards and it'd have its own gate road ... and they just worked that twenty yards. At Snibston, when I first went, there was the Yard Seam and the Lower Main which was a three foot seam and the Middle Lount and Nether Lount and they'd be between four feet six inches and five feet.

When I say stall work, a face of coal, it's solid. You just couldn't attack it with a pick and a wedge and a big hammer because you'd only break little bits off. What they used to do, they used to cut under it with a pick. Some faces, underneath it, it would have what we call a soft dirt band and they'd hole in that. And well, a stint for a holer, that was a bloke, a holer, that'd be six feet wide and six feet under. And that'd be a shift's work, that would.

Joe Webster: One day they rang up and said we were going to Swannington tunnel, that's Stephenson's tunnel, sixteen foot high, twelve foot wide. They wanted it herringboning. Well, hundreds of miners had never seen that, you see. It was a very good way of safety where there was bad ground, until they got the arches — the metal arches of different sizes and brought them in the pits. It was easier to set those. The herringboning ... took you a long time to get very far — all made of wood. If you could get the light on it, it'd look fancy. You used to start from the bottom, get the bottom solid and then get up as high as you wanted the road and then come in to the top until you met. It was about all foreign wood in those days, until the war.

Fred Betteridge: On one occasion I saw the roof fall in off the coalface — this was another seam by the old Ibstock Colliery. When the roof fell in and a piece of stone came down, I looked up and it was the largest stone I've ever seen. It looked like the fossil of a crocodile. It must have been seven or eight feet long. The head dropped onto the floor — it was solid, as hard as iron. But the body didn't drop out while we were working. It's still there as far as I know.

Carl Brown: When Ibstock Colliery closed down, my father went to South Colliery and of course, all the pits were on short time and we used to listen for the buzzer being blown to know if Dad had to attend next day. Each pit seemed to sound different and we could hear Desford, Bagworth, Nailstone, Ellistown, South, etc.

There was a drift shaft and two vertical shafts at Ibstock and the locos travelled across the bridle path (soon to be named Miners' Way, I understand) then alongside the road, crossing it past Ellistown pit to join, I suppose, the Coalville to Leicester line.

Ernie Harris: Time was important to be regulated. Under privatisation each colliery had its own method. Most collieries had a steam instrument called a buzzer — like a train but larger — and it could be heard for a number of miles around and they all had different tones. At Desford it was blown at 6.00 a.m., then again at 6.30 a.m. when the shop workers needed to be there. The shop workers were allowed thirty minutes for breakfast from 8.30 a.m. to 9.00 a.m. The workers on the screens, their snack time was 11.00 a.m., so it blew again at 11.15 a.m. The shop workers lunch was 12.30 p.m. to 1.00 p.m. Again for the end of the mining shift at 2.30 p.m. and again

3

for the screen workers at 2.50 p.m. It was blown again at 4.00 p.m. for the shop skilled workers to finish work.

In the early days the colliers didn't work every day, probably only three days a week. It could well be that if the men went home on Monday, they didn't know whether to come in on Tuesday. There was a system at Desford that if they went home and it was decided the pit would be off, the buzzer would be blown for a long time — 6.15 p.m. if Number One pit was to be off, at 6.45 p.m. if Number Two pit was to be off.

It was also used for another purpose. At Desford we had our own fire brigade. We had our own pump and hoses. If there was a fire there was to be one long blow and two short blows. There was a locked cupboard with a glass panel with a key in. The first man to arrive and break the glass, got the key out. There was a two and sixpence reward for him, to induce the speed, of course.

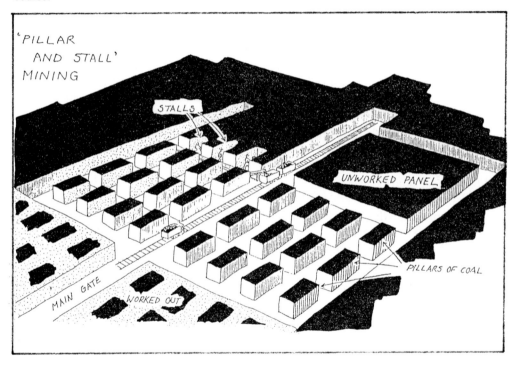

'PILLAR AND STALL' MINING

STALLS

UNWORKED PANEL

PILLARS OF COAL

MAIN GATE

WORKED OUT

Jack Adcock: The men, they'd start underneath the coal. The coal face, it were like same as you'd see a brick wall and they'd start taking the dirt out from underneath the coal with a pick. Then when they'd got as they couldn't reach anymore with a pick then they'd what they call 'slot' the coal. That was, break it off to make themselves enough room for their body to go underneath. They'd take about three inch of dirt out with a pick. Then they'd slot out another foot or so of this coal to make enough height for their body to keep going underneath the coal, keep getting the dirt out. Of course, the farther you got under the coal, you had to shove the dirt back with your hands and then you'd keep coming out to clean that up to give you room for some more dirt coming back. You'd hole, what they called holing, beneath this coal 'til you'd got underneath it, a matter of six foot. And then, as you were going underneath it you'd put a bit of timber ... a piece of a prop the size you wanted underneath so the coal didn't drop off and bury you ... then that'd stop like that until you were ready for blowing it down. And when you'd blowed it down, you'd got to fill it in the tubs. You bore a hole in the coal. Then they'd put some powder in and then a fuse that'd be in the powder ... you'd bring it out the hole, you'd cut it off outside the hole

4

... this fuse went then from outside the hole right up into the end of the coal ... might be four foot, might be six foot. Then ... they'd light this fuse and you'd go out the road so you weren't in any blast or anything and then when it exploded it'd blow this coal off the coal face.

Len Bramley: The explosive was called John Hall powder and the chargeman would get it from a ... type of corner off-licence shop. The type of shop that sold paraffin, beer, everything and even this explosive. I know it was sold in them places because I'd not only heard my dad talk about it, I've heard others talk about it. Then in the thirties the pits actually started supplying the explosive which was a type of gelignite explosive. In them days, when a shot misfired in a stall, the stall would be fenced off and them stallmen would have to go home for the day. Nobody'd be allowed near it and the reason were because it was a naked fuse and when you'd lit one of them you can never be sure whether it's still smouldering. It weren't an electrical charge, a detonator, it was a fuse you lit with a match.

Harry Sheffield: The district where the explosion was at Whitwick, that's all sealed off with barriers and no-one ever wanted to go by them.

He used to thread three bobbins of powder onto the fuse and shove it right back to the end of the hole, you see, and then fill it up with clay and then you had to get away, perhaps twenty yards, a fair distance before he lit the fuse and he'd come away quick. This morning, he was going to light the fuse. We borrowed a candle — we worked with candles then, just candlelight then, no lamps. He was going to light the fuse and then all of a sudden there was an explosion on the top of the coalface. It was frightening, really, because it was a pocket of gas. Actually, it could have caused a major explosion. There wasn't supposed to be much gas about, you see. If they'd have known gas was there, of course, we'd have been working with lamps, and no-one wanted to work with lamps. A lamp used to be alright for the first two or three hours, then gradually it got smoked up until you couldn't see a yard in front of you. You would be more or less in the dark.

Fred Betteridge: When I worked down the pit everybody worked with candles — those who were on the face or doing repair jobs. Apart from candles, those who were travelling (ponies or men going to their jobs) had a little lamp with a handle on with a little paraffin wick in it and glass on the front. But if your paraffin didn't last out all day, you would carry a little candle in your pocket, cut a bit off and stick it in place of the wick. You had to buy your own candles and in the early days they were not the white wax candles as are around now but green, tallow candles with thicker wick ends.

Jack Adcock: They got tight for officials [1926] and they kept begging me to go on as an official ... you went either shotfiring or deputying. I was deputying straight away. Well, I was in charge of all the men in that district ... all the facemen as were filling coal and all the men as was getting it away or supplying them or whatever it was. At one time of day I'd got one hundred and twenty-seven men working under me.

No, it didn't make any difference to your wages. If you'd got a district only half the size as I'd got you'd still get the same wage as I did because it was a fixed wage. I think it was three pounds odd a week. That was before wages got a big increase, before the war.

There were ropes in the pit, a haulage system. The empty tubs used to be sent into the work, near the coal-filling and then the rope coming back again brought the full tubs to the pit bottom. An endless steel rope. The tubs were fixed to the rope by clips. There was a clip with jaws on and then as you pressed the handle down the jaws went together and gripped the rope. The rope was moving all the time. Previous to the haulage system it was all done by horses.

They were always willing to set you on because they wanted you as a pony boy. You went half a mile or a mile out underground before you got to where the men was getting the coal, then you

5

would have this here pony and an empty tub at the back of him. You'd take it into the stall where the men were getting the coal and then you would bring the full tub out. They were kept near the shaft bottom. It was a big stable, about seven foot high. It wasn't only ponies, but workhorses, they were about twelve, thirteen hands.

Ted Kerry, hostler at South Leicester Colliery

There'd be a hostler in the stables, all these ponies used to be in the big stables headed out underground. Every pony would have its own stall, all the ponies were separate but in one long stable. This would be made to hold up to thirty or forty horses because they were there for different districts. The hostler harnessed the pony and it was ready for you when you went to the stables to bring it out to get to your work. You'd got to get into your district ... the haulage rope that brought the empty tubs in and took the full ones out — from the haulage rope you would take your pony, take an empty tub on the stall and then you'd bring the full tub out as the miners had got off the coalface and filled into the tub. That was their work all day long, getting this coal. The pony boy fetching as much from them as was possible. You used to send twenty five tubs, but if you'd got longer distances to run you'd happen only get twenty out.

All you'd got was a little lamp, what we called a bulls-eye lamp, and that just used to shine straight forward. And of course it was a lamp about six inches tall. Wherever you wanted to go you'd got to shine with this lamp. It wasn't a very good lamp but it gave you enough light because everything was pitch dark. If you blew your lamp out you couldn't see an inch in front of you. It was complete darkness so you'd got to have a light all the while and these bulls-eye lamps as you used to carry in your hand, they'd give you a bit of a light for about six foot. You'd have to fill the vessel with oil and then put the wick in and light the wick ... in a specially made lamp. Instead of a plain glass it was a protruding glass, because if it had been a flat glass you'd have

6

broke it, with hitting it. So you had to have this bulls-eye so you didn't smash the glass. In the pit bottom where the air was good and no danger of any gas or explosions, they used to have these flare lamps, same as they'd have on stalls at the wakes and that [naphtha lamps]. That was the lighting before electricity came in.

My first wage as a pony boy was five shilling a week for five full days, eight hours and then a short shift on Saturday — six hours. There were no meal breaks, you took your bread and butter or whatever. You'd happen have a sit down for five or ten minutes if you was in the stall. What they call 'have your snap'. Most of them took tea but of course it was cold then when it came to drinking time. You had to be down the pit before seven o'clock and then you came up again after three. You had to have your eight hours below surface. It might be a quarter of an hour before you got to your work ... in the district.

There were no toilets in the pit but of course you used to bury it. But the stable muck, that was loaded into tubs and sent to the surface. But it was always good ventilation you see, because they were near the pit bottom. You wouldn't get any stink or anything. The stables were always clean and washed down.

Fred Betteridge: At South Leicester I think there was sixteen ponies in the top seam and then in the bottom seam another sixteen or eighteen — getting on for thirty or forty ponies. The ponies only came out of the pit when there was a strike on, they never brought them up unless they were worn out and then they'd bring them out of course. Then you'd got the odd 'un, they were cruel to the ponies, you see ... I liked ponies ... some didn't. They wanted the money, they didn't matter how they knocked the ponies about. Sometimes when they were short of ponies some of the poor old ponies had to go out again and do a double shift you see, the hostlers didn't like doing that, but you couldn't avoid it sometimes.

I would love you to have seen them stables, they were nice down pit. They lived pretty well all their lives down the pit. Oh, you got to know them, I mean if you had a long period in that particular job you mostly had the same pony every day, you'd get to know him, he'd get to know you and you'd hardly have to speak to him, you know, the routine going in and out. He'd stop, he'd turn round soon as you'd saddled him up with a little coal wagon, he'd turn round and go and walk in front of the other one. You'd never say a word to him and he'd do that all day long. As soon as a job was finished the old ponies knew. You didn't have to take them back to the stables, they knowed the way in the dark, a couple of miles, but you still had to follow them in and unsaddle them and give them a drink of water and tie them to where they were feeding.

Sim Woolley: I'd be probably five, six, seven, or eight [1920s] and my father used to work in Ibstock Colliery then. Well, we used to see the pit ponies of course and there used to be a family who lived at the bottom of Colliery Lane and at the bottom there used to be a man, his wife and two sons, who used to be what they called the hostler, and he used to look after the pit ponies. I can't remember his name but one of his sons still lives in Heather. Although they were only children they used to look after the pit ponies.

Anon: My father [John Hutchins] worked in the stables at Snibston pit from about 1923 until he retired at the age of seventy in 1953. We used to listen to my parents talking about the strike [1926] and I was quite concerned about what was going to happen to the ponies.

As my father was in the stables, the daily talk at home was to do with stories of various ponies. We knew most of their names and their likes and dislikes. They were loved by all the men and boys who worked with them and they were well treated. Apples were regularly taken down the pit to give to the ponies as a treat and they also shared the men's snap. We children used to be very upset to read about supposed cruelty to 'shaggy, blind pit ponies' because we knew that blind ponies were not used down the pit. They were also well groomed.

When the strike became fact, my constant question to my dad was, "What is going to happen to the ponies?" I was very relieved to be told they were all to be brought to the surface. Soon afterwards Dad came home and told us that the ponies were to be brought up to the surface the next morning and were to be taken to be grazed in fields behind South Leicester Colliery for as long as the strike lasted.

My mother was told to wake my sister and myself at a very early hour one morning to watch the ponies going by on their way to the fields. I remember sitting at the window, wrapped in a warm blanket for what seemed an age, waiting and looking out into the very early dawn. Then we heard the clip-clop of many hooves coming down the road. The ponies came by, heavily blinkered to guard against the coming daylight.

I had always been told that the ponies were little, so in my childish mind I had imagined them to be like Shetland ponies but they stood as high as the men's shoulders and each man was leading several by the rein. It is a sight from my childhood that I will never forget, nor the sound of the hooves as the ponies trotted along. Through that long, hot Summer, the stablemen took turns every day, sitting in the fields with the ponies and my mother often packed tea and we took it to have a picnic when it was Dad's turn to be with them.

Philip Gill: Then I progressed to pony driver. The stables were only just a couple of hundred yards away from the pit bottom. Once I had a tummy upset and the hostler gave me a bit of some horse medicine.

I went pony driving and you used to get some ponies that they wouldn't walk in the rails, they'd walk out of them. They'd have tubs on the back of them and they used to come off and you'd curse and swear. Then, some ponies, as soon as you started to put the limmers on them — you used to have a harness on the horses and then a frame that went round the back of their legs and down the side of the bodies — you used to fasten them on but ... they'd start kicking their back legs up and if you weren't very careful you got kicked. There used to be a limmer cock — a shaped piece of steel. You used to fit one end into the limmers with a limmer cock peg and then there used to be steel couplers, that's two hooks with about a couple of links in between and you'd fix them in between the tubs and you used to take them into the districts. Mostly it'd be arches and wood bars and lids for the facemen. There would probably be about twenty in the stables, in about 1951.

When you used to take the ponies into the district, if you didn't tie them up they used to make their way back to the stables in the dark. And they knew the way! Some of the supply lads, they used to have a bit of fun and ride on them, ride on the horses. There wasn't much room between the top of the horse and the gate road ... I've even seen a pony ride on a belt. Some of the supply lads used to bring carrots and grass off the verges as they came to work in the morning, take them down for the ponies. They used to enjoy that.

Outside the stables there was another building, (we used to call it the hospital) for the horses if they got injured, which quite frequently they did. The trolleys used to run onto the back of their legs and cut them. And the safety officer, he turned it into a mushroom farm. He started growing mushrooms in it. I don't know whether he did get any out of there or not, I don't know.

Frank Smith: I remember we had one called Creamy ... he was a beautiful horse ... like a show pony. As soon as they put the tackle on him he started to kick, he used to kick tubs, kick walls, kick the roof, all sorts of things. I couldn't do anything with him. A fellow named Arthur Shaw could quieten him down by just speaking in his ear ... Arthur Shaw was the only man. When he finished driving he [the pony] came out of the pit.

Name or situation of stables _No. 5 Pit_ Date _Nov 8th_ 1939

Name or Number of horse. (1)	Time at which taken from stables. (2)	Driver. (3)	Entries in Columns 2 and 3 certified correct. (Person certifying to sign in this column.) (4)	Time at which returned to stables. (5)
Day Shift				
4 Blake	7am.	F. Straw	J. Clamp	12.30
14 Gipsy	"	G. Cook	"	"
Afternoon Pony				
5 Linnet	2.30	H. Heward	T. Andrews	9.30
Night Ponies				
16 Billy	10.30	G. Scriven	T. Andrews	6.0
18 Skipper	"	G. Beson	"	"

Pony records, Whitwick Number Five pit, November 1939

Herbert Blake: Well, this chap, he got a pair of glasses, he'd only had them a week or two, and they got broken, and so, of course, he had to go for another pair. He had to go and have his eyes examined and tested again. So, whoever was there, filled in this great form, you know, it was all forms and such like that, and said, "What happened to your previous glasses?" "They got broken." "How did they get broken?" "A pony stepped on them." Actually a pony had knocked them off and stepped on them.

Eric Hunt BEM: When we were filling there was another chap that used to fill with us occasionally. Owen Halfpenny was his name and he were an Irishman. We all used to take our sandwiches in snap tins. This particular day, Owen, forgotten his snap, went in the canteen and he bought some bacon sandwiches out of the canteen in a paper bag. He was pulling our legs because we'd got jam or cheese in the tin and he'd got bacon. We hung our coats up in the supply gate road that led to our face, went on the face, done half or three parts of our work, come off for snap and Owen couldn't find his jacket. Eventually the supply lads came up with a pit pony, and one of them, Ron Mitcheson, started to laugh. I asked Ronnie what the bloody hell he were laughing at and he picked a sleeve up off a coat. Owen says, "That's my bloody jacket." And that's all that was left of Owen Halfpenny's jacket. The pit pony ate the jacket and the bacon sandwiches.

Jack Rush: My brother had a pony called Gypsy and it used to kick all the while and nobody could drive it. Anyway, my brother went up the stalls where my father was. He got two full tubs of coal and he'd put the horse on the limmers. Well, off he [the pony] went and down the hill — the maingate — and he went through the siding and he got in the pit bottom and it had got right down the centre of it (some pillars) and he cleaned them all out and the stone come down and buried him. So Mr Rowell came. He says, "Ooh, he's a dead 'un! He's a dead 'un!" But they got him out, took all his tackle off and when they took it off, he run like hell to the stables!

Jim Eckersley: We moved because of pit closures in Lancashire ... I finished up at Whitwick pit where I worked all the time I was here. I'd never seen a pit pony before, and the first thing I saw when they sent me into the district, down underground, was manure in the middle of the road. And I thought, that's been left by a horse and I realised there were ponies. They never had them in Lancashire where I was and I never even saw one because they took them out of Whitwick pit the same time as I arrived. So I never even saw one. Oh, yes I did! I nearly got killed by one. I was going to open the air doors, they used to rush out you see, when they'd finished work, the ponies ... they used to come like mad, charging out. And they used to have big wooden doors, which are called air doors, from one tunnel to another, and this door just literally flew back and missed me by a fraction ... and this pony went flying past me and that was the only time I ever saw one down the pit. It just went hell for leather back to the stable.

Ernie Harris: One blacksmith was kept pretty well fully occupied making pony shoes and going down the mine and shoeing the ponies. The blacksmith that went regularly underground for some reason or another wasn't at work so another blacksmith who could do the job (but the ponies weren't accustomed to) went underground to shoe them. The stables underground were very warm. He took off his waistcoat and he hung it up near the manger where the pony stood and he shoed the pony. When he went to get his waistcoat it was all in shreds — the pony had chewed his waistcoat, eaten his watch and chain and everything that was in it. And the pony was called Merryman and ever after that, this blacksmith, they gave him the nickname Merryman.

Len Bramley: Once they went down they stayed down. But later, after nationalisation, they used to turn them out for the holidays. Well, I don't think they turned them out until 1953. That was the first year we ever had a fortnight's holiday. The last pony at Snibston was one called Sandy and that went out the mine in 1968.

Ernie Harris: When they were turned into the field they were provided with eye shields because of the extreme difference in the light. They'd gallop around the fields and be really wild for a while and I can remember stories that at the end of the week the men who looked after them had to go and round them up, bring them back and send them down the pit one at time. Some walked onto the cage quite calm, no trouble, but others, the moment they reached that cage, would start to kick and shy. And I can remember one that got away and it took them all day to catch it again. It was when I was at school. In the field at the back of where I lived, some of the young men were challenging each other to ride the ponies and they didn't go many seconds before they were like bucking broncos and off they'd come.

Reg Thomas: Mice have always been part of the pit life — arriving underground in the pony feed, hence a lot of fat cats around the stables and the pit bottom — and the need to keep your

Pit ponies, annual holiday 1956, Ellistown

snap in a tin. Sitting in a quiet return air-way eating your snap, mice were a common sight and often provided a bit of company. Many are the stories of snap which had only been wrapped in paper having a neat hole cut through the middle of the sandwiches ... and who hasn't had an apple eaten out of his jacket pocket by a pony.

The situation began to turn ugly with the arrival of the rats. I had never seen, or heard of a sighting of, a rat down the pit until I was doing some surveying work down Number Two drift at Merry Lees and, crouching to look through the theodolite telescope, I saw out of the corner of my eye the fleeting glimpse of a large rat — seemingly tip-toeing past me down a drainage channel. I think my sighting was first treated as a bit of a joke but there was sufficient concern at the implications and the Market Bosworth pest control officers were told.

It was the Friday night shift, the pit was virtually deserted and I was alone, taking monthly air samples ... there was a tremendous scuffle — such that I thought that the road side was collapsing. It was a large rat which I had disturbed from its perch among the road-side stone. I don't know who was scared the most ... having crawled down that coalface, I emerged at the main gate to be confronted by what seemed to be a neat circle of seven or eight crouching rats — it was an uncanny sight — before they scattered in all directions ... Doing some final surveying in an abandoned district — I think it was called Maryland — the main road was crushed almost beyond recognition and it was some problem crawling along, up and down over the heaps of fallen roof ... as my cap lamp beam lit the way ahead, I saw two similar lights coming towards me. Who on earth could be crawling about a smashed up, abandoned roadway except this crazy surveyor? As the lights got nearer, I was soon to find out ... a rat which appeared to me, in that confined space, to be as big as a dog, shot over my shoulder — the lights had been my cap lamp shining in its eyes.

Don Connolly: My father was pretty unique among miners because he was a tramp collier ... he tramped the coalfields in Scotland and he used to actually walk about from pit to pit with his tools on his shoulder. He could be employed at two pits in the same day. He'd been a collier from way back.

I used to work with him at Desford. I was his mate, we worked together on the same job. He'd had no end of accidents. He'd got scars all over his body from various accidents. We used to have carbide lamps at Desford and my father was very bad with his eyesight because he had a couple of scars across his eyes. He couldn't see to clear the aperture, as the flame used to come out of his lamp. He found it difficult to find — to prog it, to make it clear and he used to ask me would I do it. What I haven't explained was, no-one can imagine the chaotic rush there used to be down on the coalface at that time of day ... during the war ... After you'd finished your task on the coalface you could go out the pit and go home. It was a good incentive to get a lot of work done ... It was absolutely chaotic ...

Jack Rush: Ooh, they used to play some tricks on them. I'll tell you one trick at Lount and they used to get the det. wire and they used to shove your [coat] sleeves up and tie them and when it came to loose-all so's you wouldn't be in front of them that'd get on the first [cage]. You'd be struggling to get your coat on. And anyway, one day I'd done a trick across one of them and they got a stall bar and they hammered [nailed] my coat all along this bar. Well, I went along to the pit bottom and I took the bar and my coat and all. The undermanager was there and he says, "Where are you going with that, Johnnie?" I says, "Have a look at it. I'm taking it home."

Don Connolly: ... Our task was to build these packs, alternately every five yards along the face so as to control the roof and let it cave in between the packs. And me and my dad worked together ... and everybody was rushing and dashing about trying to get the job done. My dad, if his lamp wasn't working properly, he would call me over to him and he'd say, "There, put your progger into my lamp, Don." We had this bit of wire attached to our hat and we used to put this progger in the lamp to make it go.

I'd get engaged in my own work, shovelling the waste like mad into this pack and then you could hear him swearing and he used to swear prolifically ... and I'd think, here he comes again, he'll be passing me lamp in a minute. And he did do and said, "Don, put your progger in my lamp again." He'd get that angry with this lamp of his — it wouldn't give a good light — he used to get it and he used to throw it right back in the waste! And he'd say to me, "Don, come and get my lamp for me." He couldn't see, anyway and ... I used to have to go and retrieve it for him. And it was an area where there were no props or nothing supporting the roof. You know, it was a terrible dangerous thing to do!

Frank Smith: You've got to have a sense of humour to keep up with the pit life, when I look back at what we had and what we've gone through.

Eli Hague: We had this large engine and the fly-wheel on the engine had cracked and required to be replaced. Trouble was, we couldn't get the old one off ... and we hammered and we thumped it and we banged it. Now, we started work on this at four o'clock on the Monday and we were still banging on Wednesday morning and they were going mad because we were getting no coal out, you see. It was the haulage engine that gets all the coal out the pit. Mr Sam McKee was the manager, a very blunt sort of chap — didn't spare his adjectives, you know, and he came up in a fury. Now, the engine was in a small purpose-built house — brickwork, nice pitch pine roof rafters, slates, the walls white-washed, I suppose, every year for about thirty years on top of the old white-wash. The white-wash was as thick as the bricks. And he [Mr McKee] came and he says, "If you can't get it off, I'll have to do it for you." Now, I was the sort of bloke that didn't take kindly to interference by amateurs and I says to the blokes, "Right-O. Let's get out. Let Mr Bighead have a go at it."

So we all came out, and it was a Summer's day ... so we all sat on the bank and had a Woodbine apiece. Now, round the back was the powder house ... and up the path to the powder house proceeds the manager. Nothing was said for a bit. He disappeared into the powder house, to re-appear a little while later with a shot-firing battery, yards of cable and handfuls of powder and a detonator. And somebody said, you know, in pit talk, "He's going to blow the bugger off!" So we went a bit further away, we did. After a while he emerges [from the haulage house] turning the cable out, connects it to the shot-firer, then he stands up and looks all around — see if there's anybody about, you see. "Right! Everybody clear!" and Pow!! Well, I don't know what Hiroshima was like but it had got nothing on this. There was a cloud of dust which shot up in the air. You couldn't see this little house. You couldn't see anything! And it gradually settled and the four or five of us wandered back, bemused, trying to hold our laughter in, you see. As we approached the haulage house, the floor was literally littered with tiles, slates everywhere, bar on the roof where they belonged. When you walked in and looked up, there was the skeleton of the rafters and the sky. And on the floor, without exaggeration, there was six inches of white-wash and the bricks of the walls were all red and as clean as the day they'd been laid. And to add the final touch, there must have been ten thousand black beetles on their backs waving their legs about!

Now, the driver as you call him, the one who controls it, was a little bloke and his name was Soggy ... and McKee, who was a big, robust sort of a chap ... towered over him. He says, "Hey you!" "Yes," he says, looking up. "You go in there, don't you, of a night? Well, if I hear a word of this has got out in the bloody Hawley [club] I shall sack you!" And Soggy says, "I wouldn't dream of it!" which meant, of course, that's the first thing he's going to be off and doing!

13

Philip Gill: We used to have one shot-firer. He weren't very good on giving you much powder in the holes. ... We used to call him 'half-a-bag Arthur'. He used to break a bag in half to fire a top shot, where four ounces would have been a lot better for us. It made it hard work for us. Oh, yes, he was the one to decide how much powder you wanted in it.

"Mighty" Jim Wardle and John Hubbard

Jack Adcock: They'd got a stand. It used to be about ... four feet. There'd be two sections, one fit in the other. Then, according to the height of the roof you'd extend this so's it was tight fitting from floor to roof and then you'd put this drill in. Your stand would be about two foot away from the face to start. Then you'd have a small drill, fifteen inches and ... you'd keep winding it ... with a handle ... and, of course, it was turning this here drill and shoving it into the coal all the while. When you'd used the half a yard drill you'd take that off and put a yard drill on. Then you'd take that off and put a four foot six drill on, you see, and that was taking the hole into the coal farther ... then the chargeman, he'd come along. He'd put enough powder up this hole and ... a slow burning fuse and you'd ram the hole with clay so as it made against the powder solid ... so it didn't backfire down the hole ... if you had a mis-fire you'd done it wrong. Then you'd got to lay off for two or three hours because it might have been alive and you wouldn't know.

So you always watched, as you cut your fuse, ... you'd cut it at an angle and twist it as the angle was facing the powder so when it came up the fuse, when it got to the end, it made a spark to go into the powder and exploded it. If you'd done it wrong and you'd put the fuse the wrong way round instead of getting to the powder it was blowing back on its own fuse. So you had a mis-shot then. Of course, then you'd got to get out the road and stop out of the road three or four hours.

And, of course, some of the men, if there'd be ... racing or anything on, they'd happen to do it on purpose because they knew they couldn't work and they'd got to come out of the pit!

Len Bramley: When he [his father] left Ellistown, stall work was just being finished with and they were bringing a belt in. Well, a belt, it was the whole length of the face and what happens then, they cut the face with a cutter! Well, in them days, they'd always cut it under the seam. In later years they'd mount the cutter on a skid and they'd cut it in the middle, you see. It was a machine but it didn't actually cut coal. All it did was cut a slot in it. ... The jib on the cutter, it was four foot six inches and it'd go along the face under-cutting four foot six inches and the next day, while the face'd be divided depending on the thickness, it could range from seven to ten or eleven yards. Say the face was hundred yards long there'd be ten men on that face and they'd have ten yards each. Adjacent to them was a belt and ... they'd break it to where the end of that cut was what they call 'up to the solid' ... while the fire shots bring it down, and they'd load that on the belt which was directly at the side of them. And that belt, that went to the main gate. There's two gates, what they term the main gate and the supply gate. Well the supply gate is really usually the return air-way but they take timber and supplies up it. The coal never went down there, it went down the main gate. It would go on a short belt down the road and then it would be loaded directly into, well some call them 'tubs', some call them 'dannies' some call them 'hutches' which are little trucks and different pits use different sizes. If it was for that work it was bigger tubs than if they were using it for 'hand-hole face' in which the actual tub went onto the face. In fact it would go up to the face, that would, and the pony driver would unhitch them and he'd roll them over. There was enough room on the side and he used to tip them over, what they call 'rolled over' and he'd attach two full ones and go he'd take them out to the siding and in the meantime there'd be two blokes in that stall, that they term 'fillers'. They'd fetch one of them each and when they shoved it on the face there was a steel plate on this floor and they'd twist it to go on that plate to line it up with the track on the face and just take it in the stall where they wanted to fill it. ... before they actually put belts on, cutters had come into being which had done away with the holers which, depending on the type of coal, it could be a very slow process holing in that coal. And you can't get coal when it's solid, you've got to get a cavity under it in order to either break it down or prise it down.

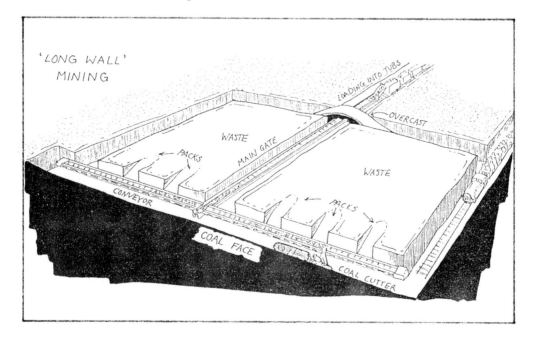

When I worked at Snibston, in 1945, there was a face there of ten stalls which would be a two hundred yards face and they, so they told me, were the last hand-holed stalls in Leicestershire. And there wasn't a bit of power up there. The only electricity of any note was the phone. There was no power cable at all ... and it finished a week before Christmas 1945.

You supplied your own light. You'd buy your own lamp, acetylene lamp, which were called a 'shooky' ... they were in use, and, well, at Snibston, electric lamps come in September 1948. After nationalisation we were still using Shookies for over eighteen months and well, when them Shookies were being used smoking, was openly carried out.

Philip Gill: I went ... packing, where you dismantle the belt and the Panzer and then advance them into ... where the facemen had filled the coal. We used to put them in there. And we used to have to put packs in the waste ... it's like a square block and you used to make a stall and then fill it all in with all the stone out of the waste. I wasn't keen on that. I got a bit more frightened if you'd got a waste that were dropping down and that, I wasn't very keen on that ... it used to be like a solid stone with the coal took from underneath and then you used to take the supports out and blow that down and then used to have to fill that in the waste, in the packs.

Len Bramley: For being a chargeman, I think in them days he [his father] got a shilling extra a shift than the other men in the stall and also I've heard it said the chargemen on a Friday used to draw all the money for the stall and he'd pay. They'd be in groups in the pit yard and he'd pay those in the stall. Well, blokes who wanted to get on the face, who wanted to earn more money, they'd go in the stall, filling ... and on pay day the stallman would give them a sum and, well, they'd never question to see the sheet, what were on it, see whether they were getting a just reward because if they quibbled about it they knew they could be out and back on a day wage job which would be lower paid so they said nothing about it. They accepted it. In fact, I did hear my dad say he had never twisted anyone. He said, "I always showed them the sheet." It'd show the gross amount paid for what coal they'd sent ... say they were earning two pounds ... well that'd work out two pounds each if they were going to be fair. Plus a shilling, which he were entitled to, for the chargeman. But, what they'd do, they'd grab a few bob off the fillers and wouldn't show them the sheet and them fillers wouldn't question the chargeman because they could be out the stall and somebody else in and they'd be back on a day wage job and they'd be out of pocket that way. In fact, my dad, when he left school he went to Whitwick pit and I heard him say when he were filling in the stall at Whitwick that's why he left to go Ellistown because he knew the chargeman was diddling them. He weren't showing that sheet.

Don Connolly: They used to call it 'being on contract'. What used to happen was that a gang of men would apply to the management to do this particular job and in some cases one man out of the gang would go to the manager. They would arrange a contract to get a certain job done for a certain amount of money. So there was occasions, for instance, when through abnormal conditions you'd be there much longer, you'd be late, you'd be two or three hours after your shift finished and you didn't get any extra for it.

It was the latter end of the butty system. I worked on the butty system at Desford Colliery and, in fact, some gangs, the butty — that was the chief bloke in the gang — he used to arrange with the boss how much you'd get paid and he used to pay out the money. Sometimes he used to get paid all of the wages and he'd pay it out in a pub. You'd arrange to meet in a certain pub on a Saturday night ... and he wouldn't pay everybody the same. He'd pay people according to how he thought they'd performed and, of course, very often personalities used to come into it. If he didn't like somebody he'd make any sort of excuse not to give them their money. It used to happen ... maybe, a pound or two pounds off their wages! The management used to encourage that because it gave them control, through this butty. During that time there were some terrible

Miners' pay day

things happen, blokes going into a pub at the weekend, might have been a few minutes late and he wouldn't get no wages! Not until perhaps on Monday, when he'd see the bloke in the pit yard.

Later on there used to be a tin box outside the lamp cabin and it would be arranged that your number would be on the tin box and you'd just pick it up and scoop the money out. That was there for you, there was no dockets or tickets to show you how you'd got your money. You simply scooped the money out of the tin and put it in your pocket. That was the paying out system.

Different areas of Britain there was different systems of blokes. In Leicester it was a very backward system. It was the 'blue-eyed boy' system. If you were well in you got a good place [on the coalface]. It wasn't even left to the vagaries of blokes who worked there to decide, it was the management. It depended on how well in you were.

Reg Thomas: George Rayworth, bless him. Now he was the colliery bricklayer at Desford and could do anything in the building trade. I remember George being involved in a splendid example of autocratic management ... Mr Butterley took George to a location in the colliery yard. With minimal instruction ... he asked George to construct a small stone building. And he agreed a price with George ... he built this place to his satisfaction and he called on Mr Butterley for his approval. So he responded to George when George says, "How's that then, Master?" He says, "I don't like it there. Knock it down." George looked at him a bit perplexed. "How much for knocking it down, Master?" George said. "Same price knocking down as putting up," replied Mr Butterley. And that's how things got done in them days.

Anon: He [Mr Torrance] was manager of Ibstock Colliery ... he came to Ibstock in 1917 from South Wales where he'd been managing a colliery there. The attraction was that being comparatively young at that time he was quite well versed in mining machinery and he was

17

employed with the idea of introducing coal-cutting machines and conveyor-belting into the colliery at Ibstock. He left Ibstock in 1924 and moved to Whitwick Colliery which he proceeded to organise along similar lines. I don't remember much about Ibstock Colliery itself but I can remember going around Whitwick Colliery, usually on Sunday mornings, and looking at the various shafts, numbers one, two, three, four, five and six. Number four was just a ventilation shaft. And being quite impressed with the steam engines which were used to keep the shafts working. There was no engine on the number one shaft. That was just a shaft used for pumping water and when anybody went down that, they sat in a bucket and were lowered down slowly to do repairs to the shaft.

I did go down number three shaft once, on Sunday morning, when I was aged about nine and this, I think, was because my father wanted to see how some repair works were being carried out ... so I went with him. They weren't, of course, being Sunday morning, they weren't turning coal at that time so I didn't see any of the actual coal production but only walked along the roads in the neighbourhood of the bottom of the pit shaft ... I don't remember being afraid of going down the pit. It was possibly a nice ride. Maybe at that age you don't visualise all the things that might possibly happen underground.

During the period he was at Whitwick he would possibly go to work dressed in clothes suitable for going down a mine, either once a week or occasionally twice a week. He wouldn't go down the mine every day by any manner of means. This role was carried out by two undermanagers. One was called Mr Price and the other Mr Percival.

On occasions I have been in his office and about half past two in the afternoon both of them would come and give a report of what had been going on underground during the day. I feel that as manager his job was largely to plan things and the two undermanagers went down the shafts every morning, saw the men to their respective parts of the mine and looked after what went on down below. He would comment on the problems that arose. He would come home grumbling because it was a mild winter and consequently they weren't able to sell enough coal and problems of this sort. He couldn't sell coal from Whitwick Colliery to the Gas Works, which at that time was down the road. They insisted on having coal from Yorkshire because it produced more gas. But problems of that sort just had to be accepted.

The collieries were often working short time and it was very seldom that they were able to work a full five days a week ... During the 1930s the collieries were often just working three days a week. They were able to produce as much coal as they could sell at that time.

I don't know what my father's income was but I should think that he would be on a salary and as a result of that he would get a pay every month. The way the collieries were run in those days was that there would be a group of coal owners. At Whitwick there were four of them who used to come and have a meeting once a month. They were always held in the Victoria Hotel which was adjacent to the colliery ... Dad, as the colliery manager, would go along and give his report on what had been going on at the pit during the month. As would the colliery secretary ... Mr Sales, whose job was to sell the coal ... I know nothing as to whether they got a bonus for what they did but I should imagine that the agreement would be that they had a fixed salary. Of those four directors, one, a Mr Whittaker, was a mining engineer and consequently would understand something of mining. Two of the others were people who would presumably be quite financially well-off. They would be the owners of the machinery and everything else that was used in the colliery. But their role in life was to run coal selling firms and one of them had a whole series of offices around London ... train loads of it would go to London and be unloaded and distributed from their coal distribution yards ... when anything new was required at the colliery such as pit-head baths, it was Dad's role to put this problem to the Board, these four chaps, and get them to agree to spend the money on it ... Also they had the unusual facility which has gone out of fashion now, in that they installed an ultra-violet lamp. And when the miners would come up from the shaft they could have their bath and go and stand in front of this lamp which gave a somewhat sun-tanned appearance and was meant, at that time, to be considered to be beneficial to health. In point of fact it's doubtful that it did benefit their health, except psychologically, except that they would look less pale and peaky. Later he persuaded the directors to build a canteen which was started well before the war and people were able to get food there. All these things were provided by the coal owners, who were the source of capital for the colliery. He lived in a house which was provided by the colliery and like all the miners he got free coal.

On the whole I would have thought that the relations between himself and the directors was good. Certainly he spent a lot of time in the evenings drawing graphs showing the output of the colliery and the number of men employed and the so-called 'output per man shift', with an occasional comment that he hoped the directors really understood these graphs!

Ernie Harris: It was the Desford Coal Company who were the owners. They had a managing director stationed at the colliery as well as a colliery manager. The managing director was a member of the board of directors, who lived in Leicester and in my early days he was transported from Leicester in his own private vehicle with a chauffeur. Before my day, the story goes it was a horse and cab that brought him. When I got there he would probably be in his late sixties or early seventies. They were remote from you, I remember in my early days, every day he walked from his office, around the surface. His name was E E Bramhall. He would occasionally make visits underground. We understood he was a very clever engineer. For instance, the winding engine signals were produced from his invention. Quite a number of things in the colliery were of his own invention, in fact, he first tried radio underground but apparently there was too much interference. I was told he helped in the sinking of the mine and he worked alongside the men.

Reg Thomas: It was the practice in underground surveying to make use of the magnetic compass to provide a reference bearing ... the amount of steel that was usually present made it difficult to find a place that was 'magnetically safe'. It was necessary for the instrument man to remove all traces of metal from his person — give up the cap lamp and use a candle — it was not a gassy pit. It was a long, tedious wait for the compass needle to settle itself ... we repeated this process several times. The loneliness of sitting at the end of this tiny hole in the ground became claustrophobic ... and to add to the feeling of doom, there was an incessant buzzing sound — just like a bee hive. In the murky light of the candle I could just perceive ... smoothly drilled holes in the wooden props — about half an inch in diameter. I was always uneasy on the many occasions it was necessary to use these locations and my unease turned to near terror one day when, about to enter one such roadway, I was hit by what looked and sounded like a swarm of locusts! I shook myself clean of them ... and proceeded to finish the job.

As we stood at the canteen counter having a cup of tea the buzzing sound took off from under my collar and flew around the room — now everyone else had got the wind up. We all gave chase and eventually took it alive on a window ledge. It was a vicious looking creature, powerful wings, tubular body about two inches long with two wicked looking jaws up front and a bright red tail and a menacing inch long spike at the rear — it looked as if it could kill an elephant! A Mr Gregory of the Leicester Museum was geological adviser to the colliery company at the time and he came to visit the thing. He drooled over it: "This is a lovely specimen." It was a wood-wasp and to our disappointment or was it relief, it was completely harmless. It drilled those lovely clean holes in the timber with those wicked looking jaws, deposited an egg into the wood with that menacing spike. The eggs became wood-wasps which emerged from props underground — simple! But I remained uneasy always about what such a creature might yet be able to do to me in a tight spot down the pit!

Philip Gill: While I was doing ratching, I went to night school to take my shotfirer's and deputy's papers. I done that off my own back. In later years they used to send them from the mines on the day releases ... I took my exams at Coalville Tech and practical at Whitwick Colliery, on the shotfiring and the deputy's ...

They used to have a gallery in the Coalville Tech. They used to have holes and it were done with imitation powder and dets and they used to tell you how to ram it and check the holes for breaks in it. If there was a break in it you weren't supposed to fire it but if you ever went by the rules and regulations of the Coal Mines Act you wouldn't turn a lump of coal out!

Then you did the gas test. And you had to read the gas caps on half a dozen lamps. They used to have managers from different collieries asking questions on different aspects of the district — what did you find wrong with the district? How many tubs were there? Did you check the first aid canister? I think the minimum bandages should have been eight in the ambulance canister because eight's the most you could use on a fractured thigh.

There used to be first aid canisters. They used to be about six foot long and eighteen inches by a foot and they used to hang in districts. I mean, you'd got all blankets and a stretcher in and splints and that and finger bandages. They were all equipped and they were down the mine and they used to advance them as the faces went along. On the pit top, they used to have morphia. In the ambulance room you'd have morphia and oxygen and all other equipment needed. I took a lesson in morphia. I used to have to do that once every four years, the exam. Used to have three lectures ... and then on the final one you used to take an exam. All you done, you used to put a pad on your partner's arm and you used to have like a little syringe with distilled water in and ... you used to stick it into the pad and tell the doctor what you were doing. You have to squeeze every drop out. I had one chap, he used to be the first aider, he was an old chap. He was taking it and I don't know if he was a bag of nerves or what but his hand was shaking and I was hoping he was going to get the needle in the pad!

... but I didn't go on the staff straight away ... the management at the colliery used to know as I'd got them and if they wanted a shotfirer on a Saturday morning, I used to go shotfiring and get paid ratcher's money which was a lot more money. It was a good thing that was. Then I got trapped on a face. I got hit by a steel girder which shot out and knocked me onto the Panzer. I think I had twenty odd stitches round my eye ... After that I decided to go on the staff. I'd had enough of the face work. Then I done twenty years on the staff.

Your responsibility was the safety of the men, the jobs they had to do, looking after the supply lads, seeing if they'd got all the supplies they wanted for each particular district. ... they more or less wanted you to keep the district going, turning coal, or getting development and advance heading and all that. Mostly, your responsibility was the safety of your men. That was your first priority. All you used to have was your knee pads and helmet, a hard hat. Sometimes, the old miners, they used to have a cloth cap. They never did wear a hard helmet.

Llewellyn Griffith: At Corah's I met a woman, lady, my future wife Mary Hemsley ... I proposed to her during the war and in 1942 got married and came to live ... my home address then became Ellistown. And my father-in-law, he was the organist at the Ellistown Church and he was quite a lively person in choral music. He had a very well known choir that toured round large houses giving concerts. He was the organist there for sixty years .. he was also blacksmith at the Ellistown Colliery. So when the war ended, I came back, well, the money they were offering me in the knitwear wasn't very interesting ... my father-in-law asked me if I'd like a job at the pits. I said, "Yes." So I went to Ellistown pit. I went as a blacksmith's striker with my father-in-law ... the blacksmiths then, there wasn't much welding, electrics or acetylene welding, it was nearly all done in the forge. I mean, if they had to make chains they used to make their own chains up in the forge. My father-in-law was also responsible for the cages and the conductor wires and the winch wires. We used to have to cap those — make the running metal into these caps to hold the wire ropes in, so that the conductor could stay in position on each corner of the cage — that sort of thing. He used to do the rope splicing in the blacksmith's shop itself, there was a lot of pit work — making various things ... they used to make their own cages ... there was a terrific lot

Blacksmith, Snibston 1957

21

of rather heavy welding — and hold them in the forge — it was quite ... true blacksmithing. My father-in-law, he was also the farrier. He used to go down the pit, he used to make the ponies' shoes and the horses' shoes and shoe them. All the shoes would be made on top and he'd go down and shoe the ponies down the pit. But, of course, the large horses that were on top, you would do on the colliery bank.

I wasn't in the pit all that long, I came out of the pit in 1949 and I took the Ellistown Post Office.

Ernie Harris: I went into the tub-shop repairing the little tubs that had wooden sides that went into the pit for the coal to be put in. The boards used to get broken, the wheels used to be damaged and there were three men and myself repairing them. Later on, of course, all the wooden tubs were made obsolete and steel tubs came into being in 1936 or 1937. After that there were no men employed in the tub repair shop but there was extra work for the blacksmiths because if they got bent the blacksmith had to mend them.

At that time Desford Colliery had six blacksmiths ... they were very busy men. Desford Colliery was almost self-contained — made their own cages, railway crossings, repaired their own wagons. They had over a thousand wagons and there was a lot of ironwork on the wagons that got bent and needed straightening.

When I left school [1928] I went straight to the mine to be on the surface, on what were known as the screens. The screens were moving steel belts on which the coal had already come over various steel riddles onto the various steel belts so it was in various sizes, and these were small, little cobbles where the boys went — the men — the larger sizes. You picked out the little pieces of dirt and they were thrown into a large heap and men came later to remove them to the dirt tip. The coal that went into the wagons was clean — no dirt to be allowed to be amongst it.

There was very little shelter, there were open sides, the wind and rain could blow through. The story was told that this matter was once raised — couldn't there be more shelter? — and the managing director replied that the men were to move to keep warm. You took every opportunity to run errands to get away from this monotonous picking out of the bits of stone — you did errands for the manager, perhaps to the shops, also for the engineer, probably up to the village to get something they wanted. There were plenty of volunteers and often it would take some time!

There were always two boys chosen to come very early at the pit to give out the tallies. They're the little discs that register the men going underground. These boys were in a little office on the surface. There were two shafts known as Number One pit and Number Two pit, so there'd be a boy giving out tallies (sometimes they were called checks) — one to one pit and the other boy to the other pit. Perhaps as many as two to three hundred going into each pit. Having done that you marked it down in a register and the final bit was, you went to the banksman who was the man letting them into the pit to tell him to record how many men had gone on that particular shift. It was also recorded again when they reached the pit bottom. There was a timekeeper there who took those tallies and put them on a board and they were there until the men came out at the end of the shift. This lasted until about half past seven and then you went back to the screens. But one advantage of it was, boys were taken into the workshops and the two lads who were the check lads were often chosen and given the first opportunity to go into the workshops. So it was a progressive sort of thing and you were very pleased to be accepted into the warmth of the workshops. You started work there at 6.30 a.m. and worked until 4.00 p.m. but you learned a trade ... I wouldn't say there was rivalry but perhaps a little bit of jealousy at times. But you didn't have a chance to complain, you accepted what was offered. They did periodically ask boys if they wanted to go underground and, of course, having perhaps had one or two winters, they elected to go underground.

I got paid twelve shillings at the beginning. You got paid a little bit of overtime for doing the tallies — half of one day's money per week — not a lot but the opportunity to go into the workshop ... there was no particular union rate, you were paid perhaps according to your wants. There would be a basic rate and I remember the first time I was offered work as a fitter — to have my own tools and be responsible for my own work — I was offered threepence a day more, for doing that. If you could get the blacksmith in a reasonable mood, he'd make you some tools but you had to provide your own.

At Desford there was a big reorganisation scheme. One huge vehicle known as a mine-car was used, to be filled by conveyors and automatically loaded onto the cage and automatically pushed off at the top. It went into an automatic tippler so they weren't touched by hand at all. They were loaded underground at a loading bunker and each contained three and a half tons ... it was quite an advancement. It came into the washery plant where the separation of coal and dirt wasn't done by hand, it was done by the density of the stone and the coal floated and the stone sank. Then the clean coal went over a screening system, over various conveyors, either into storage bunkers or into wagons or lorries, whatever transport. So very little was touched by hand in a modern washery.

I should think there were times when there were a thousand men at Desford Colliery, doing all the various jobs as well as producing the coal. They produced their own electricity by two huge turbines and they had nine Lancashire boilers producing steam for the winding engines ... another great invention, as we thought in those days, the turbines were driven by the exhaust steam that came from the winding engines — it was all economy. Men worked very hard in the boiler plant, producing the steam for driving the fans for ventilation, the lighting ...

Whitwick screening plant 1958

The winding engine had a real change — new ideas for safety — they were fitted with new cylinders and new drums with steel scrolls. The winding gear had over-speed restriction gear for men and over-winding gear for coal so it was pretty near fool-proof by the time I left it.

Aubrey Peace: I worked on the surface all my life. I started on my fourteenth birthday [1940]. Yes, I was very fortunate. It was during the war, I wrote to Leicestershire Education Committee and I'd already got a provisional job and they sent me notification as I could start work. I left school on the Friday and started work on my fourteenth birthday.

I shall always remember it, that morning, you know. It was a dark November morning — blackout — proud as you like going down the road, the old cap on, tilted at an angle, you know. Got my pit head locker — 616 — I shall always remember it, same number I had all the while. And they said, "Shall you report to the bank foreman?" So I reported to the bank foreman and he says, "Hang on a minute, Aubrey, and someone'll come and pick you up." So, somebody came and picked me up and took me to my first job. I shall always remember it, very calm, you know, 'til I walked in — they'd got a gangway up the screens and all of a sudden the screens kicked up and I thought I were going to Hades. The row were terrible!

We had a wonderful record at that colliery [Snibston]. We used to do a hundred runs an hour [of the cage]. One day we done three consecutive hundreds and they came to modernise the pit top. Westinghouse came and timed us and he timed us, we were ten second ... coming onto the cage ... and off again. And we were just ten seconds. And there were four tons went off there.

... the old steam winder was a credit to us. It used to be a ritual, you know, me duck ... any shift, Saturday morning, Saturday afternoon and Saturday night, the engine was split into three sections for the three winders. And we used to take one, the cylinder, one take the middle and the other one took the other end. And they used to compete against each other to see how nice it looked. It was holy of holies to get in the winding area. You couldn't get in. They used to clean the floors three times a day.

Day shift, it were more or less we used to get the supplies and men in. Then afternoons it used to be more or less running men out and night shift just the same. I was there with the old steam winder when we were winding coal up the shaft. Oh, wonderful engine, wonderful. If we'd got ninety pound of steam pressure we could do anything. That was an old tank engine from out of a ship, you know. Yes, an old ship engine that was. You can see it on the pictures the old eccentric rods going. But that's how it was and ... they used to clean it and made a design on the old eccentrics, you know. It was a credit to us that winder was.

There used to be three winders and a spare man. The spare man used to do the day shift with you, with the ordinary winders. Well, if the night man didn't come on the afternoon, one's got to stop. He's got to stop because there's no relief man.

Ernie Harris: The headgear that we used for the winding wheels and so on were made of pine and in 1927 the company introduced a reinforced concrete structure. An engineering firm erected the headgear around the old headgear while the pit was still working. It was the first in this district. The colliery winding engines were built by John Woods of Wigan and the turbines were built by a firm known as Westinghouse.

I progressed into the fitting shop. Steam boilers had to be inspected annually by a separate boiler inspector. Therefore, for a visit of the inspector, it'd got to be stripped down so he could thoroughly inspect the whole structure because one hundred pounds steam pressure could be a dangerous thing. He was more or less like a government inspector and everything had to be clean. I've seen him turn away because it wasn't clean enough for him. So that was a job that kept you occupied — breakdowns, rough jobs, dirty jobs, nevertheless all the time you were progressing.

Tony Turner: My dad worked at the pit and he got you a job there, sort of thing, boiler cleaning, fourteen when I left school [1941]. Clean the boilers, chip them, clean the inside, clean all the flue dust out. The one at Speedwell was ... fifty foot high, the one at Number Three, they were Lancashire boilers, the ordinary sized boiler with the two fire boxes in each boiler.

In the Winter when there were a lot of snow they always had a stockpile of slack for the boilers down there and if they used it up in the winter, you know, they renewed it in the Summer ... and I started down there emptying the wagons — two on us — while we were down there emptying the wagons, we heard this water break in on the shaft side.

It [the pump] used to drain all the pits in Leicestershire this 'cutta had, it were essential that it were kept going, sort of thing. A big beam engine — the fly-wheel were sixty ton, just the fly-wheel on it — magnificent machine — Calcutta. [Calcutta] that were the name of the mine, when it were a mine. Apparently it flooded out and they couldn't do nowt with it, too much water. They just had to leave it. Well, they used it for a pumping station. The pump itself were a magnificent piece of machinery ... they cut it up, I think ... in the fifties. Normally they only run it from six in the morning till four in the afternoon — that were the normal run of the mill, but when they had this water break in they had to go on three shifts, you see. Every time it come up it pumped two hundred and fifty gallons and it done five revs a minute.

At the cottage, at the bottom below 'cutta, there were an old bloke lived there in this cottage, named Obadiah Smith. We pumped that much water out we drained his well (he used to have his drinking water out of the well, down there), drained his well. Just below 'cutta, between Obadiah's cottage and 'cutta itself, there were a spinney that were all fenced off and there were a shaft dropped in there. We took that much water out of it, they found two shafts as nobody knowed anything about. Well, there were no toilets down there. If you wanted to do owt you'd got to go into this spinney. That were the regular procedure. One of the shaftmen, he went in one day and come out and said, "I've just heard a dog barking." The dogs used to come out from Swannington and Thringstone, running the rabbits, you see. This dog had gone through and he were down the shaft, actually. One or two of these shaftmen, they got a rope and went down and fetched this dog up ... about thirty feet it had dropped it.

There were a brook down there that run into the Gracedieu brook, we pumped millions of gallons [into the brook]. I think we were on this job somewhere about four month before they got the topside of this water ... no modern electric pumps in them days, 1943/45.

I were pretty lucky. I think about two foot-nine were the lowest seam I ever worked in ... we drove a head from Whitwick to Old Smokey — the Snibby Shaft. I worked on a machine called the Samson Stripper. It were very successful at Whitwick but it were about the only pit that you really made use on it ... We were going along one day with the old Samson Stripper and it started to go into the floor and we backed it up and looked and there were a great big hole underneath ... they got the plans out and apparently there'd been a seam of coal took from underneath, nobody knowed about it. It weren't really recorded.

[The Stripper] were about five yards long and it'd got a jack in the middle and you used to set this jack up and it used to rawm into the coal and literally brute force it off ... it loaded the coal on the belt. My job at that time were snaking the Panzer over. Now they do all that with hydraulics but I used to do it with a ten-ton jack. Well, the Panzer is a metal conveyor ... we used to take coal away and my job was to jack these over, ready for another run back.

Lena Gee: I used to love to stand and watch the men with the elephant feet. There were two men, I know they lived on Moscow Lane near Shepshed and everybody called them the Moscow brothers. And they'd got round feet like elephants' and these round boots with laces up ... the old fashioned laces ... and tied in a little bow. I used to stand fascinated looking at them. They

A Dosco mining machine and belt loader showing signal line for stopping the belt

used to come every day fetching the coal ... you had to pay for the coal and then pay for them taking it back. There were lots of them, like private dealers. These two brothers ... had got a donkey cart and they used to draw it down the front of the mine ... and they used to have to go on a great big sheet of metal ... and weigh the cart to check it. And they called him the checkweighman. They paid him, the private dealers, that's why it was 'check' and 'weigh'.

Joyce McKinnon: My father's shop was on Belvoir Road, Coalville and he started in 1927. And it closed ten years ago [1982]. Leonard Coleman's ... solely ironmongers. Tools for the miners. The shovels, the wedges ... the shafts for the wedges and pit axes. Carbide for the lamps and we used to sell the hats which they used to put the lamp clips on the top. And also tool rods. They were about eighteen inches long and they used to drill their tools and they could put them on this rod and then there was what they called a key at the end which they put a padlock on. It held them all together.

We lived behind the shop to begin with and then in 1937 my father built a house up Greenhill Road. It was very good living accommodation for being behind a shop. Eventually, as trade grew, my father took one room then the other for stock.

You'd open at half past eight in the morning. The staff would go home for lunch time, staggered and then they'd go home also for tea. They'd have a tea break. And we'd open 'til half past seven at night. On Friday and Saturday it was half past eight, nine o'clock. We sold powder cans ... and snap tins, which was for their lunch. I think they had them on a belt, round their waist. For a long while there were only the two ironmongers in Coalville and we really specialised in tools. It was a typical ironmongers and domestic stuff as well. The miners, they would go amongst these, they called them the pit axes, shovels. They'd go amongst them and pick them up. They'd weigh a little bit different. They'd go amongst them, to see which one they liked. You'd just leave them to it. When it was nationalised, the Coal Board bulk bought the tools. We still sold odd ones but on the whole, then, they used to go to the colliery and buy their things.

We had an office staff. That's where I was mostly to begin with, in the office. Growing up with the trade it just came naturally to you. My father ran it, then when I got married ... with myself having no brothers or sisters it was talked about and my husband decided to come into the business. Unfortunately he died in 1964 and I carried it on.

The pits bought things from us but it was the miners that came for their own tools. Especially Whitwick Colliery and Snibston Colliery which were the two in the town. One time, it was in my father's time ... there were lovely enamelled tallies that Whitwick Colliery ordered from my father for the miners. We used to do credit. But for the tools, no, they didn't ask for credit. Of course, it was a low wage in those days, really, compared with now ... If they had credit for anything, they were good payers.

It was a regular occurrence to buy carbide for their lamps. That would be a weekly thing that they would come in for. When we ordered this carbide it was two or three tons at a time, in small drums. They used to have long thin drums, the miners, for this carbide and they'd go and fill it themselves. The drum was near the end of the counter.

They liked to have allotments and we used to sell the seeds and seed potatoes and onion sets. They were great gardeners. Our customers, a lot of them were miners. Of course, you got to know them ... in those days, shopping was one to one with your customer. You really got to know them.

Elizabeth Whatnall: The Co-op run it at the time, not the Coal Board ... well, Mr Hill, his brother married my husband's sister, and he suggested, "Why don't you get a job in the canteen, Lizzie?" ... I went and had an interview and that's how I got the job. About twenty-seven years altogether I did in the canteen. Twenty-four at South and three at Whitwick ... I put my whole life in that work, I loved it ... I had to do some homework, sort of, and a bit of training — we used to go to Skegness, the miners' cripple home ... we used to go to Coleorton Hall a lot ... the money wasn't very much, you know ...

Hot meals, breakfasts — bacon, egg, tomatoes or beans in tomato sauce — good meals every day. Nearly three hundred a day I used to do. When I went to Whitwick, it was more there ... We used to go to Coleorton Hall for the fete and gala ... it was lovely. The fete and gala was beautiful, selling food, and games and everything, tug of war ... we used to live for that day — on a Saturday it was. Sir George Beaumont kept Coleorton Hall at that time. The gardens at Coleorton were really beautiful.

They'd order their dinners when they were going down the pit ... between two and half past they used to come up. We used to have their dinners all ready for them in the hot plates, oh yes ... Cups of tea for tuppence. Dinner, sweet and tea — half a crown ... breakfast — one and six.

Just before I left the Coal Board, the miners came over from Scotland ... and we used to have to pack boxes of food for them and make bottles for the babies, ... get there for six in the morning and welcome these Scotch people ... In fact I went up to Scotland last year to one of the ladies who used to work under me at Whitwick ... after all them years, thirty odd years ago.

You used to see cockroaches and hear the crickets, you know ... oh yes, used to have one or two mice running across the floor ... they always said the miners' canteens were cleaner than anywhere else and they were clean, oh yes ... I forget who the gentleman was ... if you was doing the tables or you'd got a brush in your hand and the miners were eating, he'd come to me and he'd say, "That staff's not supposed to be doing that in eating quarters, catching the dust on the food." He was very strict, very strict. I used to have half a dozen staff under me and then there was the night duty ... there used to be two on nights but, of course, they didn't have the work to do as we had. But they used to get them bacon sandwiches ... nice bacon sandwich for sixpence. They used to come up at such a time and we should get them a meal and fill their flasks for them and they'd take it back and go down the pit again.

There was a deputy and he swore. I had to come back on duty that night because one of the night staff were off and he came in ... but, anyway, he swore at the counter, he used the 'f' word, you see. And when he got to me, of course, he used it again: "Give me an effing cup of tea." So I picked up the cup of tea and chucked it all over him. I says, "You've got your cup of tea now. Will you go and see Mr Neath, the manager?" Oh, he had to come and apologise to me. That was the only bad instance I ever had through all the many years I worked for the Coal Board.

[For Christmas] we had turkey, they always had the best of dinners, turkeys and roast pork and stuffing and they always used to have all the diddly bits as had to go with it. We used to have to do, as a matter of fact. We used to have orders from Coleorton: "It's so and so day today. Are you putting a special menu on?"

We used to say, "Just look at the pots in the sink." We hadn't got a washing up machine, you know, in them days. We did at the finish. We had baskets. They were big baskets about the size of the top of a table and we used to fill that with mugs, wash them and ... fill the sink , sterilize them that way. Same with the old coppers. We used to boil these puddings in the coppers and that was it. You know what the favourite pudding was? Apple pie. They used to love apple pie and custard ... Never had no complaints. Always got on very, very well. They were honest girls, that was everything ... you'd got to be honest ...

We used to sell towels, shoes for the baths ... these rubber shoes for the baths, soap, everything we used to sell, hot water bottles ... sweets and everything ... and trays and trays of cakes that

Leonard Coleman's shop, Belvoir Road, Coalville

Jack Miles, one of the first customers, Whitwick canteen

used to come. We used to have them from the Co-op ... but at the finish I think they came from Rawdon. There was a big canteen, you know, at Rawdon ... it was altogether different ... it was strict after the Coal Board took over than what it was ... in a good many ways. You'd got to order properly. It was no good ringing through and saying you'd run out of cheese or anything like that. You'd get told off over it. When the Coal Board took over you'd got to send your order in every week and you'd got to make that order last you. They didn't like you to borrow from another canteen. We used to have a man come in in a morning to do the floors for us, in the canteen. Of course, in the kitchen we used to do those ourselves. I used to make the pastry and prepare the meals ... and set the menu for them ... we used to sell cigarettes, ice cream, everything.

I remember fetching a cylinder of pudding out the copper one day. I'd made jam roly poly and, you know, I'd picked up the cylinder and the jam all run out and run down my leg. By gum, didn't I squeal. They heard me on the bank. Had to go to the Royal. My leg was all right afterwards.

We used to go to the miners' home in Skegness. It's a disabled home but we used to go there for the weekend and stay ... we used to go on a Friday, come back on a Sunday ... the staff hadn't used to go, just the manageresses.

Len Bramley: I'd take four sandwiches. Well, I wouldn't always take it from home, I'd go in the canteen and buy something. Well, you got extra cheese rations during the war but cheese, it gets a bit boring and they'd have meat sandwiches in the canteen and I'd go buy some of them. They were ham or beef which you wouldn't get at home. I've forgotten the price of them, but they were very cheap.

Sir Derek Ezra (Chairman N.C.B.) and Ronnie Oliver 1973

Philip Gill: I was about seventeen and a half when I went there [1950]. I think if your father worked at the mines you'd got a good chance of getting a job there. I started on the bank. I was shoving tubs round on rails where they used to tip them up onto a steel conveyor and then the men used to pick the stone out and the bad coal and the good coal and fill them in wagons. In the Winter we used to have a burner, a big tin, and burn coal to keep us warm and we used to do a bit of toast in the morning...used to be seven o'clock and I think I used to work 'til about quarter-past, half-past two then.

Then I went down the mine with the tally man. Used to collect the tallies on the pit top. They used to send them down, they used to put them on a board and then they used to collect them as they came out the pit. So you knew if anybody hadn't collected their tally they were still left in the pit or lost in the pit. The first day they told me to go and clean some windows, but there were two little windows in this tally office as we used to call it.

I wasn't frightened ... I think you're born to be a miner and that's it. I wasn't frightened, it was a good experience. You'd have electric lights in the pit bottom and then where you went out of the pit bottom into the gate roads it was just pit darkness...you got used to it. If you were frightened of small places you were no good being a miner.

In the pit bottom there used to be two rails where all the tubs used to come down with the coal in. I started working there, scotching the tubs up. Big tubs. There used to be ton of coal in each one...a matter of two hundred yards from the pit bottom, from the shaft. You'd be getting one coming about every thirty seconds or a minute and we used to take them down, a string of probably twelve or fifteen. You used to have a bar, about a six foot bar... there used to be two grooves each side and you used to put these grooves on the rails in front of the tub wheels...and then we'd take them down to the pit bottom. Two men at the bottom, they used to let a lever go and two tubs

31

used to roll onto the cages. Then they'd wind them up and send them round the rails on the pit top and tip them onto the steel container and then they'd come back down again. Eventually they did bring the belt right down into the pit bottom and they changed to skip winding later on. In the pit bottom, when I was a lad, we used to send our billycans up and somebody on pit top used to go across to the canteen and fill them up with tea, then send them down. But nine times out of ten they banged them down that much as they spilt the tea. I can remember times, the undermanager, named Street, he used to have one and we used to drink his tea and then tell him it got tipped up! He wasn't a bad gaffer, he wasn't.

Len Bramley: I didn't go to the pit to get the job, I knew the bank gaffer and I knew what pub he went in, in Coalville. He were a bloke named Bill Keeling and he was boss of the surface on the pit side ... the coal processing side. I knew he went in the pub Friday nights and I was fifteen and a half, 1943, and I used to go in the back room in The Red House, which is The Steam Packet now. I went to him and said, "Good evening Mr Keeling, any chance of a job at your place on the surface?" and he says, "Have you got your cards?" So I says, "No, but if there's the chance of a job I can get them within a week." He said, "Well then, you get your cards and come and see me again." So the next Friday I went to the pub and he was there and I think he'd forgotten who I were, but he said, "Come and see me half past six Monday morning." I went and saw him in his office and I signed a book and after a while he took me down this belt and he showed me what I'd got to do. I went in a wagon with a lad named Robinson from Thringstone, learning the job.

This bloke, a very old man from Belton, he'd pick lumps of coal off the belt, put them on this board and you used to have to take them off and stack them in the wagon. Not chuck it down, it was quality coal what they used to send off somewhere. It was handpicked coal and you would just keep stacking that coal in that wagon. I've often thought how many wagons I used to stack in a day. It'd be something like three wagons a day. In them days nobody wanted slack, they wanted lump coal ... it was handpicked and it was advertised as such. It was Middle Lount coal which was very good house coal, a soft coal. There were two wagons what were 'best coal' and that was Lower Main and that was first class coal. That belt was four foot wide, moving slowly, and by the time it had got to the end of its run most of the lumps had been picked off and the smaller stuff then'd be brought to the screens where it'd be mechanically graded into cubes, cobbles, down to slack.

It were either called stacking or setting. My hands were very, very sore. I'd got really soft hands and it did play on them. Once they got used to it I didn't mind it. In fact I put gloves on to lessen the impact on my hands but gloves on that job, they didn't last five minutes. In them days, pay was fifty bob a week. In fact, when I left Clutsom and Kemps, that was twenty six shillings ... when I went to the pit I doubled what I was earning and, well, they always said pit were poor pay but it was certainly a lot better for me.

I stopped on that job, well, it'd be September when I went there, and the following May ... I went down ... working on the cage. They'd send this coal up on the cage and it was a double-deck cage and there'd be four tubs on the cage, two on each deck and when they run on the cage they used to push two empties off. Them two empties, I used to push them then to a creeper, which was like a chain what used to take them to the top of a hill and they used to run down to the haulage where they'd be distributed throughout the mine. When you started, 'til you finished, you was on continuously. In fact you was like a clock. In the Winter, very, very cold. That shaft bottom, it could be uncomfortable because water was dropping on you all the while. Dropping on your hands, making your hands sore, damping your clothes.

I became a ropeman and I stayed a ropeman for something like thirty years until I finished. It was rope splicing...steel rope. It's a job that if you ever see it done it looks like a Chinese puzzle. But when you know it, it comes effortless to you. This is down the mine. Endless ropes and direct ropes, towards the last twenty years they were used really extensively. There weren't a roadway hardly in the mine without one in. What it is, it's a haulage drum and you wrap it round the drum, run it in round a wheel, back and round a return wheel and join it together by splicing. Then you'd tighten it up and it'll pull equipment, tubs, supplies. This equipment, it was really heavy. It was beyond horses and you'd got to have some mechanical means of doing it. You'd got to have ropemen for repairing them and keeping them in tension. They constantly wanted watching.

Fred Ketcher: When I left Bardon quarry I moved to a job with Dick Wheatley, up Ashburton Road, Hugglescote. We had two lorries, one was a Model T Ford. I was running coal from Nailstone Colliery up to the Cliffe Hill Quarry which was highly mechanised. You only carried about a ton to twenty five hundredweight, that was your weight for a Model T, so you made journey after journey to Cliffe Hill to supply the narrow gauge engines, the steam lorries and steam diggers. This was 1932 and I used to think as I come out the gates of Nailstone colliery how long the coal would last. And I've seen it run out, haven't I? I've seen it run out.

George Clarke: I started at Nailstone Wood Colliery in 1940, as a lad. Mr Maxwell Turner owned Nailstone Wood Colliery and all the farms belonging to the colliery and every time he used to come over on holiday to the White House, that's what they called it, we went out on a shoot. And I was one of them as used to go round beating, beating the hedges, for the rabbits and the pheasants to come out.

On my last job I worked in the outloaders ... the lorry used to come under the screen and I'd press a button and it'd lower a belt down ... and the lorry would go under this here belt and I should start the machine up, the belt up and the coal would come along and it'd drop in this lorry until it's full. Well there's a big hopper at the belt, nearly as high as that church steeple ... and that gets full with coal and that's where the coal drops onto the belt and into your lorry. ... and I used to sign the ticket, sign my name on it and they had to go down the weighbridge to weigh it over, then they come out up the Crown Hill. I've loaded them from all over the country these lorries. Some of them used to come in for a load of coal for the prisons.

Up the hopper ... on the girders round the top of the hopper, high as that church steeple, there were pigeons all round there. They call them 'homers' — pigeons as have lost their way ... I bet if you went there now you'd find no end of pigeons up in those buildings, up in those hoppers.

Edith Roberts: My father was a deputy at Ibstock Colliery and that closed in 1929. Then he went to Nailstone Colliery which they always called 'the wood'. He went as deputy, then he was overman and he finished as training officer. They used to call him Major Sharpe because in the 14/18 war he was a regimental sergeant major for the 8th Leicesters. Very, very strict but he said a spade was a spade and we all adored him.

Although my father had a good position, it was very poorly paid ... The mines then were owned ... privately. Well, Maxwell Turner from London was one of the people who owned Nailstone Colliery and he was like a god. And everybody really had to bow down to him. And the wages were terrible, really. They were really terrible.

Leslie Roberts: My father was the sawyer at Snibston Colliery and as far as I am aware he worked there for forty-five years. His work was cutting all the timber that was used down the pit to size and seeing that the orders that were sent for went down to the pit on the day they were ordered. He'd got men that brought timber to him — pit props and things like that, that probably wanted shortening.

As a child I used to go down, especially school holidays. I liked to make it on a Friday because Friday was pay day and there were the odd men there that would slip you the penny after they got paid. I'd only be about ten or eleven [1934] when I used to visit him and then walk home with him at night. [Where he worked] it was dark, very, very draughty and noisy because the saw and a lot of the machinery for the fitting shop, which was next door, was driven from the one motor — all overhead shafting and belting. So it was noisy, dusty and very, very dismal.

The biggest one that we used (I went to work with him later in life) was a forty-two inch circular saw ... and he used to sharpen all his own saws .. he'd do one a day. The saw bench would be about six feet long and three feet wide — a massive cast-iron thing ... no safety devices. When I went to work there, on one occasion, we were in the shop and there was a terrific explosion. The free pulley which was going round all the time ... one of the wheels had just disintegrated and shattered all over the shop ... nobody hurt.

I wanted to be a carpenter. Tommy Heap, the headmaster said, "No way! I've got a job for you." I went to work at this place [insurance brokers]. A little office — gas light — and the first thing I'd got to do when I got there was sweep the place out, empty the fireplace, light the fires, polish the brass plate outside before we started doing the office work ... I only worked there for about eleven months and I left of my own volition and I went to South Leicester Colliery and got a job there. I'd already been sent to Whitwick Colliery by the headmaster, to get a job there. There were two of us went from Broom Leys School and the headmaster said, "You ask for ten shillings a week." Another lad from another school asked for seven and sixpence and he got the job.

I started as office boy. Well, first you had to go to the Post Office and get a big leather sack which was locked in the Post Office and take all of it down to the managing director's house. He lived on Ashburton Road in Hugglescote. That was Mr Canner. The mail had got to be on the chair in his conservatory at half past seven in the morning. Then you went home, had your breakfast and went back again. By that time, there'd be two bags. One was the general mail for the office and the other one was all the orders for the railway office. You had to drop the general mail at the office and take the other down to the railway office — bike over a couple of fields down to the railway office — dump the bag there and then come back and start your general office duties.

You were the run-around for all the office staff. Mid morning you had to go to the shop at the corner [South Street, Ellistown] owned by a man named Newbold — it was an off-licence. Well, one or two of the old boys there, used to have a half pint ... old Mr Harris who was virtually in charge ... he used to like his half pint of beer. He always used to keep it in the safe. Some time later, when we had a new office boy, he went to fetch the beer and it was a very frosty day and he skidded and fell off his bike, the beer went ... the cork came out and spilled. This lad didn't know what to do so he nipped into the toilet and filled it up with water ... dinnertime came and Mr Harris had his sandwiches and his half pint of beer. He says, "I don't know what it is, my lad but the beer tastes a bit weak today." He was an old boy and he used to bike it from Ravenstone to Ellistown every day. He was full of arthritis — could hardly walk.

There was no smoking in the offices or anything like that. The pens and pencils were kept locked in a cupboard. You went and asked Mr Harris for anything like that, even to a pen nib ... you couldn't use fountain pens because of the very thin columns in the wages book — there was only room for the very fine pens. No-one was allowed to smoke during working hours ... they used to wait for Mr Canner going out at lunchtime or when he went home — about four o'clock — we went home at five — as soon as they heard his door click, one of the old boys would climb off his stool ... he used to peep over the frosted glass partition and say, "He's gone up South Street." Or he'd probably gone through the colliery yard and over the fields — walk that way home ... then they'd light up. They'd always be peeping over the glass to see which way the boss

34

had gone ... If he went through the colliery yard and down by the railway offices, we would ring the railway office to let them know he was on his way so Tommy Shaw, there, would put his pipe out. Being in the railway office, you could smoke all day down there. That all changed when we all came back from the war. We were all a bit bolshie, I think, then and they used to smoke in the office and didn't take much notice of rules and regulations.

Reg Thomas: When I left school [1941] I quite frankly didn't know what to do ... mathematics and all that was my strong suit ... There was a requirement at Desford Colliery for a young surveyor lad ... so I was invited to go for an interview for that. And I was accepted. Those things happened funny in those days — if somebody liked you, you got the job ... You had to be the office boy at Desford Colliery before you did anything. When I was getting the coal in, in the winter, for the clerks in the office, I used to really fret — what have I got my school certs for, just to get the coffee and fetch sandwiches from the canteen and make the fires, come early in the morning and fill the inkwells up, stop at Bagworth Colliery to get the post — never come on the bus because you had to get the post — and I was miffed about that in a sense ... this usually happened for a year. You had to be the office boy.

I remember one day, I was making fires up in the office, Mr Butterley's office, and he got a helmet off his peg and he stuck it on my head. He says, "Well, Reggie, my lad, I think you're ready now." That's when I stopped being the office boy. They set a new office boy on there and then which I had to take in hand for a couple of weeks. I gave him a good hiding every other day. I was power mad then. But then I became the apprentice surveyor. I was the only one and it started from there.

Billy Sargisson ... he was the land sale office clerk ... and it was a scene from Dickens ... very high sloping tables with a very high stool. He was a thoroughly conscientious servant of the company. I thought he was over a hundred when I was the lad in 1941. His office door was always open ... one day we were snowballing in the colliery yard right outside — the office staff were snow fighting the electrical shop. A shower of wet snow balls poured down on Billy Sargisson's ledger and Billy was not at all amused but being the ardent churchgoer that he was, he had a lot of difficulty finding the right words to express his tantrums.

Every quarter the surveyor has to go down the mine and make a map of exactly where they are on that date ... to map the underground workings. But you also map them in relation to the surface, so also you've got to correlate the surface with the underground and this is very high tech surveying. And then we have to link other collieries to ours ... and then drive tunnels between areas underground and other collieries. And we're advancing, exploring headings all over the place to get new territory opened up in different seams because there were seven or eight seams. You have to be a bit of a geologist because occasionally you lose the seam you're in and have to go looking for it. It has geological fingerprints that you go looking for.

Tom Biddle, a splendid character, getting towards his sixties. He was the overman at Number One pit ... in charge of the whole underground workings ... I always felt totally safe underground when he was with us ... he could shout the men out of our line of sight when we were surveying ...especially going down the coalface. If we asked them to shift, they'd tell us (ever so politely!) to come back on the night shift ... he was capable of a violent temper at times. But he was also a devout Jehovah's Witness and I never, ever heard him swear but, I tell you what, his alternative vocabulary was vast. What he could say without swearing, you wouldn't believe!

I had to do air sampling. You used to fill little like footballs up with a pump at various places at the pit, the coalface ... you'd pump up a little balloon with air and it'd be sent off to the laboratory. They'd test for methane gas and carbon dioxide and oxygen.

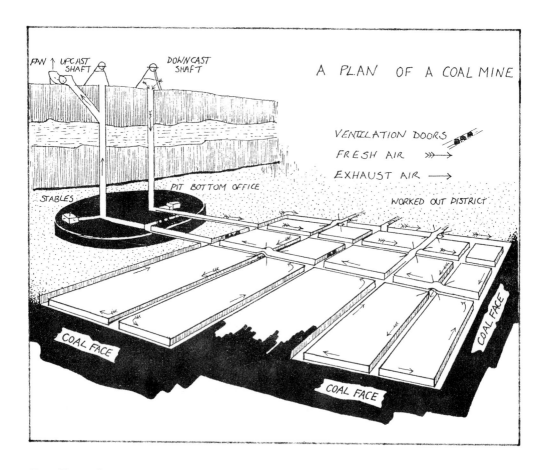

A PLAN OF A COAL MINE

Len Bramley: They'd only use canaries if there'd been an explosion and they wanted to test for gas. Well, there's two types of gas. There's black damp and methane. Methane's high explosive and, well, I don't think that knocks a canary off its perch. The gas that knocks them off their perch is what they term black damp ... I think it's air that's starved of oxygen and it makes you feel tired and want to shut your eyes and if you ever do that, you'll die. That's fatal, that is. In fact, there has been accidents where somebody's gone into a disused road which they shouldn't go in and there's damp and it's got them. Very dangerous stuff because when you're in it you don't feel any unpleasantness, it just sends you to sleep, makes you sit down and nod off and you just die.

Reg Thomas: When we got Merry Lees as well as Desford Colliery, I used to disappear down Desford shaft about seven o'clock of an evening, go twelve miles underground to every coalface with these great piles of balloons — bags — on my shoulder and come out at Merry Lees about six o'clock the next morning. The finest experience I've ever had in mining was to come out of Merry Lees drift after being air sampling all night, on my own, to smell hay being cut. I tell you, that's magic.

Mr Butterley sent me off to Cardiff University for a week's course to do the actual analysis. We had an analysis laboratory at Desford ... instead of sending our air samples to a central lab, I did them ... that's how Mr Butterley prompted me to do things — that was very encouraging.

Air measuring, that was just a case of making sure the quantity of air moving within the various parts of the coalmine were enough for the purpose. The Mines' Inspector would always want to look at your air sample quality and your air ventilation quantity. So they were very important features. And you had to take dust samples every month throughout the pit.

Jack Adcock: All the collieries had two shafts. Now, one was called the down-cast shaft and the other the up-cast shaft. On the up-cast shaft at the surface ... there was a big fan ... The down-cast shaft was for the air going down and then coming up the up-cast shaft, going through the pit and coming up. That provided fresh air all the while ... It was a big fan wheel — I should say a ten foot wheel — spinning round and round and pulling air out of the pit.

Reg Thomas: I went to the Coalville Tech to learn surveying but then Mr Butterley (splendid, kind man to me) he fixed it. I went to the University of Nottingham one day a week ... I had three years there ... I sat my exams in 1945 and passed them. I was a qualified surveyor at twenty-one — the minimum age.

In the time of the Desford Coal Company ... there was this thing called the excess profits tax ... they thought they'd open a new mine — Merry Lees — on the excess profits ... and so we sunk Merry Lees drift. Mr Butterley cut the first turf, I remember Mr Skelding cut the second and I jollywell cut the third ... We saw that project through, of course. And in subsequent years when I'd got Desford to myself, while Mr Skelding was away, I had my 'Channel Tunnel' ... I was surveyor on the tunnel that joined the two together ... That's a frightening prospect for a lad of about twenty-two or three for his first big job. This was going to be the main transportation route between the two collieries, hence its importance in alignment and level. The day before we were due to break through, Harry Mee sat with me at the Desford side of this tunnel and says, "I reckon as if it will come out about there." and he pointed his stick about four feet off the centre line. Well, I was worried sick ... of course, I needn't have worried because it came through the next day absolutely dead on line. But he chuckled no end, the way he'd put the wind up me that day.

I was given surveying at all sorts of places — Nailstone, for a very short time, Snibston, from time to time, South Leicester also, New Lount, Whitwick (when their surveyor left). But when I came to apply for the Whitwick job properly, I was accepted for it and to my horror, Mr Torrance [the manager] vetoed it. This made me very cross, so cross I was almost going to write him a letter ... but he had better things in mind. A week or two after, the Area Chief Planner called at Snibston to see me ... told me I was required to go to Coleorton as a group planner which was above the job I'd lost at Whitwick.

I left the Coal Board to be the project planner of a new town. Nobody could have had it better than that. I'd have done both jobs for nothing.

Eli Hague: ... I sat down and wrote a letter to the manager of Snibston pit, never having been in a pit in my life before — but engines to me were engines, don't care whether they're on a ship or in a cotton mill or in a pit, you see. Eventually a gentleman from up the road (used to work in the Snibston offices) ... he called in one day and he said, "Mr Emmerson would like to see you ... he's the agent for the colliery and for South Leicester colliery."

So I went to South Leicester where this Mr Emmerson ... he was there along with the manager, Mr Sam McKee. He asked me one or two questions ... then he says, "Why are you leaving Pegson's?" It seemed an innocent enough question but I sensed something or other than requiring an answer just to that simple question. I said, "What do you mean by that?" "Well, I'll be frank with you. Is there any reason why you should leave?" And I says, "Yes, there is a reason. I want more money and I want some coal." "Well," he says. "I just wondered why a man with your background wants to come and work at the pit." He said, "You've been through the pit yard. You've seen the dirt and the dust. I wonder why a man of your qualifications should want to come and work at the pit." "Well," I said. "That's rather intriguing because about a month ago I went to the court and there was a man up for committing some offence." (I'd gone up because I'd

37

committed an offence, you see — we'd had a little bit of horseplay at Pegson's and we'd damaged some woodwork and they wanted to sue us ... and Emmerson was the magistrate, you see, and I remember when they had found him [the other man] guilty they gave him a choice of sentence. He could either go to prison or opt to join the army or go down the pit ...) I reminded him of this and I said, "It seems to me that you equate the pit with prison ... Is pit work so degrading that you can equate it with ...." "Oh, no, but there are people who've been brought up to expect to go in the pit and you're not one of those, are you?" he says. I says, "No, but I think it's a job of work and presumably it's going to get better." Anyway, I got the job. It was like any other job. They made me the assistant engineer so that I very quickly had a nice little promotion. I worked underground and on the surface.

Anyway, there are jobs and jobs and after a time I found that the job was getting a bit monotonous. Quite honestly, to work at a pit is a kind of inherited thing. Fathers work at pits and sons go to the pits perhaps because that's what they expect. They love it. I don't know why but by the time you've slobbed about through the slop and the muck and the mire on a pit surface (we had no pithead baths, you see) I began to get a bit fed up. So I looked for a job and strangely enough they were advertising one at the Tech. to teach engineering, mining engineering. Well, I thought, that's ideal, just down my street. So I applied for the job and the funny thing was, it was Emmerson who I'd fallen out with many times on points of policy, was the chairman of the governors of the Technical College and I thought, well, that's my chance gone for a burton.

But I remember, Emmerson, he said to Mr Burrows [the principal], "Well now, I can't appoint this gentleman. I'm only here in an advisory capacity but if I was the principal, I would have no hesitation in doing so. But don't let this influence you in any way." And I thought, I've got this job! And, of course, I did and I spent twenty-five years there.

Peter Smith: I spent thirty years in the coal industry, 'til 1987 ... My first job was in the Cost Department at Coleorton Hall, which was the Area Headquarters. Then I moved into the Capital Expenditure Office for five years and in those days there was millions of pounds being spent on reconstruction of the collieries of Leicestershire, and at that time South Derbyshire. South Derbyshire merged with the Leicestershire coalfield during the 1950s and so it meant that in addition to the nine Leicestershire collieries there were also nine taken over and controlled from Coleorton from South Derbyshire. A number of these collieries were geographically in Leicestershire but as far as the coalfield was concerned they were designated as South Derbyshire. For instance Measham, Donisthorpe and Rawdon ... so it meant that it was an interesting job. I enjoyed it in capital expenditure because my job was to look after the major projects, which was generally the complete reconstruction of collieries following nationalisation in 1947. A lot of money had to be spent in order to modernise them. It wasn't spent haphazardly. You had to prove that it would be a worthwhile project and this had to be approved by Hobart House in London. So you didn't just go ahead and spend, spend, spend, it was controlled.

At that time Leicester was a profitable coalfield, therefore you were putting money where it would be to the advantage of the National Coal Board in the longer term. They certainly didn't want to put in millions where there was doubt about the colliery's future. Obviously, errors were made because you can never tell, geologically, whether you were going to meet hazards such as water or uneven faces or falls ... all these things. Despite all the bore holes you can sink it can still prove to be wrong in hindsight. But at the time all were thought to be sound. The one glaring example where millions was spent and never recouped was the Cadley Hill colliery where there was a major reconstruction. Cost almost half of what it would to have sunk a new colliery and yet due to geological conditions Cadley Hill never really took off in the next twenty odd years and consequently closed with reserves still underground.

Coleorton Hall, N.C.B Headquarters

One of the major items on the surface was the treatment of the coal once it came to the surface, and the coal preparation plants were one of the major items of capital expenditure. To screen and wash the coal and ensure that there was a viable product to sell at the end of the day ... because obviously coal straight out of the bowels of the earth is not in a fit state to sell to customers, in particular our major customer, East Midlands Electricity Board.

Not all our collieries had got a pit head baths and canteen of reasonable standard. In fact, no pit head baths at all at some places, and so they were built. Also, the winding gear. Again, it had to be electrified ... which was partly underground, partly surface. And, of course, the change underground, the faces, from being hand-filled as we called it, which meant that the men had to go with pick and shovel and hew it out and it had to be moved by tubs probably pulled by a poor old pony. That was changed to a mechanical face. Whereas in the past you'd have dozens of men working on the face, it then resulted, with mechanisation, with machinery, down to as few as ten men who could produce as much coal as a hundred or two by the hand-filled method. But, of course, this all costs money. Roof supports as well were important ... and of course the haulage systems ... were electrified and the pit pony became redundant. Plus, the pit bottom area. Again, that had to be reorganised in order to cope with the increased volume of coal which resulted from mechanisation.

In the old days there was just the colliery manager and then he would have an undermanager and then there'd be the overman and then a few deputies and a few shotfirers on the staff side. But with mechanisation you'd then got to have a colliery electrical engineer, a colliery mechanical engineer, deputy managers — 'planning'; deputy managers — 'production', in order to oversee this change from manual work to mechanised.

There were less jobs, certainly, from the days of hand-filling. This was one of the reasons for change. When you did change from hand-fill to mechanised you'd got to prove that it was going to be viable financially and, of course, the main item of cost was labour and so it would save so many jobs. To compensate that, partly, it meant that in the old days there was probably only the day shift which was the main coal-turning shift. With mechanisation it meant you'd got to use this machinery more often to get the maximum benefit out of it and so you would certainly have an afternoon shift turning coal and in some cases also a night shift turning coal. But you've still got to have time for maintenance. That's an important aspect. When you've got machinery it's got to be maintained, and so you had to allow time for maintenance but this was mainly carried out at weekends.

The machinery was British. Yes, some famous names such as Dowty who were associated with the Desford Colliery Band. The props and machinery, almost exclusively, would be built in this country. Also, the Coal Board would assist these suppliers. At Bretby Engineering we had a testing and design centre where equipment could be tested and ideas passed to the suppliers of mining machinery and materials in order to constantly improve the standards of the machinery and the materials.

Well, when I left Capital Expenditure after five years, I applied for a job in Internal Audit. Internal Audit was a statutory requirement of the National Coal Board following nationalisation. There had to be a department of internal check. There were also outside auditors as there always had been and they were to continue.

This type of work interested me. It would mean that I would be visiting every colliery in the area and Coleorton Hall became the centre not just for Leicestershire collieries but, in the 1950s, South Derbyshire were merged and came under Coleorton's control and in 1967 the Warwickshire collieries merged ... and in 1976 the Kent colllieries also came under the control of Coleorton. So it meant that being in Internal Audit one had to travel to, not only the nine collieries in Leicestershire and the nine in South Derbyshire, but also the five which were then in Warwickshire and the three down in Kent. The reason that Coleorton took over Kent was that we were the nearest to them still in operation.

It was our job to ensure the N.C.B's assets and resources and materials and finance were not being misappropriated and so when I first joined in 1962 every colliery had to be visited each year and audits such as sales of the coal, road and rail, wages and salaries, the cashiers department, canteen and the pit-head baths and the stores, the purchasing and usage of materials, and the mobile and surface plant and also underground plant. All of these had to be checked systematically to a particular programme to ensure that as far as possible things were being run in accordance with the Board's agreements and instructions.

As with mechanisation at the collieries, so into the Board's systems in the later 1960s was introduced the computer. From a department ... which had fifteen people, by the early 1980s, that was reduced to just two because the computer could reject most instances if there were plans to misappropriate the Board's assets or finances, and it didn't require the individual person to be checking that this was so. And so ... I was made redundant from the Audit Department after eighteen years, in 1981, and for the last six years of my working life with the National Coal Board I was at the Central Workshops at Swadlincote.

I went to Central Workshops as the assistant to the workshops' accountant, mainly on costs. The workshops, their function was to repair colliery machinery underground and on the surface and they'd got to do it competitively because the collieries were the workshops' customers and they

wanted not to be ripped off, so workshops were set up. In fact, prior to the strike — of 1984 —
there were twenty-six workshops around the country. After the strike, within a very short time
that had whittled down to eight.

Ernie Harris: When I started to work in 1927, most men either walked or cycled. A man
called Arch Wright had a lorry that he carted coal on during the day and he had a contraption that
he lowered onto it to make it into a bus and he did that specifically for fetching miners to work.
He gave it a name and it was called Llewellyn. I remember one winter morning, there was ice
and snow and rain and we set off at half past five and we didn't get out of the village, the lorry
went all the wrong ways despite his efforts. We tried to walk but we kept falling down and never
did make it to work.

Don Connolly: There were no buses went to Desford Colliery [1940s]. You had to go down
to Merry Lees ... and you were still in your black, there were no baths or anything. You'd have
this problem of getting on the bus in your black when there were people there, ordinary passengers.
They used to look really down on you, to get on the bus black-faced and so on. Very often you'd
have your helmet on as well, you know. That bus would take you to Western Boulevard in

A miners' bus

Leicester. We used to catch the Corporation bus then, outside the West End Club, to the Clock
Tower. One day (me and my dad invariably sat on the seat next to the entrance ... and the seats
used to face inside) me and my dad would get up, maybe, coming down High Street in order to
get off the bus first, and as we got up this old lady, she put her hand in her purse and give this
shilling to my dad. She says, "There you are, old chap." She says, "That'll get you a cup of tea."
She thought we were a pair of tramps!

Jack Jones: It was not until the middle sixties that miners, to any degree, started to acquire motor vehicles. The motorbike and the push bike sheds were absolutely full in those times. There used to be several double decker buses come from Leicester and bring miners. Very, very few cars indeed. And it was something of a pleasure for miners to travel to work in a motor vehicle. We used to share the costs of running that vehicle between us.

The Leicestershire mines are not deep mines and so one can get very cold places. Also, by the same token, depending on the amount of work ... bearing in mind that most of the work in those days was of a heavy, physical nature, you did work stripped off with what was termed a sham — that was just a vest and a pair of trousers ... in a colder area you did require a pullover and in some places, actually a jacket as well. What we used to wear then, was moleskins — moleskin trousers which were the miners' uniform. They absorbed the sweat. They were strong but used to become very stiff when they dried out but they were warm and they did keep quite a lot of the wet out.

There were no facilities at Desford at that time [1950s]. You got wet through going to work and you worked in the same conditions. You had a wash down because there was no real bath facilities in the Council houses at those times.

Carl Brown: The miners' trousers were all patches ... carbide lamps were the order of the day on the bicycles (it did stink when you dropped it in a puddle) and should the water freeze for the lamp — I leave you to imagine what the men did to thaw it out (or so I was told).

Lena Gee: My husband worked on the coalface. Moleskin trousers ... were far too expensive so we saved everyday cast-offs ... these had to be 'faced and arsed'. The facing was a large deep patch of strong material ... almost like canvas and it was hard to sew ... a patch starting mid-thigh and reaching well past each knee. The bottom of the patch would be hemmed and left loose so that the coal dust, when they were kneeling, could fall through it. The other patch had to be large enough to cover the backside. We used to buy special thread to sew them up with. Pit breeches and patching were the bane of miners' wives.

At Home

Arthur Bale: We used to go up to the golf links at Swannington on Saturday ... we used to go caddying, my cousin and myself. I should be about eight or nine ... we didn't do it for nothing — perhaps threepence or sixpence, it depended ... of course, that was quite a bit for us in them days. One of the teachers used to go down there regularly.

I think it was about 1914, Good Friday. Of course, the Co-op bakers used to come round then and they used to blow a whistle and you used to have to go out and get your bread and such like. On this Good Friday they'd got the hot cross buns on as well. Later on in the afternoon there was such a commotion. Bakers were coming round blowing the whistle as hard as they could ... folks were running out to see what was the matter. "Don't eat them hot cross buns if you bought any this morning." Somebody had mixed them with engine oil instead of cooking oil so folks chucked them out of the road.

And then to cap the lot, Burgess's factory took fire that same day ... poor old chaps had to go to the Council yard and it were just a trolley affair with the pumping doings on and they had to run with that. There were no horse-drawn do then. They used to have to run down the streets as hard as they could pulling this here trap behind them. Good job it weren't a serious fire, else there'd have been no Burgess's factory today.

Eric Burton: The house I was born in [1920] it was in Ravenstone ... Pipey Lane. There used to be a blacksmith's shop attached to it. And I can always remember that blacksmith's shop. You could smell the old hooves burning as the smith was doing the shoes. At Christmas time, we always had happy memories of that house ... we could not afford this Christmas tree business. My father always used to hang a big holly bush up from the ceiling. That holly bush, it used to serve two purposes because at the end of the Christmas thing, my father used to tie that old holly bush on to big sticks, shove it up the chimney to sweep it ... if it got fast in the chimney my father used to put some paper up and set fire to it. Childhood days were very sweet in Ravenstone.

The water we used to have to fetch from the well down Jenny's Lane ... every day with two buckets. There was no electric light, no gas, we used to have the old paraffin lamp on the table. My father, when he used to come home from the the the pit, as black as the ace of spades, we used to have the old tin bath in front of the fire ... my mother used to wash his back for him ... My mother was very particular. As soon as my father came in ... she used to bring the hot water in a bucket and tip it in the bath.

We all had jobs to do. My job, right from when I was about seven years of age, I always had to have the firewood ready for my father to light the fire with the next morning. If I'd gone out playing and forgot, my father used to still make me go get the firewood from somewhere ... gather firewood, take a sack bag and go round the fields and collect any old dead wood up and get enough firewood to last me the week. My sisters all had their jobs to do in the house. Every Saturday morning my sisters used to have to black-lead the fireplace and they used to have to do the ironing. My brother used to help with the gardening.

Edith Roberts: You made your entertainment in the little village [Battram], that's what we did. There was a little Wesleyan church and that were everything. We used to have social evenings and all do something ... we always had tea and we used to think it was lovely because you had jelly and blancmange and sandwiches ... you thought that was great. It only cost a few pennies to go in. And they always used to get me to say a poem. Now, I was only ever so small as a child and they used to say, "Come on, come on, Edith Sharpe. You say 'Sal's Bonnet'."

I were well-behaved in home but I were a bit of a tom-lad really. With having a brother, if he did anything, I'd do it ... my youngest brother, four years older, that's the one I remember most ... he were murder and he used to put fireworks in people's locks and blow the locks. The policeman used to come — Mr Calow, he were a special constable — and he used to frighten my mum to death ... it were devilment, you see, ... anyway we'd got this old dog, Jack, and there was a hedgehog. The dog had been after it and it made the dog's nose all bleed, so my brother went and got the hedgehog and cut the bristles off ... He'd always been motor-bike mad and he went and bought a motor-bike ... for, I think it was, a shilling and he was riding through fire. He'd set some tyres on fire and he were riding through them on this motor-bike and my father went out ... he made him come in and says, "You can go and throw that now, in the pit." and he had to go and throw it in this big thing as they called the big pit, so he wouldn't ride it again ... he were only about eleven.

It were my mum's birthday ... and he'd walked to Coalville ... and he'd bought her a sixpenny teapot from Woolies. And he'd done something wrong when he got home so my mum shouted at him and he went and buried it ... anyway, he said to Mum, "Do you forgive me now?" She said, "Yes." He said, "Well, I bought you a birthday present. I'll go and dig it up."

Eric Burton: We played tremendous games. We used to have a little game called 'Sound your Holler'. Split yourselves up into two gangs. One gang used to go off and hide and the other had got to find you. Every now and again we used to shout, "Holler!" I used to jump over the back of the cemetery wall where the others daren't come in and find me. We used to make a barrow. Any old wheels we could find and make a barrow. Get an old tomato tin and nail it on the top and put a candle in it. We'd run all over in this here little truck, you know, somebody in it, giving them a ride now and again ... no toys, you couldn't afford toys in those days. We used to make our own fun.

We'd eat all different kinds when we was out, anything that were along, I mean, carrots or anything ... we used to get those from people's fields. I remember the time going round the farmer's fields ... where he'd got taters in, we used to go scratting at the roots and take one from each root until we'd got about a couple of dozen potatoes. Took them home, alright. We used to go scrumping, pinching apples, and take them home. My father didn't approve of this ... I used to get the apples and one of the old-fashioned crisp tins, square one, used to go over the fields and dig a hole in the ground and put the tin in, put the apples inside the tin, put the lid back on and the turf back on and mark it, so's I could go and pick apple out the tin every morning before I went to school.

Margaret Hedges: We were on the border of starvation. My little brother, Maurice, was born in 1926 during the general strike. One day my mother was feeding him at her breast and she collapsed over the fire-guard. And the then midwife ... came in ... and she found her and she took the baby from her, put him in the pram, carried her on to the sofa and said to her, "Have you had anything to eat today?" And she shook her head. "Did you have anything yesterday?" And the nurse said to her, "Well, if you've got nowt in your belly, how can you feed that kid?" She went up and down the row of houses ... and found somebody who could spare some bread and butter. She brought it back to my mother and stayed while she ate it. She said, "Knowing you, you'll only save it for Arthur." (that was my dad).

Mr Jarvis, the milkman from Ibstock ... in those days milk was delivered to your door in a bucket and it was measured out. And when we hadn't much money, my mother would get out the one pint jug instead of the three pint ... Mr Jarvis would push it aside and say, "That little 'un's no good. Where's the big 'un?" And he'd get his milk pail and fill it to the brim. He was wonderful. Years later, his own wife became an invalid ... [my mother] would go down to the farm ... and

44

she would bath the Jarvis boys and put them to bed and she would stay, do anything that wanted doing ... And every Christmas, the Jarvis's would have us all down there for a good old tuck-in and we could see the sides of bacon and the hams hanging on the wall. My mother used to say, " They're the best pictures to hang up." Yes, they were very kind.

Edith Roberts: For May-day, we used to make maypoles on the last day of April. And we used to get up for half past six ... and we'd walk to the blacksmith's shop and sing to them and we used to stand round the fire, singing May songs: "Here we come a-maying, through the meadow straying, maying, maying, you and I. When the blackbird sings and whistles in the Spring and the lilies grow. Here we come a-maying, through the meadow straying, round and round the maypole, trit, trit, trot, to see what a fine maypole we have got. A rig and a rag and a very fine flag. For it is the first of May ..." They all used to give us money.

Phyllis Palmer: For May the first, my father used to decorate my hoop up with all flowers and one on my hair. You'd go to one or two neighbours and sing: "Here we come a-maying, through the meadow straying. Maying, maying, you and I." And then they'd probably give us a ha'penny. It was quite the thing on May morning, before you went to school.

Sim Woolley: We used to go round the colliery climbing up the screens and the only danger, of course, was the mine shaft ... on the old colliery spoil bank ... where they used to take all the coal that was of no use, dump it on the top and let it slide down — I should say it was about one hundred and fifty foot high and occupied two or three acres by the time it was completed — as children we used to go on the top of this bank and there was an old shed there ... and we dismantled part of this shed, it was corrugated iron sheets, turned up the front and decided that we'd do a skiing effort down the side of this spoil heap. Of course, in those days it was a matter of spontaneous combustion ... it was alight and smouldering. Four of us would get on this sheet of zinc, push it over the edge and slide down ... but one day we all came off and landed in this hot ash and quite a few of us got our legs burnt.

There used to be what they called the powder house and I often shudder nowadays to think of the tricks we used to get up to and why we were not blown sky-high because when the miners used to go down the pit, they used to collect this powder from the powder house in little tins ... and they'd fill these tins and just knock it and put the cap on ... but under the door when they shut it, was powder floating about which had dropped from the tins. We, as children, used to scrape this powder together on a bit of paper and take it a few yards away and have great fun in lighting it and seeing it go phsst! not realising that it could have tracked itself back to the powder magazine. However, fortune must have been on our side because nothing ever happened.

There was a loco shed right at the end of the colliery ... and this train used to run from Ibstock colliery to Bagworth sidings ... I remember a gang of children that I was with one day, we went into this engine and the men hadn't put it away very well and we went in and fiddled with the levers and one of the lads decided to experiment and he opened a valve and he did in fact get the train going. It gave a few puffs and then ran out of steam ... probably as well that it did because it was going towards the end of the loco house!

Reg Thomas: ...Ibstock Colliery was closed and we used to play around it as kids ... we used to go and chuck bricks down the shaft and hear them splashing in the water. We did all sorts of silly things, dangerous things, like that. That is of particular interest to me — chucking these bricks and hearing them splash — because later in life I was, in fact, for a certain time the surveyor of Nailstone Colliery and I went down that Ibstock shaft because they de-watered Ibstock shafts to help the safety of Nailstone ... I went with the manager of Nailstone Colliery down Ibstock shaft in a bucket and actually stood at the bottom of the shaft on the bricks which I'd chucked down that shaft many years ago. It was a thrill, it really was ... it was a sad thrill because my dad worked at Nailstone Colliery ... and he got the sack because of an infringement of the Coal Mines Regulations that he was totally unaware of...

Margaret Hedges: ... One day he was called to the managing director's office — Mr. Jock Robertson — and he was accused of breaking one of the mine's safety rules. My father didn't know what it was all about ... it was a rule that when a cage came up the shaft you couldn't have men on the bottom and materials on the top ... pit props, girders and things. Men always had to travel on top ... For some reason this cage was raised with men underneath and materials on the upper deck. It was a misunderstanding between the man on the bottom and the man on the top ... but my father wasn't aware of it ... my dad pleaded ignorance but he wouldn't hear of it. Then he pleaded that he had my mum and three little children ... he said, "You get out of my office and I don't want to see you again." And worse was to come because my step-brother also worked in that colliery and he dismissed him too.

Mr Butterley was one of the leading people for making arrangements for the nationalisation of the colliery ... one day, this gentleman came into the office from a neighbouring colliery — he was a managing director — to talk about his colliery to Mr Butterley and I was introduced to him and I was given his name — Mr Robertson. Little did he realise as he made a fuss of me then, this little, young secretary, that I was one of those children who suffered because of what he did to my dad, all those years ago.

Harry Sheffield: At about eight [years old] we transferred to Holy Cross School at Whitwick because we were Catholics. I always remember one afternoon as I was at Christchurch [previous school] ... the headmaster called me out after the assembly in the afternoon .. I wondered what I'd done wrong ... the whole school were assembled and he says, "I'm going to tell you this — Matthew Henry Sheffield — he's never been late once for school and he's never missed a class for a whole year." So he gave me five shillings. I don't know who was the most pleased, my mother or me when I gave it her. I gave it my mother. I think it paid the rent.

Reg Thomas: We were attending the Hugglescote School ... there were three of us, my mother had three of us within virtually three years ... throughout the school we appeared to show a bit of form ... and naturally the eleven plus came up. Well, Margaret passed hers, then mine came up the next year and I passed mine and we could do nothing with them because we'd not got the resources at home. At that time Joey Garrett, the headmaster, was starting to make a few noises about the Thomas's being so well prepared educationally but couldn't do anything with it. And that caught the headlines, literally. The Coalville Times took it up, of course, and the Leicester Mercury then picked it up. I can see the picture now — my dad with us three in the garden and the story about us .... my mother wanted no part in it, really. She was a very retiring woman. My dad, he saw the opportunity, I think ... then the Daily Mirror picked it up — POVERTY MAY BAR THEM — that caused quite a stir ... and we had all sorts of strange enquiries. There was a mysterious enquiry from Guernsey to take me to ... there was some worry that I was being asked to be taken to Guernsey to become — we thought there was a German influence in this — and I was being taken away to be brainwashed into being virtually a spy. And my brother, separately, thinks the same.

The Leicester Children's Society (Mr. Smith) got in touch and because of that, bearing in mind that Margaret was now thirteen, beyond the age of going to the Grammar School, they paid for her to go to Clarke's Commercial College in Leicester. Myself, just one year over the odds ... they let me go to the Grammar School with Maurice — Coalville, King Edward VII. ... Now we were embarked on the Grammar School ... I was in 2A and Maurice was in 2B ... Mr. Rigby, the headmaster was reading the results out in the hall ... and he says, "I see the Thomas boys are up there again. Thomas One, top in 2A, Thomas Two, top in 2B. What happens when they come

Maurice, Margaret and Reg Thomas 1937

together in 3A?" The gospel truth, we were joint first. After that guess where I was? Second, second, second. Guess where he was. He was always top. That was highly encouraging to our parents obviously, but must have been for these people of the Society. I beat him once, he was about twenty fifth. He broke his leg and I went top of the class.

With Margaret, she went to Leicester, you see, to college, so they gave her a season ticket for the train and every Friday she had to call and see a Mr Smith ... and he would give her ten shillings per week ... they paid whatever the costs were of the college. She was mixing amongst quite elite people at college ... people of our class didn't go to those sorts of places, and when they queued up to buy books and materials they would just have it booked to an account which was rather toffee-nosed in those days. Now this Mr Smith made sure that Margaret also got it charged similarly to an account to save any embarrassment. In spite of that when there were various outings that the college went on she never went. Mr Smith found this out and he chastised her for not going. He said, "We will always fund it." But she never went, in spite of him insisting, she never felt she should do it ... and the ten shillings a week must have been to give Mother, I would presume.

In my own case, what it cost to go to the Grammar School, they paid directly to the school ... Mr Rigby, the headmaster, always used to buy my caps. And one day ... his secretary came to the classroom and she asked the teacher for me to go and see Mr Rigby. I thought, what on earth? When you've been sent for by the headmaster it's usually for a flogging. And when I got into his office things didn't improve because as I walked in he says, "Come in, Thomas." ... and he started peeling his jacket off and I thought, my Lord, what's going to happen to me now? He said, "Take your jacket off, Thomas." which I did and he said, "Try this on." He was giving me his jacket. That was nice.

Maurice and myself made friends across the entire class, as it were, and it was very revealing because even at that level of class, the place they preferred to be on a Saturday and Sunday night was down at our house because Mum made apple pies for them. It was a marvellous leveller, was that. ... Other children went to the Grammar School and made their way despite being poor but I think the problem we had that there were three of us within three years, made the whole concept of a child's future very difficult.

... Now Maurice was being separately financed by a mysterious Mr Berry ... and he was a clerk in the Education Department, Leicester (living with his mother) ... he did for Maurice what the Society did for me. The difference was, being an educated man himself, he sent Maurice to Cambridge.

Florrie Harris: I had to leave school earlier than I should have done. I should have stayed until I was fifteen but I was the eldest of five and I'd grown out of my tunic (and that was the day when we had to go to school in tunics) ... Mum couldn't afford to buy me another tunic, so she went to school and saw Mr Hill, the headmaster, and asked if I couldn't be allowed to leave because she needed me to earn some money. Mr Hill begged of Mum to let me stay but eventually they granted me permission to leave. I had to leave six months earlier than I should [1930]. I was sad but whatever Mum and Dad said, that was the word. It had to be obeyed.

Mum said she knew of three places that I could go for an interview for work ... the first place was the Wolsey offices in Leicester. There were about fifteen of us and we had to have an examination ... I was the one that was given the chance of a job. Mum said, "How much will it be?" — ten shillings. Kendal's umbrella shop wanted a girl to assist behind the counter. The question came up: "How much will this be?" — just ten shillings. Mum took me down to the factory then, and the factory offered me ten and six and Mum said, "Well, that's it." Just for sixpence. Out of that ten and sixpence, I had to pay five and nine a week bus fare ... I didn't like it at all — making men's suspenders. I would have much preferred an office job. Mum regretted it afterwards ... I've seen her almost in tears because my younger sister did get on better and I wasn't allowed that chance. But it didn't do me any harm.

Harry Sheffield: We were taken to church from when we were babies. Never missed Sunday morning mass. If it was snow up to the windows, we went to church.

Leslie Roberts: My mother was brought up a Methodist and she always went to Belvoir Road. My dad used to go as well. They tell the story that on one particular Sunday, shortly after they were married, that they'd got three ha'pence between them ... and they went to chapel and my dad put a penny on the plate and Mum put the ha'penny and that was the sum total of what they possessed.

Of course, my granddad used to go. He was there every Sunday morning. I can remember him going every Sunday morning. Very, very strict, Granddad Swain. He was a well known football referee in Coalville. He'd go to chapel on a Sunday morning and after going to chapel, he'd come and visit us and my auntie who lived in the next yard. But woe betide them, at their age — in their forties and fifties — if they got as much as a needle out on a Sunday. But he wasn't averse to having half a pint if Aunt Beat'd go and fetch it from the corner shop.

On one occasion, I think I'd probably be about thirteen or fourteen [1937/38], my dad was called out on one Boxing Day with a few others. They'd got water in the shaft [Snibston]. It was susceptible to a lot of water coming in and they couldn't stop it. They were there for over twenty-four hours. They worked all the time, non-stop, to try and stem this flow of water. Mr Emmerson — big chapel man that he was — sent across to the pub and had coffee made and had some rum put in it because everybody was soaked, working down in the shaft with the water coming in all the time.

Frank Smith: My dad was a Primitive Methodist and my mother was a Baptist, so I had to go to Sunday school — Primitive Methodist. My dad was predominent, he wouldn't have the Baptist life. I had to go to the Prims. It was all coal miners who were teachers, readers of the Bible. Harry Springthorpe were my first teacher. He was only a small fella but he held you in awe because the fear of God ... he'd put the fear of God into you with his fervour about religion. And he was a pitman ... It was hell fire and damnation kind of teaching. There were a lot of preachers you know, came from pits, worked in terrible conditions and then on a Sunday spent all of the day telling you about damnation ... they'd been through it all week. There was a inborn faith in miners. I think there had to be, to work in those conditions. To work underground ... in close, claustrophobic conditions and stygian blackness, you've got to have some faith.

Men swear underground, sometimes because of the frustrations of the job or the conditions of the job ... but these are exceptional circumstances. If a man uses blasphemy underground the men will walk away from him, or will crawl away from him ... because generally speaking we are a religious bunch of blokes, miners. Whether it's the fear of the work and the constant conditions under which they work, I don't know. I think it's a contribution of both things. From the moment you get on that cage your life depends on the good fortune throughout the day. Take that as fact. And so you've got to have some faith in somebody, you know, to keep you from that fall of coal and from being run over. You'd got to have a faith and your alertness of course. And fellas that hadn't got that were exceptional, the blasphemers.

Leslie Roberts: The various collieries had got their own little churches. A lot of the Snibston Colliery people went to the Wesleyan Chapel on Belvoir Road where Mr Harrison, the manager was a leading light. Whitwick Colliery went to a chapel in Whitwick Road. The South Leicester people used to go to the Hugglescote Church of England — St John the Baptist ... you can draw your own conclusions ... When most of the bosses go to one church a lot of the followers used to go there as well ... When I worked at South Leicester, the people that used to go to church there, I don't know whether they were particularly religious or whether they wanted to be seen to be at church where the bosses was. Because Mr Canner [managing director], I think, he was a sidesman at the Hugglescote church ... Old Tom Shaw who was in charge of the Railway Office used to spend more time in a pub called the Castle as he did anywhere else and yet he'd always be seen in church on a Sunday.

Ellis Walker: There was victimisation if they knowed a man went for a drink and didn't go to church or chapel ... if you offended any of them, you carried a stigma and you was out of work and you was poor.

Florrie Harris: The Sunday School Anniversaries were great days. I went to the Baptist Sunday School, that was between the villages of Bagworth and Thornton. I used to go round to lots of different churches, singing, from the age of fourteen up to a few years ago. I used to do solos ... if there was anniversaries coming up, people would come from different churches inviting me to go and help them which I did and I loved that sort of thing.

We used to have what we called socials at the chapel on a Saturday night. We would have little party games ... such things as 'Hunting we will go', passing the parcel ... we'd always end up with an epilogue. And it's amazing how many couples used to go to this as single people, young people, and they used to get friendly and eventually they get married. Lots of people found their partners like that and they were very, very happily married. In fact, I found my partner like that.

The farthest that I think that I went ... it was a friend of mine at Broom Leys School, invited me to go to spend the day with her at the Traveller's Rest at Griffydam. I had to go home and ask my mum. She looked at me and said, "That's a public house." I said, "Yes, but I'm only going to Sarah's." With a lot of persuasion she did let me go.

49

Stan Moreton: I started singing at Chapel, Sunday School, right from when I were a boy, five years old. I were a singer ever after. I carried on (when I were seventeen/eighteen) and went to the adult services and I asked if I could be in the choir because I knew I could sing, I knew that. ... they were pleased to welcome me. I went to afternoon and evening services ... I also went to practise at Ibstock [Church of England] ... I preferred chapel because it were more simple. It were just the hymns at chapel, you see. Church, you get the psalms which are very complicated.

In the pub, I always used to sing ... when I got, you know, unnervy — I were nervy for a start and shy. I got used to it and people used to ask me to sing ... and I always used to sing my favourite songs ... I did have one that stuck out in my mind, my favourite, and it was called 'Friend O' Mine'.

Edith Roberts: You always had a new dress ... Battram is only one street and there was a girl named Edith Jacques who had a hairdressing shop in the front room. For the Sermons my mum used to give me a shilling and let me have my hair Marcel waved ... and I used to sit up in bed all night so it wouldn't fall out for the next day. And we'd never tell anyone what colour [dress] we were having so it was a surprise to everyone. But we really used to take care of them clothes because they were our Sunday best. And then the next year you wore those for the Saturdays and you could go to school in them but you always kept one lot of clothes for Sundays ... and the clothes that you bought were from the Co-op and you used to pay so much a week and buy cheques and that's how you bought your clothes.

Arthur Bale: The sermons. That were one of the highlights of the Sunday School, really. See, there were three important dates in the Sunday School Calendar. That was the prize day, the Sunday School treat and the Sermons. Well, if you went to Ebenezer Chapel in them days, if you wanted to go at night and you went at half past five, you wouldn't get in. It used to be packed ... We used to borrow chairs from the Y.M.C.A. ... but we couldn't get them 'til after ten o'clock on a Saturday night because they had a whist drive there on a Saturday night ... One of the local coal dealers, he'd got a horse and dray and he used to let us hire that and go and fetch these chairs across ...

We used to have hymn sheets ... we'd got to learn the words ... you'd got to stand there and sing without the sheet. They used to start about a month before the Sermons were due and they used to use the Sunday morning school for practice time and then perhaps twice in the week. Then on the Sunday before the Sermons they used to have a general rehearsal with the orchestra. Of course we used to have the violins and the cello, the brass ... adults in the band, proper musicians, you know. They used to come of their free will and help us out.

If anything went wrong it was always me ... we used to get a piece of paper and put on it in big letters 'kiss me' then stick it on a girl's back. Otherwise we'd perhaps put 'kick me' on some of the lad's backs ... One of the best, when we were in the chapel ... we'd got our gallery at the side and just below us were one of the deacons and he were bald headed. So when it came to the long prayer in the middle of the sermon, we used to roll little bits of paper up ... and we used to drop it over and see if they would drop on his head ... We used to sit there like little angels. We'd perhaps stick a pin on the seats with the point sticking up.

We used to have classes in the afternoon ... There used to be a shop in Coalville, Margaret Street, they sold snuff — long-delayed snuff, they called it — so I fetched the snuff out when the Superintendant started the prayer, and said, "Anyone want a bit of snuff?" They wouldn't have it, it would make them sneeze. "It don't", I says. "Right-oh we'll have a bit." So it went all round the class and just about the time the Superintendant was finishing his prayer, they all started sneezing. He came down off the platform. "What's wrong here?" "He's give us some snuff."

50

He gave me a clip aside the earhole. And that weren't the first time ... he'd clipped me a time or two. Anyhow, we got through alright.

Coalville Ebenezer Chapel — that's where I first met the wife. We got married there. We were baptised there, both of us and the kiddies have all been brought up there as well. That were the turning point in my life because before then I was one of them little rough lads in the Sunday School. If anything went wrong, it was always me. One day, there was a new family come into the church ... and the two youngest come to the Sunday School and they used to sit on the girls' gallery opposite. I noticed these here two girls and I thought, hello, that's my wife there — I was ten. It wasn't long before we got to know one another, so I told her, "I'm going to marry you". "Oh, no you won't," she said. " You're not big enough, you're not old enough." She was ten. She was half an inch taller and three months older than me. I said, "We'll see." And it didn't matter whatever were going off anywhere in the district, we always seemed to be running into one another, so eventually we got married, 1925.

Ellis Walker: I was brought up Baptist ... the first minister as I knowed there, very nice fella, very reserved. He didn't believe in ... he used to preach hell fire and all the rest of it, about abstaining from drink and all this, that and the other. He expected you to join the Band of Hope, so you wouldn't drink. I used to go down there. I'm sorry to say it's been broke a good many times. After that there was Mr Gregory ... I used to go to church regular, as a young man, up to seventeen and eighteen. I remember this Mr Gregory ... I'd started going out with the ladies and I'd missed Sunday School for about two or three weeks. I had to go this special time and his first words were, "You're like a bad penny. You turn up any time." So I says, "If that's chapel, I'm finished." And I didn't go no more. I was beginning to learn there were better things in life.

Reg Spencer: There was The Grand and I can always remember a fella named Joe Bowley used to stand outside on Saturday afternoons shouting, "Tuppenies and fourpennies this way!" We'd go in for a penny, you see and were separated, if you were tuppennies and fourpennies, towards the back. There used to be dances at Father Degen's, which was the Catholic Church ... St Saviours Catholic Church. He used to have monkeys on the outside ... as kids we used to tease the monkeys. I always remember the band. It was The Arabian Nights and the signature tune was 'The Sheik of Araby'.

Lena Gee: I had two close friends and we used to go dancing at the baths as used to be at Coalville (it's the ambulance place now, I think) and at Holy Cross at Whitwick and Thringstone Clubhouse and, of course, we went on the Monkey Walk on the Sundays. You used to go up Coalville. You started at the Grand and you walked slowly from there right up to the Forest Rock Public House, up London Road and over the bridge and then you'd turn back. You did that all night, but you'd be stopping all the while talking to the boys. The only mischief you got into was if you went into one of the shop doorways, used to be Lashmore's was the one, and you got the coppers saying, "Come on, move out!" And they'd perhaps say it two or three times all the night. Sometimes you'd get walked home and you'd get to know the chaps. But honestly, you were too much in dread of the workhouse and that, and you really didn't know what they were talking about anyway. You weren't so well informed.

Eileen Smith: Our courting would be done round the Altons. You go to Ravenstone and right round the Altons and back on the Ashby Road. Then the pictures, of course, on the back row. We went with a party to the Ashby Statutes. It's a fair that's held right down the street and it's been going for years. It's forty-three years since we first met there. We all went in a gang. We came back by taxi and Pete then asked me out. We've been together ever since.

Reg Spencer: I met my wife ... first met her when she was about fifteen. I was riding round Peggs Green and I think she was waiting for the bus to go to chapel or somewhere like that. That

Advice for Miss 1927
By Father Joseph Degen
ST. SAVIOUR'S, COALVILLE, LEICESTER.

Please Keep this Leaflet in your Hand-bag for reference

MOTTO FOR THE MODERN GIRL

"Let God be your Companion and Guide in your hours of leisure and amusement, as well as in the more serious affairs of life."

TEN COMMANDMENTS FOR MISS 1927

I-Do not parade the main thoroughfares with an all-dressed-up-and-nowhere-to-go air, waiting to be asked to take a walk with the first nice-looking boy who happens to be passing along.

II-Always tell your mother where you are going and with whom, and return home not one minute later than she suggests.

III-Do not accept gifts of jewellery, money or clothing from men. Indebtedness creates an obligation and destroys independence.

IV-Do not let fellows treat you to intoxicants, especially at a public bar. The hot blood which courses through the veins of youth is stimulant enough.

V-Avoid demoralising dances where there is little or no supervision, or where couples are permitted to seclude themselves in obscure corners inside or outside the premises.

VI-Beware of the "something for nothing" type of man, who offers you a joy-ride in his car-especially if you know nothing more about him other than that he has a tooth-brush moustache and scented hair.

VII-Hockey, lacrosse, tennis and dancing are healthier forms of excitement than street flirtations, which are always perilous.

VIII-Beware of a man who after an acquaintanceship of only ten minutes, wants to put his arm around your waist. Do not make yourself cheap, even to a duke's son.

IX-If you have found a really decent boyfriend, be true to him and don't flit like a butterfly from one to another. Take him home-introduce him to mother and father. Make the choice of your future husband a matter of earnest prayer.

X-Do not expect to go through life attired in silk and chiffon waited on hand and foot, and never doing any hard work, Few men can afford to keep a luxurious and expensive fashion plate. You must learn to be useful as well as ornamental.

AN IMPORTANT FORGET-ME-NOT FOR THE WHOLE OF YOUR LIFE.

Mere natural morality, uninspired by religious motives might stand the wear and tear of everyday life for a short period, but it is bound sooner or later to break down hopelessly. We cannot avoid sin nor can we advance in virtue without keeping ever in view a supernatural vision.

Leaflet issued to local young women

was when I first met her but I didn't go out with her. I met her actually in Coalville years later ... probably on the Monkey Parade. It used to be from The Grand to the Station and back, on one side of the road, the side of the road opposite what is Woolworths now. They used to parade from The Grand to the Station ... Occasionally the police used to have a bit of a round up, for obstructing the footpaths. It was really crowded ... you just walked from one end to the other and got talking to the girls, if possible ... that was the aim.

It got so that, I suppose, everybody more or less knew everybody eventually because it's not that big a place, is it? You usually stood talking to them and asked if you could take them home or something like that. That's what usually happened anyway. I know quite a few that were summonsed for obstructing the footpath. They used to have a swoop now and again ... you see, you used to stand in shop doorways and all sorts. You did that when you hadn't got enough money to go in the pub, usually.

Sarah Whittaker: At a dance at the Adult School in Coalville, I really met him then. Well, he'd seen me before but I don't remember seeing him, that was a year or two sooner. He was a miner. He worked down the pit at Ellistown. He did that for a little while after we were married, but not for long because I really wanted him to come out of the pit. Well, I thought he'd be better out and get a job in the daylight. It was dangerous, I suppose that was about it. So he worked on Midland Red Buses. He was an Inspector in the finish. He worked there nearly forty years. I can't remember what he did get, his wage, we struggled on. I didn't go to work after we were married.

Harry Sheffield: I was born in Park Road, Coalville[1901] and I am the thirteenth child of a family of fifteen. My father worked at the mine, in Whitwick Colliery, and worked there sixty-two years down the mine. Every one of my brothers worked at the same colliery, the same pit and where we lived ... a few years after I was born we went to live in Albert Road which is a road running along side of the colliery and we could see the men, the cage coming up, you know, and the men pushing the tubs and all that sort of thing and we knew straight away if there was an accident of any sort because we used to see the ambulance go up to the pit top and we were all wondering who it was that had got trapped. It was seven brothers and eight sisters and I had brothers-in-law, as well, as worked down the mine.

It was a little terraced house. But, my brothers were getting married before the others were born, you see, so ... we weren't all seventeen in one house. All the lads used to sleep in one room and the girls in another and mother and dad where they could, I think ... three bedrooms, two fair sized ones and then a little one and my mother and dad always had the little room to themselves. No heating or nothing, you know.

My sisters all come in from the factory about twelve, half past twelve to one, she had to get a meal for them and some of the men as were on the night work, they used to have their dinner at that time. And then there was us coming from school about four o'clock and we used to have a hot dinner ... How she did it, I don't know.

There were two sitting-downs at the table. We had to sit back, the younger ones while the older ones had the first course. Then we had our meal. We used to generally start off with the puddings, the dumplings and all sorts and rice puddings. Always used to have the sweet first. Then all sorts of things for the second course. That could be potato pie, potato and meat pie or stewed meat and everything was marvellous ... we always had good meals. I never knew us to be told to cut down at all. I remember for breakfast before we went to school we used to have extra big cups and used to toast some bread and we used to put the bread into the cup, sugar on top and pour tea on it and that was our breakfast ... almost everyday. Sometimes we should have a bit of bacon and egg.

We never all came home together ... those as were working on the roads in the pit, well they were up first and were at home perhaps half an hour before those as worked in the stalls because they'd got to walk right from the stalls which sometimes were two miles away from the pit bottom before they could get to the pit bottom to come up. So instead of being up the pit at half past two it'd perhaps be half past three or four before they got up. So we were never, hardly ever, together.

Barrack Row, Ashby Road, Coalville

Lena Gee: It was lovely living down Ashby Road. When you went out at night the pit was all lit up. Well, they'd only got the winking gas lights in those days and it used to shine like a big beacon and every time you went by you could hear the banging, the talking, the singing, the whistling. Look up at the headstocks and the wheels going round.

When I look back at it, it was just like one great big happy family. All the terraced houses. Everybody had got families. Everybody was good, kind and helpful. Got any children ill and they'd come in with a basin full of beef tea, they called it. You'd only got to knock on the wall if you were in trouble.

Frank Smith: My father was a miner. My mother did hosiery work. Naturally, I followed him in the pits ... he spent 56 years in the mining industry. He followed his dad, of course, my grandfather, Arthur Smith. It was in the family, everybody worked at pit. All the Smiths worked at pit, all his brothers ... and on my mother's side, my grandfather Cooper, he was a miner of some distinction, he got quite a name for himself. And all his sons and he had, I think, five sons who all worked at pit, all from Whitwick.

We lived, until I got married, in a little cottage ... two rooms down and a pantry. Three little bedrooms and a sixty yard long garden. A delightful little cottage, my mother used to keep spotlessly clean. The front room we had to go through to get to the kitchen. We only stopped in the front room for ... Sunday teas or anniversaries or if friends came. We had a coal house inside and we had a ton of coal a month and that had to be carried through the house, with paper spread on the floor, to be put in this coal house.

Dr Sheila Lee: Up to the end of World War Two a collier's life was pretty awful, it was very dirty. I lived in Liberton, Edinburgh, which was sort of the south east borders of Edinburgh. Then beyond that there was the Lothian coalfield ... so I was quite accustomed to seeing colliers. ... but in those days, a collier's job was low down. But by the time I retired and the pits stopped here, they were quite wealthy compared with office workers and shopworkers.

Len Bramley: My father was a miner and in my boyhood days he worked at Ellistown pit. The thirties although I didn't realise it then ... were called the hungry years, depression years. And well I always had presents at Christmas and I can honestly say I never went hungry.

In 1919, his mother and dad, they bought a house down Highfield Street and my dad bought the one next to it. He bought that house for two hundred and fifty pounds and he borrowed a hundred pounds ... some Leicester firm of solicitors did the turning over and the turning over in 1919 — the fee — was seven pounds something. Well, my dad, for saying he bought a house in those times when money was really tight — they reckon nobody could afford anything — well somehow he bought this house and he was still single. He didn't marry my mother until 1924 and they were living in a rented house in Ellistown and the bloke who lived in his house was an undermanager, a bloke named Henry Brierly from Clutsom and Kemp ... he left and I think they moved in in 1926. When I was born they hadn't been living in that house that long. But nevertheless I've never lived in a rented house in my life. Well, they say very few owned their own houses then, well I suppose my dad bought that house probably because his mother and dad bought the one next to it. Up until then his parents had lived in rented property. Well, my dad, I do know he was always on the higher paid jobs at the pit. I mean, when he was at Ellistown he was a chargeman ... for being a chargeman, in those days, I think he got a shilling extra a shift than the other men in the stall.

There was no water on tap. The drinking water was a well at the end of the yard and that answered for two houses, in our case and the two houses next door they had got a well for two houses and next to them a family named Bancrofts, they'd actually got one well individual, used exclusively by them. The toilet arrangements was a privy at the bottom of the garden. They were emptied at night time by the council. You could hear them sometimes in the night and they were termed 'night soil men'. Those arrangements lasted up until, I should be somewhere around nine and they put drainage on and they put piped water on. But in those houses, even now, if you walk along them you can still see some of them privies what were used in the early thirties.

Dr Sheila Lee: The Greenhill Estate started in about 1950, 1951 and Stone Row and all of Mammoth Street except for the Tompkins' house, ... they were what you might call evacuated up there. And, of course, then there was no difference between a collier's house and the other, because it gave the wife a decent environment and she became as house proud as anybody else. But I'm really just talking about Stone Row, Mammoth Street and then what was known as Ashby Road on the left side, it used to be called Long Lane and ... that was all cleared ... in the early fifties.

Ken Bowley: My father worked at Nailstone Colliery. Then he went for another job at Ellistown Colliery partly because there was a house that went with the job. He was a miner all his life ... [My mother] was a cleaner at the colliery offices, so we were all tied up pretty well with the colliery at that time.

It was a terraced house... they're all knocked down now. There were three rows actually, three rows of terraced houses. One, one side of the road then two the opposite side of the road with a gap in between ... I would think that everbody who lived in them, the men, worked at the pit in some capacity. They were owned by the colliery ... Ellistown Terrace. Mr Ellis, who I think had a lot to do with the sinking of the pit at Ellistown, before they all became nationalised and, of course, the brickyard, Ellistown Pipes, Ellistown Bricks, and the town and most other things just carried his name. It was Ellis' Town I suppose. It was just called The Terrace. Well, we all called it The Terrace. It's right where Ellistown Colliery is, well, at the bottom of the lane where Ellistown Colliery is now. On the main road through to Bagworth. All the houses have been demolished now. The top two rows were affected by subsidence.

Tony Turner: [I lived] in Church Lane, Whitwick, with my mam and dad ... oh ah, pits kept going under Church Lane ... no end of houses knocked down up there, through subsidence, they actually tumbled down, some of them did ... they gave them the equivalent value to go somewhere else and that. They've built it all up again now.

Edith Roberts: The Battram house, where I spent my childhood, it were constantly falling down with subsidence ... you'd wake up one day and the ceiling'd start to crack again ... and you couldn't get out of the door ... It was terrible because we hadn't got a house to lean on to. We'd got a house that stood on its own.

Fred Betteridge: When the old Ibstock Colliery closed ... they closed it because of water. In 1954 ... they drained no end of water out the old Ibstock pit but it was at an incline. It went up at about, I should think, thirty degrees for getting on for half a mile then it went into the old Ibstock seams. They would still have had quite a lot of water but they managed to work the seams because the pumps were so powerful they contended with the water. It was good seam coal, good high seams, eight foot high a lot of them. But it were nearer the surface you see. You went down the shaft to the pit bottom but then ... you were climbing ... all the while you see, all that way out. And all those houses, when they got the coal ... they were coal owners' houses, you know, for the miners in the old days. Everyone of them, it shattered them. All the door frames jammed, the roofs cracked, they had to put new door jambs in and all the roads went all up and down. Eventually it settles, you see, it does settle ... but the deeper you are the less sign there is of subsidence but when you get seams nearer the surface naturally you're going to get more subsidence.

Tracey Ridgway: Our house in Donisthorpe is one of those that's coming down ... it's subsidence ... through the Coal Board. In a sense I feel disillusioned because the little girl starts school after the Summer [1992] and unless we're moved very soon, she's going to have all the upheaval of moving. As regards the property, it's very, very damp and really it's not habitable ... it's not very good, healthwise.

There's a lot of people in the same position. All the houses have got subsidence and damp. The glass in our front window, a couple of years ago, all of a sudden we heard this crack, got up to have a look and we'd got a hairline crack in the window ... the Council said, "Oh, it's subsidence. Nothing we can do about it." So I says, "Oh no. That's your responsibility." Eventually they did have to come and do it because over the months it just cracked right down 'til it was almost coming out. It's been going on for years. The houses were put up just after the war, I believe, but the subsidence has got worse. We've been here six years and we've noticed a big difference. You can actually feel the movement ... I don't thing we've got a poltergeist, although I sometimes wonder ... You can get up in the morning and walk down the stairs and they seem really steep or your doors will close for no reason ... sometimes you can't even shut the doors.

I think there are twenty-three or twenty-five houses coming down, the rest of the houses are going to be repaired ... underpinning. We could be rehoused in a week, a month or it could be two years. We're just living from day to day. I won't be sorry to leave the house but I'll be sorry to leave the area ... You spend a lot of money improving things to find you're going to have to start again.

I should say a good seventy-five per cent of the Avenue ... obviously most of them have spent their lives here, they've grown up here, they've probably always lived in that house or in the village. I suppose it's going to to be very devasting if they have to move out because ... you have memories. It's going to be a big upheaval ... just to walk away and leave everything ...

Elizabeth Whatnall: The houses where we lived in those days ... there used to be a lot of cockroaches. Say if the room had been in the dark, been no lights on and you switched the light on, you'd see them running up the wall. And my mother, she wasn't a bit afraid. She'd pick them up and drop them in the fire. I remember once my husband's work coat had got wet, it had been a very wet day. He worked at Nailstone at the time and I thought, well I'll hang his coat over two chairs in front of the fire when I go to bed. And I always used to pack his snap up at night. Put a mashing of tea in the tea pot and all as he had to do was just mash. Well, he never used to step off the step at the bottom of the stairs. He always put the light on first and he said the ruddy table were alive with cockroaches — never thought anything. Gets to work and they were all in his snap!

Lena Gee: I went to live at Thringstone. We lived there with his mother and his dad mining and his brothers mining — the same as in dozens of houses throughout the district. As one lot of workers went out, say the dad went, well perhaps his son would be coming in from nights. Then the girls would be going to the factory. Then they'd come home from the morning shift, somebody, and the girls would be in at tea-time from the factory. As soon as you'd got one meal ready you'd got to start getting another one. You'd never done washing up!

Harry Bancroft: I tell you what we used to have for breakfast more than anything when we were little kiddies. We used to have a basin of sop, as we called it, but we used to have cocoa and break us bread up in it and sugar it well and that's what we used to have more often than not for breakfast. Sometimes a bit of toast if you wanted it. But you could always have some bacon if you wanted it because they'd got plenty of bacon.

We used to have two dinners really as boys because we used to have a dinner about twelve o'clock when we come out of school and when our dad come from work about three o'clock or half past there were another dinner for them and we should get a bit of that as well. It were ordinary meat ... potatoes and vegetables. We used to have allotments, two allotments. Oh yes, we grew our own.

Lena Gee: Nearly all of the miners had back gardens and allotments where they grew their own root vegetables and cabbage, sprouts, carrots and peas. So, of course, this helped a lot. No need to worry if you had not got a garden — neighbours would never see you without. That was how the people were on Ashby Road.

Gwenda Taylor: We'd got our own back garden and allotment. We grew all our own vegetables. My granddad had a piece at the top of the garden where he grew his own flowers and he'd got that fenced off, that was his patch. But the rest of the garden, it was raspberry canes, blackcurrant, gooseberry. Then my dad used to grow caulies and all that sort of thing but on the allotment it was more or less new potatoes and cabbages and beans and all that sort of thing.

Joe Webster: Gardening ... I lived in the garden. Plenty of exercise keeps you fit. I've shown everywhere. The undermanager here asked me to go over to Derbyshire. I went over to Derbyshire and they put a big show on at Gresley Town Hall and I was at Snibston then putting the big show on at Coleorton Hall and I went over to Gresley Town Hall early in the morning and to their show. We won that cup, came home and when I got back the tannoy was going and my name was shouted out. I went and I got that cup. That was for all the best produce on the show. All mixed, everything.

Robert Stewart: We had a big garden where we came from. I loved gardening and walking the dog. I had the dog twelve years. I walked it so much its back legs went! I used to walk down Moira, through to Donisthorpe, Oakthorpe and back to have a couple of pints down the Tavern — twelve miles that was.

Edith Roberts: You could get wallpaper from Coalville market for half-a-crown a roll. Well, the rooms are so small you only needed about three even if it was a matching wallpaper. And there was an old soul down Beresford Street, named Win Middleton, and she could paper a ceiling in two hours. And she was absolutely brilliant. One day I tried to do a ceiling and I'd spoilt some paper and I started to cry and Les said, "Stop crying. I'll go and ask Win to come across." He went and asked Mrs Middleton to come and she said, "You get to work," — because at that time I was trying to earn a bit of money for some Christmas things for Judy. I was working at Cascelloid's at night, I think it was four hours on night shift and if you worked there you could get dolls and a pram cheaper ... and I got her a lovely coach-built pram for about four pounds and a lovely doll. I went to work that night and by the time I'd come home she'd done that ceiling and everything were clean ready for us to do the walls the next day. She used to go papering houses and she only used to charge about ten shillings.

Some of the men did [the papering]. My father never did anything like that. My father did gardening, like Les's father ... because after they'd worked all the time in the mine and because it was hard work and my father was underground all day, most of the day. I guess they wanted to get out in the fresh air. They didn't want to do things inside. So we'd always got a marvellous garden. A beautiful garden.

Sarah Whittaker: My father was a miner — on the belts, winding or something, at Ibstock. I was the youngest of nine. It was always a lot of plain food, good food, cooked at home. We always kept a pig and some fowls so we used to have plenty of eggs and kill a fowl. About every year a pig was killed and everything on that was eaten up — sausage, bacon and pork pies. All made at home.

Sim Woolley: In those days they always used to keep pigs. My grandmother, at Ellistown, always had pigs. And, of course, they wouldn't kill them 'til there were about twenty score. Nowadays I think it's totally different ... They used to have them on the back yard, they used to call it the causey ... they used to get the pigs on the trestle, tie them down and just simply slit the throat, put the bucket under and let them bleed to death.

There was a pig killer that I remember very well, he was very well known in Ellistown, called Smedley. He was an Ellistown man ... I think he used to send shivers down my spine when I saw him in the street because he was a bow legged sort of man. He had an old mac on and an old trilby that had no shape in it and we used to know him as the pig killer. He put the fear of God into us whenever we saw him. Nevertheless he used to roll up, he used to say, "Put the copper on and let's have some hot water." They'd fetch the pig from the sty at the bottom of the garden. They'd get it on the bench with a lot of squealing and struggling, tie its legs down, then it would happen. He always used to bring with him ... a low trestle, about two feet high and they'd get the pig on it, however big it was ... there was no stunning it. It was usually a team job. The man came along with a knife, sharpened his knife — I can visualise him even now — stuck it in the pig's throat and cut it. My impressions of that as a child of about five, six or seven wasn't very nice. It wasn't very happy for me.

Then the next week the whole household and the neighbours were busy cutting it up, cutting the various joints up, cleaning all the wraps, pig intestines. This all used to be done in the back kitchen and, of course, they used to scrape the pig and clean it all down, cut it into sections and hang it up. They would cut the thing up and all the meat that had to be disposed of quickly, they would share with the neighbours so that when the neighbours killed a pig on another occasion they would get a loin of pork. But the hams and the sides of bacon, they cured them and you could always go in a house along that street and see several hams hanging up and sides of bacon. So you were never short of a meal in that respect.

Eileen Smith: Of course, when we had pigs that kept us going for meat. You used to hang the pigs on the wall and the riper they were, that means the older the meat, the better it was. My dad loved a slice of ham and it had very thick fat. You'd put it in the frying pan and sizzle it. We used to have bread dipped in the fat and it was delicious. My mother used to make faggots and chorl — that's the face of the pig. Then chittlings, that was the intestines. But the miners used to have their half pigs. You couldn't use it all and there were no fridges then, so we used to pass it round to the family and the neighbours and they all used to have a fresh piece of pork.

Dad grew potatoes during the war in the front garden and at the back of course. All flower beds had to come up. Maybe it was during the war that Dad was most active in his allotment. Of course, they were too old then to be called up but the fuel was vital.

Tony Turner: The war was on when I was at school and everybody had got to 'dig for Victory'. Well, Pat Downs, at Holy Cross School at Whitwick, at the back of the school there was allotments and he decided to extend them and get all the lads to dig this for growing vegetables. My dad would say, "What you been doing at school today?" "On the garden all day." "Well, if you're going to go on the garden all day you may as well stop at home and do mine." So, I finished up stopping at home for about three weeks doing these allotments of my dad's and one day the School Attendance Officer came and asked my dad why I wasn't at school. He told him and the Attendance Officer said, "Send him tomorrow to school." When I got to school next day, while the lads went out gardening, Pat Downs sent me in the sewing class with all the girls.

Florrie Harris: My father was a deputy at Desford Colliery. When he first worked at Desford Colliery we did live at Barlestone and they used to have to walk to Desford. And then they built some houses specially for deputies and officials near to the colliery and my dad was offered one of these and I remember moving in November — a very crisp morning and Mum pushed the pram with the little children and I walked along the side. I'm not sure how they got the furniture over there but I know there was a wheelbarrow used for a sack of potatoes!

We went to this house and we thought it was absolutely marvellous because we had a toilet just outside at the back door where we used to have to walk right down a yard ... and we seemed to have modern facilities. I remember we had a little porch on the front of the house where Mum used to let us children play and we used to decorate the walls with a clock and pretend it was our little house. We'd have a net curtain put across and it was great.

One of the highlights of my father being a deputy was at Christmas time when the deputies were given a brace of pheasants and that, to us, was absolutely wonderful. You didn't have turkey and that unless you were very rich, not in that day, and to us a brace of pheasants — we were in heaven. Desford Colliery management gave them to the deputies, the miners didn't get them but the deputies did.

They weren't all deputies that lived down there. There were some electricians, of course ... I think the friendship in that day was absolutely wonderful, it really was. We used to have a field at the back of the houses and the men used to play the ladies at football, cricket, we had sports, there was a swing. We used to have a bonfire party, even a party in the canteen at Desford Colliery, on Boxing Day. The men paid ten shilling a week, which was a lot of money then, I think for the last few weeks and then all the people down Heath Road had a huge party. They called it Desford Colliery village. It was between Bagworth and Desford village but the buses

59

used to have a title 'Desford Colliery Village' ... there's nothing there now, nothing at all, no houses, nothing.

At the time when we got married, my mum and dad, plus the rest of the family, had been promised a house a little bit further up the street. And they'd made that into a shop, so that the shop would be open before half past six in the morning so that the miners could come in and get a little refreshment and whatever they needed to take down to work. My mum and dad had that position and when we got married we went into Mum and Dad's house.

I used to help Mum in the shop. If the men wanted any sandwiches making because that was before the days of the canteen, I used to help with the sandwiches. The men used to come in for cigarettes but they weren't allowed to smoke really but the men came in for cigarettes in the early morning. Mum had a list with the peoples' names on and they used to say, "I'll pay for this at the end of the week." They did. The majority of them did.

It was Mum and Dad's own business. They didn't own the house or anything like that. But then when war started and we had to have ration cards and points for this and points for that, it got too much for Mum. She couldn't quite fathom all these things out and she carried on a while but eventually the canteen was built and the men could get meals at the canteen so Mum said that it wasn't really worth it.

There were nineteen houses to start with, then another five were built after. We did get tradespeople down. We used to have a lady come from Desford with a lorry ... and she used to bring vegetables and different kinds of groceries on the back of this lorry. And we used to look forward to her coming because when she came we had one pennyworth of toffees between the five of us children and Mrs Weston ... knew Mum had five children and she used to put twenty toffees in a brown paper bag and we used to share these out. So that was four each, for one penny. That's all we could have in a week ... We used to have an ice cream man come down. He used to shout, "Okey-Pokey." I remember that distinctly. His name was Mr Milnes and he lived in the village of Bagworth. He used to sell half-penny cornets but Mum couldn't afford to let us have those ... very seldom, that was a real treat when we did. Mr Milnes still came after we were married, so we did patronise him then.

Then we used to have a Mr Miles. He was the butcher and he used to have a little shop in the square at Bagworth. When we were first married I didn't quite know the joints of meat and I used to say to him, "I'll have a half a crown's worth of beef please." and he used to bring us a lovely joint of beef for half a crown.

We had no modern conveniences for cooking. It was just a black-lead fireplace with a boiler at the side that we had to fill with water to get some warm water and we had a ladle ... to get the hot water out again. We had a copper at the side where we had the hot water to do the washing and also to have a bath, in a zinc bath in front of the fire, until we got modernised and we had a bathroom ... it would be 1953 when we had hot water put on ... we had got a bathroom but no hot water. When we became modernised we had a Rayburn, which was marvellous for cooking.

But these black-lead fireplaces with the oven at one side and the boiler at the other, a coal fire to heat the oven, they used to make lovely cakes and pastries. You sort of got used to it very quickly by just putting your hand inside to how know hot it was. You used to have to gauge things for cooking that way. Well, it was [economical] to us because we had such an allowance of fuel. Every miner had twelve tons of coal at that time and we used it in a year because every room apart from the bathroom and the pantry had a fireplace in, even the bedrooms.

[Coal was delivered] by horse and cart. It would be the same chappy every time, his name was Ted. They used to tip it up at the front gate and if the menfolk were at work you'd see the womenfolk getting the coal in. Or if the men were home early enough they used to get it in. We hadn't got a coal house ... out the back the coal was put just below the window. We used to have to go outside, no matter what the weather was, to get the coal in ... and if we thought snow was coming we used to make sure that we'd got plenty of coal in because the snow would cover it. We used to have cardboard boxes or wooden boxes and fill them up with coal to make sure we'd got plenty of fuel in. Gradually the menfolk started to build their own little coal sheds, just under the window. For safety's sake we used to try and get it in because it was put on the path and there were no street lights. If it was there in the dark it would be very, very dangerous. So we used to leave whatever we were doing and get it in ... If there was anybody poorly and they couldn't do it or if they got a little bit too old, the younger people would help them and get it in. There was a wonderful friendly atmosphere, you know, in the whole of the street.

Thinking of the difference of today's properties and the properties that we lived in then, I counted the concrete steps that had to be scrubbed every week. We had two down from the front gate ... you used to swill them down every week. One up into the front porch. From the front porch another one. Along the tiled passage, red brick passage — all this had to be scrubbed! Down into a pantry, four steps with the red brick again and the whole pantry floor ... then the kitchen floor would be red tiles and a black-lead fireplace, four steps down into a bathroom. A bit further along, four steps down onto the back yard and one step up to the toilet. And all of that had to be scrubbed. And it was a wooden seat in the toilet that had to be scrubbed, as often as you could really.

When I got married it was like that, you know, black-lead fireplace and a copper to get the hot water. My husband was in a very dirty job then in the fitting shop and he used to get his overalls very, very greasy. In fact, you could scrape the grease off. But we used to put them to soak in a big sink ... in soda ... and soak as long as possible and then we used to scrub the overalls and eventually boil them in the copper, when you'd finished all the other washing. We used to start the washing very early on a Monday morning by filling the copper and getting the water hot. We wouldn't be finished the washing then 'til about five o'clock because it was the punches and the dolly peg. No washing machines then, so it was very difficult. Then we used to have clothes lines in the kitchens if it wouldn't dry the clothes outside ... because we'd got a nice coal fire and it didn't take them long to dry. But we only had a mangle, no driers.

The railway lines ran at the bottom of the garden and on a Monday morning when we'd got the washing out on the lines he used to bring the train down to the bottom ... and the steam and the smoke came off and if the wind was our way he used to blow it on purpose and then scamper the train back down the line. And he were laughing and waving to us because we were there shouting, "Go on, with your dirt!"... if they were whites. If they were dirty pit clothes it didn't matter quite so much!

The men at the colliery were always gaming with one another and trying to play tricks on one another and I recall one day when I saw a group of workmen working on the railway lines — I don't quite know what repair they were doing but you know, they all look alike in overalls and a cap. I saw this group of men, and it was a cold morning, so I shouted, "Is Ernie there?" And they said, "Yes." I said, "Come across and I'll make you some coffee." They sent one of them across and I made six mugs of coffee and they carried them back on a tray and they all had this coffee and brought the things back and they were laughing. I said, "What are you laughing at?" They said, "Nothing — Ernie enjoyed the coffee!" When Ernie came home from work he said, "What have you been doing ... sending coffee across to those chaps?" "Well they said you were there." And he said, "Well, yes, there was an Ernie there but it weren't me!"

61

Stan Moreton: My mother died in 1940 ... I've never been married — always a women-liker but never been married. Most miners are married. I think you've got more privileges when you're single than married ... I didn't do cooking and cleaning. My eldest brother done all that. He were good. He was good as a woman, you know, for the home. He were the only one in our family that didn't drink. As long as he'd got ten cigarettes, he were happy.

The Beniston family, Coalville

Eileen Smith: My dad had his own property ... and it had a bathroom but the only problem was that the copper which boiled the water was in the kitchen. ... and you had to pump it up and you had to use it on wash days but to get the fire to go, oh it was a problem. My mother used to get up at about five or six in the morning to get it going for wash day, so what it would be like if my dad wanted a bath — well! So they used to bath in the kitchen. I can't remember whether they had a tin bath ... but when the pit head baths were built ... my mother thought it was seventh heaven, for the simple reason of no coal dust in the kitchen, no dirt. I should think they were built in the late 1930s. Around the bottom of the trousers they'd put string round and whether this was a leg pull or not, my dad used to say it was to keep the mice or the rats from going up the legs ... but when they undid it all the dust would come out!

My dad insisted on my mother having a washer. She didn't want one but he insisted and that was seventh heaven again. It was hard work, even with this washer but it was better than it was before.

Harry Sheffield: It was just the pancheon, as we used to call it, it was a big bowl in the sink. And I always remember once, I think there were two nuns come begging and I was at the sink because I'd got my shirt and everything off, just my trousers on and I think it was my mother said, "Are you coming in?" and she opened the door and as soon as they saw me — they flew! They'd never seen a man like that before. I should only be sixteen or seventeen.

I left South Leicester in 1940. I wasn't too satisfied with the money I was getting at South so I went to Whitwick Colliery where I was well known. They'd got the baths at Whitwick Colliery as well, you see, and that was a big improvement in mining conditions. You didn't take all your filth and stuff home. You went home clean. That's the only pit round here that had baths at that time. It was nearly after the war before any others had pit head baths.

There was no pleasure for a woman with a miner taking all his clothes home. Some were fairly clean and I used to have a regular bath because we'd got a bathroom at Ravenstone ... and that used to be my first thing, strip off and get in the bath. But some of them had never seen a bath from one year to another! I can remember one chap getting hurt at South Colliery when I was working there. He got his leg badly trapped and he said, "Oh, don't let anybody see my legs, I ain't been washed for a long, long while." He didn't want folks to see his legs!

Edith Roberts: We never had electricity when I were a little girl [1930s]. We'd got oil lamps. We'd got no bathroom. We'd got a wash house ...across the yard — we used to call that the causey — and you went across the causey into the wash house to wash you ... My old dad, he used to work mornings, afternoons and nights ... so at night, when he used to come home from working afternoons, (I so remember it) we used to stoke the fire up, we used to put saucepans of water around the fire ... he used to wash him in the pancheon because it was bigger. And we used to leave all warm towels because he worked, mostly, in water ... and he always used to have clothes drying, overnight, round the fender. I always used to leave him a little letter. After my mum had put all the water round ... she used to cook him some thing and put it in the oven and leave the door ajar so it wouldn't burn. And I used to write and tell him the same thing every time: His food was in the oven and his water was boiling. And I'd put Good Night and God Bless. It were a lovely atmosphere. We'd got nothing, yet we'd got everything.

And the pancheon was a great big round pot thing, but it was high up [the sides] and he could wash him better, to get his arms in ... because he used to get absolutely filthy. We'd got no bathroom and you couldn't send him out across the yard into the wash house at that time of night because there was no fire or anything in there. My old mum used the pancheon to make her own wine. We'd always got barrels of wine in the pantry on the big pantry thrall. But my old dad would never leave it long enough ... he used to want to drink it all the while because he loved his wine and he loved his whisky. They used to make elderberry, parsnip — you name it, they made it.

My mother used to have to get up every morning at quarter to five because she cooked breakfast — bacon and egg — every day ... by half past nine, ten o'clock at night, my old mum were really and truly tired. I realise now, how hard she must have worked.

Gwenda Taylor: When they come home, they'd got to have a good strip wash, you know, and they used to put the pit trousers over the guard. You were never, what should I say, really clean. There was always the pit clothes around, you know, and there was always dust on the pit clothes and when they used to come home, they used to bring these beetles home in their clothes. It was something you couldn't stop ... black beetles. And you used to be killing them, shaking the trousers out. And there was always pit coal dust around the house, where they put their clothes. It was terrible 'til they had the pit baths, it really was.

All the housewives, it was habit, on a Friday they used to do all their cleaning and they always used to wear, miners' wives, what we used to call a coarse apron. It was either made out of sacking or what we called hessian and they'd wear that to clean in. But on Friday afternoons, on pay day, they always washed and put a clean apron on ... and it was a joke that they put this clean apron on to hold it out for their husbands to drop the money in ... most of the miners tipped all their wages up in those days, to their wives ... it was automatically handed over to the woman of the house.

Fenella Frearson: When my father worked in the pit, wages were very poor and they didn't bring enough home to look after the families properly. So the mothers, even if they had big families, in the village they used to take in people's washing, such as farmers' or anything like that. They used to take in the washing and they used to get about half a crown a day for washing, ironing and taking back ready to wear.

Ernie Harris: My mother was at home as many other women. My mother used to do washng for various people to supplement the income. I well remember that she did a huge basket full of washing for farmers, people like that. It would take her the whole of the day, using the old fashioned dolly pegs and the old fashioned mangle. And for that full day of washing she received two and sixpence which was a great help to the family finances.

Eileen Smith: My mum had boarders ... to make up for the wages that my dad had — it was a very poor wage then but we never went short. She had boarders, which meant sometimes they were builders. The builders would come from away and would have to have lodgings and so they opened up their homes for extra money. And policemen ... my mother had her name put down at the police station and anyone that wanted lodgings, then they would contact my mother to see if she could put them up. She would cook for them and wash for them.

Elizabeth Allen: I never went to work ever. My husband wouldn't allow me to and I had no desire to go out to work. My family and my husband, that was my life. It was a hard job but I did a lot of dressmaking and I used to sole and heel their shoes, even that job. They never went short of anything. My husband was a wonderful man. And people, when my children were growing up ... they looked down on me, "You poor soul, having so many children." But they forget the love and the pleasure that I've had out of them.

My husband always gave me a certain amount of money and I had to pay for the food and the rent and school dinners and things like that. I had to pay those and it was him that helped me if I got into debt, which I did a good many times and when he didn't know. A lady came to see me — she'd been recommended — she came to see me and she said, "I sha'n't ever come when your husband's in but I'll always come on a Monday morning." And she came from Leicester and she used to bring me all the little girls' frocks and things and the boys' clothes and ... I had to go into hospital to have my baby and, of course, this lady called. My husband paid her up! When I got home he said, "You're never again to do that — go in debt for anything like that — I've paid it and if there's extra money you want, you can have it."

At that time I only had five pounds a week to keep us all. I had that when I was first married and it didn't get much more. I used to get a little more when the family allowance came in and I had that. Later on it went to ten pounds as the wage got better.

Lena Gee: My dad ... he'd buy anything. From a bundle of rags up to the most expensive thing you could think of, even animals. We'd always got pigs, rabbits, calves, goats, sheep. And everybody were hard up down there ... And it took me years and years to think, well we must have been better off than most others because when the miners had received their money on Fridays it was spoken for. They used to go to the pawn shop. We didn't. What they wore on Sunday would be at Dickie Whitfords, as we called it, the pawn shop, on Mondays. It was in Coalville this pawn shop. Then they'd fetch it out when Friday come again to wear at the weekend. It had the three brass balls hanging outside. I've been with girls I played with. I've actually been in but we never did that ... When you used to buy clothes they were mended and we wore them. And we were taunted by the other kids sometimes ... but I used to go with a flat barrow, that's a horse and cart, with clothes on that had been washed and mended and sell them all up the back of the terraced houses, you see. They used to fight for them ... and the kids would say to me sometimes, "Where you had your coat from. Off the cart?" and they'd perhaps got things on that I'd sold their mother for a couple of coppers!

And I also was going all round those houses collecting a shilling on stuff they'd had off my dad — furniture. I'm sure there wasn't a house that hadn't got furniture off Mr Matchett! Arnolds were there then, the auctioneers, ... and my dad used to go every fortnight, buy furniture ... and they used to follow him up the yard and have these things and pay a shilling a week. I used to hear some right tales, why they couldn't pay!

Elizabeth Allen: They found us a Council house in Charles Street, just off the Ravenstone Road. Well, Lionel, the eldest one, he's done forty-two years at Whitwick ... my second son, he worked at Snibston for a period and he became a deputy and he ended up at Bagworth Colliery. He was made redundant and now I don't quite know what he does. He's got another job. I didn't mind [about sons working as miners]. They chose their own trades. I used to worry about them but they saw no fear so why should I? Then Stuart, my third son, he went to the pit.

[What did people think when you married a second time?] I think people were glad I remarried ... the majority of people that knew me they were glad because I'd had a rough life ... I had to go to work and work all hours, you know, and when I was working full-time I never had more than about thirty bob a week. And out of that I had to keep myself in clothes and look after Lionel. I used to pay three shillings and sixpence a week for him to go to a day school. I also used to send some money to London, to the grandmother who was looking after Geoffrey.

Every baby I had, I had a new outfit of clothes and a new pram for the new baby. When we lived in Deal, William would go along on the promenade with the new baby and he'd take all the children with him. He was as proud as anything of his family.

At Peril

Gwenda Taylor: The miners' wives, they were always on edge, you know, when their husbands had gone, they always seemed to be watching the clock when it were time for them to come home, in case they didn't. I mean ... I've heard my mam say that one of the other miners come and said, "Lew won't be home for a bit, Florrie ... he's been helping out. There's been a fall. He's helping the rescue but he's alright. Don't worry." But til my dad came home, my mam was on tenterhooks because once there's been a fall, as I say, there was generally two more.

I've seen my dad come home and he'd have a strip wash ... and his back used to be very often all scratches and cuts. You can always tell a miner, you know, because they've always got blue marks on them.

Len Bramley: In all the years down the mine, the only time I ever went on the 'club' through injury were when I was seventeen in 1944. I always remember the date, it were a Wednesday November 22nd 1944. The rope that holds the cage, it didn't break, it overwound and it crashed to the bottom. Well, it gave me a black eye and I got stabbed in the leg by some glass and this stabbing, it bled like, well, really made my sock ... you could ring it out more or less and looked a lot worse than it was. In this accident there were quite a lot of men fractured their thighs ... dislocated ... in fact I got off lucky. Anyway, I went to the doctor's and he put me on the sick, well, 'club', whatever they call it and I had the rest of that week, then the next week I had a letter come round and I'd got to see the pit doctor on the Tuesday and he says to me, "You're alright laddie, you can go and see your doctor tonight and sign off and start work tomorrow." So I says, "I can't go tonight, it's half-day, there's no surgery tonight." Well, anyhow, when Wednesday come I thought to myself, I'm not going to see him on a Wednesday and start on a Thursday, so I didn't bother going seeing him 'til Saturday.

Harry Sheffield: I've seen scores of bad accidents really. Men buried quite a lot ... falls mostly. There was nothing like what there are nowadays (rings, the same as they are in the Tube) ... just a prop here and there and a cross bar as they called it. The stones could drop out almost any time. Sometimes big stones would bounce off the side of the wall and somebody who thought he could get out of the road ... you'd have to stop the rope that was continuous, going round the tubs, stop that and get the deputy or the overman and he'd look into getting a stretcher for you and that sort of thing, you see. It was their job to stop the tubs, otherwise I don't know how they would have carried them out actually ... they used to have a first aid box but there weren't much in it, just a few bandages perhaps. I don't remember anything else. Stretchers were in certain parts of the pit. There were no proper ambulance team, not until later on. I was a member of that.

The first bad accident I had was when they got the coal cutters in the pits ... it was 1934 or 35 before they were about. But I nearly lost my leg. It ripped everything out and just skimmed the bone, nearly took my leg off. Another few inches and I should have lost my leg. I couldn't get out of the road, the cutter was going to go up to the coalface and then, what was called the blade would have gone under the coalface to skim the dirt out, you see. There was the driver of the cutter and there was one of us each side of the cutter with the wooden bar to try and keep it in position but actually, as soon as it touched the coalface it swung round, the chap at the controls hadn't got proper control of it and it swung round and all but cut my leg off. They rushed me off to the hospital ... it healed up fairly quick and I went on a light job for a week or two. If you weren't quite fit to do the face work they'd perhaps put you on a light job where you were just pushing buttons ... at that time they'd got the press button jobs going. There was no National

Health then, I paid into a friendly society and I used to get ten shillings a week from that but I don't think I got much else.

Anon: My father spent all his working life at Whitwick pit. This was during the thirties and forties. His name was Eric Samuel Myatt. He worked a cutter on the coalface. At the age of thirty-two he had a mining accident. This was in the Winter of 1947 when deep snow was on the ground. He was a hard-working man. At the time of the accident, he had doubled back to cover another man's shift. They say he was struck on the back by a piece of coal which cut his spinal cord and left him paralysed from the waist down. The ambulance had a job to get through to Leicester Royal Infirmary in the deep snow. He was later transferred to Sheffield Hospital where he spent two years on a frame.

They only gave him two years to live but being the man he was, he lived for seventeen years after the accident. I, for one, would have missed him dearly if he had died. I was nineteen when he died. He was a man who had a smile for everyone.

My father never received, or was awarded any lump sum of money — that had not come in at that time. I believe that all came about a year or so later, following his accident, so my father missed out on that. My mother used to collect a weekly amount of money to live on, from Whitwick pit paying office each Friday. I don't know exactly how much ... My mother's management had the knack of making a little go a long way. Our house was only rented. No luxuries could be afforded like cars or holidays. We did have a good aunt who used to keep Beesley's shoe shop. She used to buy my brother's new suit each year and my new dress for the Sunday School Sermons each year and our main Christmas present.

The Coal Board's miners' union used to give the family a paid holiday each year at the Derbyshire miners' holiday camp at Skegness each year. We really used to enjoy it. They had a special paraplegic block, there, for disabled miners.

Ron Gregson: Safety was a thing that had to be done, see. I mean, when you are an official you're responsible for everything. There's lots of things overlooked in mines, I'm not saying everyone's perfect, there's lots of chaps been killed ... there always will be accidents, there's always someone lets things lapse. It was your job as an official to make sure you saw as much as you could and did as much as you could. You were responsible for them people but, in saying that, they were responsible for themselves. If you saw a person not doing a thing right it was your job to say something. If you overlooked the point it could cause a bit of confusion because if anything happened ... "Why, he didn't say nowt, he didn't mention it."

I did have one sad occasion in 1969 when I was ... I was on night shift at the time ... the week before the July holiday ... Johnny Sheahan was the man that was killed, he was a good worker Johnny Sheahan, Irish chap he was. He'd been on the afternoon shift and he had to double back, that means he had to come back earlier than he should have done to get this job done ... they had to change a disc on a machine ... and when I got to the pit I got changed, and I was standing at the pit top and Tommy Challoner come ... he came running up and he said, "Come on, there's been an accident." I said, "Whereabouts?" He says, "Eighteens." That was the name of the district — they went in numbers you see, or letters. I just went with him and we practically ran into this district, you know, because we knew there'd been an accident. Tommy was a bit older than me, I was in front ... we galloped ... it was a long way. It must have been three quarters of a mile, and that's a long way when you're underground, running. We got to this ... we went through these wooden doors, there were three man sat there. There was Reg Smith, Charlie Stoner and Shirley Saunders, they just couldn't speak, you see. We got through these doors and Chally says, "What's up?" "Johnny." That's all they said. "Whereabouts is he?" "On the face." Chally said to them, "You three don't move here, don't move." Charlie Stoner says, "I'll come with you." We went to the edge of the road and there was a danny lying there — that was a trolley with wheels on. I started to push it up this gate road ... a low gate road, not much height, bad sides and that but we had to take it up this gate road. It would keep coming off the roads, you know ... rushing to get there. We knew there'd been an accident and we thought Johnny might still be alive, see ... anyway, we eventually got to the ... the danny dropped off the rails and I dived straight into the face. Well, the shame was, Johnny was under the machine, he was dead. He'd been putting a prop in ... the machine had caught him and chucked him under ... he was in a state. I'll not tell you in much more detail because it was rather gruesome ... his head was in a mess. You've no idea ...

Anon: His having to go to Carlton Hayes, that was caused by him being buried in the pit. He got buried twice in the pit. The roof came in ... he went down in the sump at one stage. But the first time he got buried the doctor said that if he had stayed at home and built himself up again, this nervous breakdown would never have happened. He wouldn't stay at home. He had asthma, terrible. That were through working at Coleorton — Bug 'n' Wink they called it in them days — he was working in water. And he used to go and see an old spiritualist as lived in Leicester, they called her Little Clara. She did a lot of good, she used to get him pint bottles of medicine, you know, herbs I suppose it was.

The new catering officer as came to the Coal Board ... he said, "I'll get your husband back again." and he did do, but he didn't work long, he fell down the chute at the colliery and about a month after, he died — brain haemorrhage. But we never claimed anything from the Coal Board, never claimed a penny. My son said to me, "No, nobody did anything for Dad while he was alive, why should we claim money for him now he's gone?" That's how my youngest son looked at it. Oh yes. He was fifty-five when he died. After he got buried in the pit ... my daughter always said, "Pit killed my dad." She's very evil towards the Coal Board. Because he only got three hundred pounds, you know, when he had his accident and he had to fight hard to get that.

Sheila Burns: I was absolutely fascinated by medicine and whenever I heard a siren coming I used to hang out of my bedroom window and watch the ambulance or the car, or whatever it was, coming up the side of the house and into the surgery and out again and off to Leicester, usually. I seemed to spend a lot of time hanging out of the window and listening to the telephone conversations. I used to love doing that if it was about medicine. My father didn't believe in women doing medicine so I never became a doctor.

My father[Dr Hamilton] would be called to the pit if somebody was trapped. He would have to go down and administer morphine or whatever it was they had to give them. He was fascinated by the mines really. He was very fond of the Leicestershire miner ... he came from a mining town in Scotland — Auckinleck in Ayrshire, and he always said that the miners in Leicestershire were of a very high standard. He thought they were very gentlemanly — just decent men, very decent. He was very much a Coalville man — with a Scottish accent.

Florrie Harris: One morning [late 1940s], it seemed to be a very hot summer day, when there was a siren, or a buzzer as we called it, went off and we knew it wasn't the normal buzzer. It was something that had gone wrong. And the women went out to the front gates because we were all anxious. We knew it was something dangerous. And then we saw an ambulance come down and we saw a doctor's car come down and then the word came along that there'd been a fire underground. I think it was twelve men that were burned. We weren't sure how badly they were burned but little rumours kept coming down from the little groups of women ... however, they got them all out of the pit and it was a good job that it was a hot day because when anybody's been really burned and in a state of shock ... if it had been a cold day it could have been very bad. They got them all treated and got them away to the Infirmary in good time. They were all congratulated on the way they treated these men. It's amazing how it gives concern to womenfolk, particularly because we did learn that one was a man from next door who happened to be my cousin. But they all recovered and there wasn't a life lost in spite of the serious burns. The first aid men were congratulated on their work.

Another one, a sad case, was ... my neighbour was actually killed. We're not sure what happened. Nobody to this day is sure what really happened but it does hurt when someone close to you like that is really hurt or killed. He got caught up on the conveyor belt and it broke his neck, I think ... that was a terrific shock ... people probably suffer to this day from the effect of those things.

I remember the day, it was the last day in September when this man was killed. On that day, you think back ... he was a very jolly sort of a chap and we had fun with him. His birthday was November 4th. It's very strange, I had a rose bush in the garden and it always flowered in November, a dark red rose, and to tease my husband and tease his wife I used to pick one rose bud and take it round for his birthday and they would do the same for us ... you do miss those people when tradgedies like that happen. He had a dog and he was so attached to his master. When he didn't come home, this dog would stand at the gate watching for a man walking down the street in overalls. The dog use to wag its tail when he saw somebody and then his tail would go slower and the dog used to go back in the house. If he heard a car come he would go running out and if the car went past the dog would go back in. Even a dog felt that as well. Very sad really. Little incidents like that, you know, you see the other side of the mining. This is life, it does happen. That lady and her family were in a dreadful state of shock and she had help from all areas. Even from the management themselves. They just couldn't do enough for her. He was a very loyal man.

Gwenda Taylor: My dad ... either 1928 or 29, he was involved in a big rescue down the pit. He got a big certificate and a medal, one of the highest honours he could get. I can remember the presentation, I should be only about six and my sister was only a baby ... they held it at Ellistown Council School ... my dad was in the St John's Ambulance and because he'd done the biggest part of the rescue he got this lovely certificate ... and I think it was five pounds in money and this medal. I thought it was a St John's Ambulance high medal ... it had got a black ribbon on and he never parted with that.

Well, in a pit, if there's a fall, they always say there's three, and this man was trapped and they dug him out ... the next fall came and trapped him again and they got him out, all but his heel — they couldn't budge it. My dad crawled in and he hacked his heel free. And while he was in there he was leaning over him and my dad had to keep coming out. The manager said, "Can you get some brandy to him Lew?" My dad said, "Only through my own mouth, I can't get it to him from a bottle." So my dad took it in his own mouth and got it to the gentleman, I can't remember his name. He knew my dad and he kept saying, "Tell the buggers to stop pouring boiling water on me Lew, they're scalding me." It weren't, it were the sweat off my dad, you know, trickling onto him. And they kept saying, "Lew, can you hurry it a bit? It's cracking again." which meant there were going to be another fall. In the end my dad got his heel free and my dad come out and he says, "Ok, get him out." And as soon as they pulled him free ... my dad went up what they call the incline and sat on a barrel and the doctor had come down and he looked at my dad and said, "What's wrong?" and my dad says, "'Tain't me, it's him down there ... he wants the help, not me." So the doctor went down and he gave him an injection. And when this chap come by him on the stretcher he just waved to my dad and he says, "Thanks Lew." and he got away with a broken leg.

Jack Rush: Then there were one day — nobody knowed nowt about this, ... We were coming along the level, with all the sludge and water ... two would get into a tub, one used to shove a bar

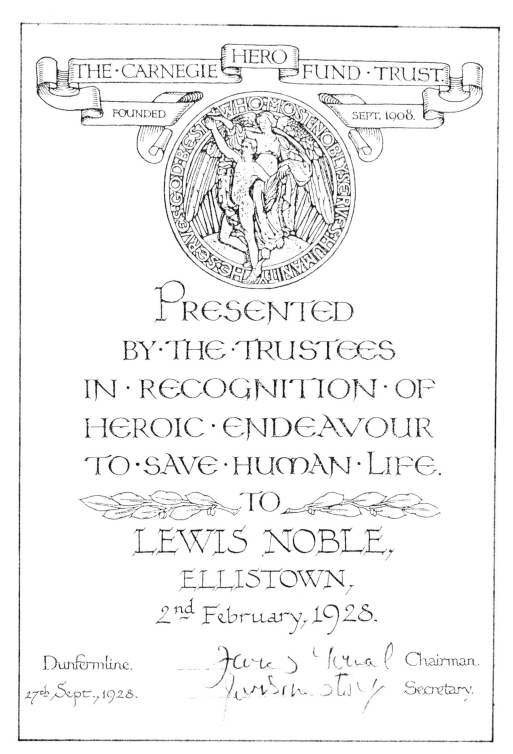

THE·CARNEGIE HERO FUND·TRUST.

FOUNDED   SEPT. 1908.

WHO·MOST·NOBLY·SERVES·HUMANITY·BEST·GOD·BLESS

PRESENTED
BY·THE·TRUSTEES
IN·RECOGNITION·OF
HEROIC·ENDEAVOUR
TO·SAVE·HUMAN·LIFE.
TO
LEWIS NOBLE,
ELLISTOWN,
2nd February, 1928.

Dunfermline.   Chairman.
27th Sept., 1928.   Secretary.

Certificate awarded with Carnegie medal to Lew Noble

underneath and sit on the buffer and press this bar down to steady the wheel. Well, instead of it going straight on, somebody had turned the switch and it were going down the bank. Him at the back jumped off ... we were going down and George Moore says, "Owd yer!" and he put his foot up into the roof and chocked it up ... that about broke his back ... Frankie Brooks says, "Ooh dear," he says. "I thought you'd all gone to the pit bottom." It would have killed us if he hadn't done that.

Reg Thomas: Sam McKee was the undermanager at Number One pit when I first started there and he was a very big and a very aggressive man, was Sam McKee, very demanding ... he was quite a frightening man ... Now, Jack Darker, the hero. There had been a very heavy fall of roof at the coalface in Number One pit and it was a very dangerous situation. Mr McKee, Sam McKee, seeing how dangerous and fraught it was, he sent elsewhere in the pit for Jack Darker. Now Jack Darker was a very experienced collier, everyone knew Jack Darker. He'd been gassed some years earlier than that, so he'd already got a sort of a bit of fame ... put it like that ... Anyway, Jack came along and got to work on this fall area ... fearfully dangerous place. And he was in the process of holding his shoulder under a roof bar so that some of his mates could get props underneath it and they succeeded in doing that while this was pressing down and these chaps got the props underneath and they succeeded but, then they discovered that Jack was dead. The pressure had fatally injured him ... Nobody knew. It had obviously fractured his neck ... and Sam McKee wept, sat down and wept ... big, bruising sort of a man, sat down and wept.

And for my part, I was straight down there to do a plan of the ... I had to measure up the scene for a fatal accident report which was one of the jobs of a surveyor. You have to go down to all fatal accidents and measure them up and prepare plans — quite a fearful job at times. I did thirty-five in my time with the Coal Board. It adds to your experience a lot.

Robert Stewart: I was packing and chocking ... I was in what we call the waste, where you've got the debris and stones to pack with and I was retrieving a piece of stone ... the roof was a yard of mush, then it was solid stone and this mush came down and buried me. There was only my head showing ... I shouted for help. One of my mates come with a catch prop — a wooden prop — and put it on my shoulder up to the roof ... anyway, I got out. I'm accident prone, I think.

I remember an accident at South Leicester. I was working down the drift ... It was a one in four drop and you used to jump on the belt and ride down ... wasn't supposed to but we used to do it. And one day a young electrician jumped on the belt ... there was a big roller at the end and a guard, and his right leg caught this guard and took it off, clean, below the knee. He was only twenty-one. He was a football player, a rugby player, a cricket player ... within eight weeks he got married ... young, you see.

Another one at New Lount, a young man, he was watching the belt, watching the coal going over the end. He must have been cleaning out some coal between the rollers and caught his hand ... pulled his arm out at the socket. He was only twenty-one. He died the same night. I've seen a few sights, terrible.

I had thirty-three stitches in my shoulder and had my leg broken three times ... I went out the mine and had it stitched at Ashby Hospital ... I was lying on a trestle and the sister came in and put a key in my mouth — to bite the key. I felt it when she was stitching under the armpit ... They wanted me to stop in hospital but I said I'd be alright and I walked home. I broke that leg. I fractured it three times and walked out of the mine. Fortunately, it was the fibula ... They were bad conditions at Lount — a very wet mine. Up where the face was rough, I was at this table end, to put timber on when they wanted it. They told us on the tannoy when they'd received it ... but one day we put some timber on and were told they'd received it and we left. Later on, a bar which had been left at the face, went up between the chocks and caught my friend in his

Desford coalface showing Dowty Props and Desford Chocks 1959

stomach, you see. They took him out and he went to hospital and they sent him home but he was in pain all night. They took him back to the hospital and they cut most of his liver away. He's alright now. Looking back at it, it nearly killed him. That was a Panzer machine.

I think, today, when an accident happens today it's more severe because of all the heavy machinery, Dowty props, everything's so heavy.

Joe Webster: I was in an accident myself. I was on a low seam, it was barely a yard and I was working with a fella named Marshall, the same age as myself and we'd just finished the shift, the last bit of coal, ready for coming home. They fired a shot at the side of us and the vibration ... down came two large stones. Well, I was fortunate, I was up against the prop and my shoulder was against that. It broke — smashed my shoulder, cracked my scapula and shoved my head to the ground, knocked all my teeth back and I finished up in the Leicester Royal and my friend at the side, it put him ... broke his jaw, smashed his face more or less and he lasted three days. And then while we was in there, the war was on and they was bombing Leicester and it was terrible — terrible lying there ... and they rushed us off to Zachery Merton Home in Woodhouse. I'd got a broken nose and they said, "Right. We shall repair that afterwards, operate." but it never came off ... it troubles me a bit but not too much. They came back to the pit and carried on as usual. But my friend died. It killed him. I was off work for two months.

I was always told ... you must go back and that helps to balance your nerves and whatever, you see. I have got a nephew who never got over it. He worked at Whitwick colliery and he was sent to a job and the overman went over the machine ... and my nephew blames himself, the overman got killed. And I said you must let him go back but he could not go back and he doesn't do anything at all now, completely wrecked him.

72

Dr Sheila Lee: I have not, but my husband's gone down to give morphia and deal with things down the pit if it had been that somebody was trapped. And I have been called to Ellistown pit, not to go down but to say whether somebody that had been brought up on stretcher was dead or not, as to what's to happen — is it worth sending them to hospital or to the mortuary? We were very involved with pit injuries. They all had got their first aid rooms but quite often we would be asked to go there to see it. You get an awful lot of arm and leg traumas ... and then of course you have people being ill down the pit just the same as they are ill anywhere. They had gone down thinking they were alright in the morning.

When we came here in '46, it wasn't so terribly long after the big mine disaster and so ... we are over a mine now — there's been subsidence here — and sometimes at night you would hear a terrific rumbling and both of us would wake up and say, "Disaster at Whitwick pit! Disaster at Whitwick pit!" So we would try not to go to sleep again for perhaps the next twenty minutes. If it really had been an explosion at Whitwick pit they'd contact us. I think just twice there was an awful noise. I don't know what it was but it just seemed to be under us. We were well aware we were sitting on top of the pit.

Philip Gill: I had about thirty odd years in St John's. And if you were in that district and somebody got injured they always used to send for you to go to the person, help them, look after the injuries and do what you can.

There was one particular chap on a face. It was a ten foot seam but they took the top half, about four foot six inches high ... when it got more mechanised this was. They used to have chocks on it and machines and a Panzer. The machine used to go down on a haulage chain. Well, this haulage chain, nine times out of ten used to run down the middle of the Panzer where the coal used to come. They used to send the seven foot bars down the face for timbering the roof up if they needed them. I were shot firing at the main gate end — advance heading. And they shouted me as I were wanted down the face so I had to crawl down about two hundred yards through these chocks and I got to this chap, his name were George King, he was sitting, well lying in somebody's lap — this other chap who was in between the chocks he'd got him ... and I says, "What's happened, George?" Well, this other chap answered, he says, "His back." I moved the haulage chain and sprang them up against the chocks. The bar had hit him in the stomach. And I said, "Let's have a look, George." and they lifted his T Shirt up and all his intestines fell out. Well, there wasn't much I could do there so I got the morphia out the tail gate end, gave him a shot of the morphia and all I could do were put triangular bandages round his stomach. I think I put about three round his stomach and one a bit higher round his chest.

We got him out, had to drag him down the face on a stretcher. It were a good job as the machine had gone by, so we'd more or less a straight crawl down the face. We got him out and the ambulance were waiting on the pit top, right against the doors. The doctor were there and they put him in the ambulance and the doctor had a look at him ... I found out as later on as they never did anything to him. Nothing they could do to him ... I found out eventually he had broken ribs, damaged spleen and other injuries to him.

They done a new treatment on him, I don't know what kind it was — it helped him recover quickly. And George thanked me and he says, "Next time I see you out, I'll buy you a pint." But I never did get the pint. I wasn't bothered, I mean, it were a job I were proud to do and help him out. It made you proud to be a first aider and to know you'd done something ... to help somebody out.

Frank Smith: I had a tragic responsibility in my thirty one and a half years as a trade union representative of dealing with every fatal accident in Leicestershire — dealing with the widows and children. The most tragic part of my job, but also the most satisfactory in a sense, was that I used to have to get compensation.

73

My first colliery accident was as a boy, pony driving. I was pony driving to a stall next to my father and I'm going to this stall and there's two men carrying a man out on a stretcher with a blanket over his head and I went by and I said to someone that were near, "What's happened to him?" "He's got killed." I went into the stall and told my dad and he put his tools down and walked out. That was my first fatal accident in the pit.

I went for a job at New Lount with my dad and we were walking in the pit yard (we walked it there — five miles from here) and we were walking in the pit yard and there was a pony and trap coming out and there's a dead body with his legs hanging over the back and a blanket over him. A man had got killed ... I can see that now. That's how they treated miners.

The accidents were more severe [with machinery] — where you'd busted a finger before, the machine took it off. The only way I can express it was that every miner busted fingers, bumped things, picking coals up and dropping them ... but with a machine you didn't do that because you lost your finger, lost a hand. And this is the severity of the accidents ... became more pronounced because of the machinery than it was. Statistically, I suppose there's less accidents now, mainly because less people work in the pits. Remember that when machinery came in, men went out, so there were less accidents.

Ernie Harris: The manager when I first went, he expanded a sick and accident benefit club. He got the miners to agree to have one penny per week deducted from their wages and he controlled it. If a man had met with an accident or had been ill for eight weeks, he received from this club the fabulous gift of eight shillings and that lasted for six weeks if he wasn't back at work. Desford had a lot of accidents at one time. Some mechanical — I remember the first man being electrocuted, that was in the early days of coal cutting machines. It was like a huge plug that went into the machine and he put his hand in to clean it and was electrocuted.

There was a room set aside known as the ambulance room. It was very primitive ...it just had a bed in it and old fashioned respiratory equipment.

Jack Jones: In the case of the less serious accidents, the NCB ambulances took the man home and presented him to his wife or his parents ... wives and mothers, particularly, always kept in the ottoman, in the house, on the chest of drawers, clean bed linen and possibly a pair of pyjamas ... always in preparation for the man of the house coming home injured ... It is somewhat of a tradition amongst the older ones that they kept the best linen and so forth for these occasions so that things looked pretty good for when the doctor came.

Anon: During the war, the only ambulance transport from Leicester to Coalville and Coalville to Leicester was provided by a group of off-duty bus-drivers. This obviously restricted the number of people who were able to travel to Leicester for treatment and most of it had to be given by the General Practitioners. Working in the Casualty Department in Leicester, a chap has come in and said to me, "Will you be finished with Joe Bloggs by half-past four because I've got to be back in Coalville to drive the five o'clock bus to Burton?"

I never had to go down a pit to attend an accident. In the early 1950s, the Coal Board employed a full-time medical officer who in theory would have done just that. His name was Campbell, Dr. Campbell and he was based at Coleorton Hall. But he wasn't always available. The first aid facilities at the colliery usually resulted in the treatment being given by the first aid worker immediately. The message would go that medical help was required and the injured miner would be got out of the colliery as soon as possible and I have gone to a colliery in response to a request to attend urgently and seen someone who has just been brought up the pit and I have done what was necessary before sending them off to the Infirmary. But never did I have to go down the pit to deal with any accidents.

N.C.B. ambulance, New Lount Colliery 1958

Aubrey Peace: The first aid in the Leicestershire mines was second to none. Oh, yes. I mean, in the St John's open competition ... there was only one winner and that was the mining team ... because they set that standard, they set a standard. I did represent the pit in the first aid competitions. I done about twenty, twenty-five years with them. Open competitions all over the country. I can say this, I was the first one at Snibby — I won the first open competition at Snibston as captain — '55-'56 time. Very rare for a workman to be in charge of three officials and I was captain of three officials.

Anon: They were called ambulance workers and they were organised under the St John's Ambulance movement and there would be a St John's Ambulance team at each colliery. There was certainly one at Whitwick before the war. After the war, other collieries had them and all the deputies would have to have a first aid certificate and some of the men would also volunteer for this. They would have to attend a course of lectures periodically. I can remember giving these lectures for various collieries.

To improve the standard of knowledge, competitions were held and mock accidents would be set up and four people would make up a team and go and give first aid treatment. Then there would be a competition between all the collieries in the area and this would be held several times a year. Whitwick would hold one. Desford would hold one. Donisthorpe would hold one and all the collieries would go and compete, one against another for a cup. In addition to that, the Coal Board would put up a national cup and the winning team from all the areas, Scotland, Durham, Yorkshire, Nottinghamshire, Leicestershire, even Kent would send teams to this national competition which would be held at Blackpool or Scarborough some weekend in the summer.

J. J. TORRANCE,   W. HALL,   S. T. BIRD,   T. J. SALES,   DR. A. HAMILTON,   B. MORRIS,
(*President,*)   (*Class Secty.*)   (*Vice-President,*)   (*Surgeon Lecturer,*)   (*Instructor.*)

J. SMITH,   W. GREWCOCK,   J. PERRY,   T. BROOKS,   N. ARMSTRONG,
                                        (*Captain.*)

Whitwick Colliery Ambulance Team, cup-winners 1937

Occasionally the winning team would come from this area. The whole idea of this was to try and generate interest and improve the standard of first aid.

They were never demonstrated to the public. They would be held in the colliery or the ... Miners' Rescue Station at Ashby or out at Birch Coppice. And the only people who came would be the visiting teams and their camp followers ... because it didn't make very exciting watching. But ... the people who were the injured parties, would be dolled up and in some competitions you would have people from what was called 'The Casualties Union' and they developed this. They would learn how to pretend that they were bleeding. They would have little beads of red ink in their mouth and they would bite on these and out would come a spurt of blood at a suitable moment.

Down at Desford, for many years I set the competition and went in and judged it. That was an annual stint ... but in addition, occasionally one went to other places. Over at Donisthorpe they would have a bigger competition that required several doctors to judge it. And if you went and judged some of those, you could get them to come and judge some of yours. ... and I've been several times to Blackpool ... to judge the national competitions. The team at Whitwick certainly won at national level ... and the team at Donisthorpe won national competitions on one or two occasions.

... the St John's Ambulance one is open to anybody, of which chiefly the police were the other competitors ... I mean, when Desford would put on a first aid competition which they did every year, there would be the Birmingham Police team and there would be people from steel works up in Derbyshire, quite apart from all the collieries from outside Leicestershire. They would all come down. That's why, as they became more popular, it was useful to be able to get some of your friends to come and help judge them or you'd be there all night.

Miners at the seaside

As a reward to people for doing this work the Coal Board used to put on a weekend trip to Skegness, which was very popular in the 1950s before so many people got in the habit of going for a week in Majorca. And on those occasions a bus would leave on Friday and take all the ambulance workers to Skegness where they were put up in hutted accommodation next to the sea. They would spend a bit of time on Saturday morning doing some first aid work. They would have Saturday afternoon and evening to themselves. There'd be a church parade with a band marching and all in uniform along the sea front on Sunday ... and you came home Sunday evening. These trips to Skegness certainly existed in the 1940s.

Philip Gill: I joined the first-aiders, St John's, after I'd been there [Bagworth pit] and I used to have to take a certificate every year. I think I done about thirty years, thirty-one years at St John's and I'm still in the St John's now and so I've done about forty years service ...

When I was first in the St John's we used to go on a Saturday morning and do first aid practice. They used to pay us half a shift. It was alright that was. They used to have a good first aid team. They won a lot of competitions. They've won at Blackpool in the area finals. I used to go out on trips with them. They'd have a bus load. They'd probably have a competition up in Yorkshire, Pontefract, somewhere like that. Used to hire a bus and used to fill it up with all the lads, and girlfriends and wives used to come. Used to have the competition, stop for tea and then come back and call at a pub on the way back. We used to have a couple of surveyors in the team and

Bagworth pit bottom, top seam 1980

they could reel it off just like reading a book. They knew it word for word. That's how they used to learn it, parrot fashion.

Jim Eckersley: Safety's always been predominant in mining. I don't know if you've heard the saying 'the Coal Mines Acts are written in blood'? Well, they did have a spell, for two or three years when all the pits in the area — I think it was nationally actually — had to put a sketch together, a stage production, on safety. It brought out the talent in mining that was hidden. I was involved. I wrote scripts actually for Whitwick for a couple of years, with help from other people. All the backgrounds and stage materials were done at the pit, in the joiners' shop and fitters' shop and the electricians'. Everyone got together. There were some very good results. We even put some words to music and it was all used in the Safety Sketches.

The Miners' Club at Coalville was absolutely packed just for that — the whole mining community. These sketches brought out all the gory details of underground accidents, which were very, very serious. There was machinery made from just fascia boards but it looked very good on stage. One sketch involved a Frankenstein image and there was stage blood everywhere! We had some notable people come along to judge them and I think it went to national level. It was an annual event. I think, because of pit closures and different complications, it just petered out. But when it was going it was very, very good indeed. They were horrifying, some of them, and funny and very ham acted in most cases!

Philip Gill: I went on the Rescue Service, had just over fifteen years in the Rescue. That was a frightening experience. I went to Cadely Hill over one Christmas and New Year. I think I was there fourteen days fighting this fire down a drift. That was scary really. You used to be all kitted up ... Then you used to have the management at the side of you telling you what to do! ... and you were all kitted up in the apparatus and they were there, well they shouldn't have been there in the first place ... It was hot. You could feel your skin actually burning, it was that hot.

There was a fire at Desford, on a crossing. Ashby Rescue Team were there first and they went in and I went in with another team ... all you can see is a red glow in the coal all above you. All the wood bars are burnt out and all you've got is a steel frame. And we had to go round the back of this fire and all the doors and the wood in the arches had been burnt away. You'd got stones hanging down and dropping down. It was quite warm. And this particular area where it was, it did belong to Bagworth but they gave Desford this coal. Actually I went down an old face that I'd salvaged and I didn't know it. It was that different, with everything being burnt out and it was a good job there was a Desford man who knew his road round there because I'd have been lost. If you get a lot of coal dust and a certain amount of heat that'll start it. And even if you leave ... coal in the waste or wood bars it all seems to get warmer and warmer ... and it just ignites. More or less all you've got to do is stop the air getting to it, the oxygen to it.

You got a retaining fee, that you used to get every year. They used to put it in your wage packet and then the tax man used to take half of it! You didn't get much out of it.

Fred Betteridge: The most serious fire we had while I was there [South Leicester Colliery] — I mean, we had little ones and managed to put them out — I think this one was in 1966, something like that. And I think they lost all the equipment on that face. All the coal cutting machines, the Dowty supports and miles of electric thick cables. And they'd gone in quite a way and they had four specialists down from the Coal Board and they decided it had all got to be sealed off. It was a big job. It took weeks to seal it off. See, what they do when you have a coalface, you have the main entrance into the coalface and then another entrance to let the air in and they'd be two hundred yards apart. And this fire had all combusted into the waste ... after getting the coal out ... so they had to seal both these roadways off to stop the air getting in ... they sealed the roadways up with bags and bags of quick setting cement.

Reg Spencer: They had an explosion at Desford. I worked on the surface and I can remember after that, all the coal and everything off the floors was loaded into tubs and tipped up on the surface and they found cigarette lighters and all sorts amongst that.

Aubrey Peace: That was the only thing, they used to try and sneak a cigarette down, that was all. Oh aye, too rigid. You see they were searched going into the pit and when they were in the pit. Well, it was instant dismissal ... very stringent on safety.

Florrie Harris: Dr Da Souza was the doctor when I lived at Desford. That then became Dr Torrance's practice. When we needed the doctor we used to have to walk into the village of Bagworth, right down to Bagworth Station and stand outside and take our turn because Dr Da Souza visited a Mr and Mrs Bowler — his surgery then was in their front room. We used to have to walk, no matter what the weather was or how we felt, how ill we felt, we had to do that. When we really needed medicines we used to have to go up to Hugglescote, which is the house where Dr Torrance lives now and again wait and he could mix the medicines up at that house ... I can't remember many times when he came to our house because we used to have to try and make it to the surgeries.

W. HALL,   DR. A. HAMILTON,   J. J. TORRANCE,   T. J. SALES,   S. T. BIRD,

A. BARRS,   G. GAMBLE,   W. HICKLING,   W. BELCHER,   T. TABERNER,   J. COWLEY.
(Captain,)

Whitwick Colliery Rescue Team, cup-winners 1938

We did have some bad times with the children, particularly the last two children. They were very, very chesty, they had pneumonia time and time — my brother and sister. One of the famous remedies then was goose fat ... I've seen my mum rub my brother and my sister with this goose fat and I've even seen her give it to them by mouth, which wasn't nice at all.

If I had a bad throat, which was quite often, my mum used to give us brimstone and treacle. And then one of the particular things that Mum used to do for me for a bad throat was, she used to get some sulphur powder on a spoon and I used to have to open my mouth and she used to blow it off the spoon right down into the back of my throat. And it did ease, strangely enough. And another thing we used to have would be blackberry vinegar if we had a cold or a sore throat. Dad used to pick the blackberries. Mum used to make this blackberry vinegar and that would be given to us with hot water added and we'd find that very soothing as well.

It was a must at our house that on a Friday night, when we'd come from school, we used to have what Mum called ... sassafras oil rubbed into our hair so that we didn't have any lice or nits or anything. Then she used to put a towel over the top. It smelt terrible! We should sit there with

80

that on for about half an hour. We would have a dose of syrup of figs. Then she'd get the bath on the hearth, a zinc bath ... we should have a bath and the last thing then would be wash this off our hair. She used to be very, very thorough that the hair was clean. Then on a Sunday morning, to top it all, we used to have to have senna pod tea to make sure that we all went to the toilet. Then we should be alright through the week because we were going to school and then on a Friday night again, the same thing again.

Carl Brown: Fevers, ringworm, headlice etc. were all prevalent and if the lice got you, you were given a balchin haircut. I believe balchin means a new born bird. Anyway the modern name is skinhead.

Eric Burton: During the strike [1926] food was very hard to come by and I suppose, it affected us all. First of all my elder brother was taken away to a place called Mowsley. It was a sort of consumption he had and they took him away to a sanatorium. And then my sister, she developed diphtheria and she was taken away ... when she came home we had to learn her how to speak and do everything again. My sister was then somewhere around eight years of age ... Then, of course, it was my turn, I should think through lack of food — they did the best they ever could for us but through lack of food, I suppose, we was undernourished — I was taken away to Woodhouse Eaves ... in a sanatorium. Consumption, I suppose. It was no fault of my parents ... My mother was great because from Woodhouse Eaves to Ravenstone where we lived, it's a matter of eight miles and my mother used to walk that round journey to come and see me ... she used to do that twice a week ... I can remember being there. We was taken as far as Quorn when they took us away. We went on a train, we got off at Quorn and they met us in a pony and trap ... Every morning when we was there, about half past ten, we always used to have to go in and have a cup of hot milk and perhaps half an apple or an orange ...

I can't quite remember how it was paid for ... whether it was through the Council ... I suppose there was a big family and they looked after big families. It took a lot of pressure off my family for us to be away, to be looked after. My mother couldn't, you know ... those days she was always doing something to earn extra money ... doing somebody's washing for them and earning a little bit of money then. A couple of shilling a week to do the washing.

Florrie Harris: I should think I would be about seven or eight years old [1923/4], living in Barlestone, when there was a serious epidemic of diphtheria and there weren't immunisation in that day. A family two doors away from us, they had little children and one of them died ... and the day that their little girl was buried, another sister died as well. So that was two in one family. I remember, in the village of Barlestone, it was said that there were other people in the same distress as they'd lost children. And I couldn't get it out of my mind. Every time I had a sore throat I thought, oh, am I going to die? We were in a little row you see and that affected the whole little row, with these two little girls. They weren't very old. I should think one would be six and probably one seven. It was a tragedy ... The mum had to go to the funeral and when she got back the other one had died.

Consumption became very bad at one point. I should think I would be about sixteen then and there were two girls in the village of Bagworth two sisters, died of consumption ... and another girl that I became friendly with at work told me that she'd had to go into the Markfield Sanatorium. She'd had consumption. But further more than that my own mother's mother and Mum's sister, my aunty, both of them died of consumption. It was a dreadful thing. It was an illness that people feared and they were put into what was called a sanatorium. This girl told me that when they went to bed at night, they couldn't have the window or a door closed. They had to have as much fresh air — no matter what time of the year, when they'd got this consumption.

I remember a little bit about polio but, of course, everybody began to get cautious of these diseases and when anything was brought out to help them, like these jabs and injections, I think the people used to take their children because they were afraid and made sure that they didn't get them.

Yes, we used to have to pay for medicines but I can tell you one thing, my sister ... when she was born was a very sick child ... I remember my Mum being very anxious because she could hardly afford the money for the medicine, which was half a crown in that day ... but she had to have it to keep her alive. That went on for five or six years. But my granddad, he by that time had got a better job in the pit, and had a little bit more money, and he used to help my mum, you know, gave her bit towards the medicine.

Jack Cooper: You used to keep the bodies at home then 'til they buried them you see ... and they carried them then, on their shoulders. There were no hearses that time of day [1920]. They carried them on their shoulders and then they'd stop half way to the cemetery and people might bring two or three chairs out to put the coffin on, you see. They'd have a little rest and then they'd carry on again. That's how it was with my dad anyway.

Lena Gee: If a miner died or one of his family ... do you know what they used to do at the pit? On the face, as they called it, at strategic points, near the offices, near the gates, they'd put buckets — sink buckets and they'd throw their money in it. Collections, they used to call it death collection. It was handed over, along with the collection that was made house to house always and it would be given to the bereaved. No flowers bought because they needed the money for the funeral.

The funerals themselves, all funerals them days when he came, it was Mr Brewin, and it's still a funeral parlour down Belvoir Road. And they came to collect the body, there were no cars you see ... but they used to come with a couple of lovely horses pulling this big glass hearse. The family themselves would have got the bearers, it'd be friends or nephews, to carry the coffin out. Now, they bring the pall-bearers, as they call them, with them, don't they? But this big hearse would draw up at the house and there'd be cabs at the back for the mourners, depending how many you wanted, and as soon as they'd stopped at the house ... the door would open and somebody would come out, probably my aunty, Mrs Peters ... she'd done what they called 'laying them out' when they'd died. They used to keep them at home and they used to go and wash them, put them a white night-gown on, usually, and lay them out. The body was kept at home, so it'd perhaps be a day before they got them in a coffin, but still kept at home. She'd have the funeral in hand you see, doing the meal when you came back. But when this hearse stopped outside, as I say ... the door used to open and they'd come out with a tray ... with glasses on with ale in it. And these men, the drivers, with reins in their hands, they'd hand this tray up and they'd take a glass off and go to the other one and he'd take one off and they'd drink it up and put the empty glass back on the tray and they'd come down, open the hearse up at the back and the cab doors ready for the coffin to be put in ... And everybody used to stop, you know, any passers-by and all the families as were anywhere near. Every man, (and they used to wear cloth caps then) every man would have his cap off, stand while it went by, never move. Even the kids used to talk in hushed whispers. It was as if everybody shared everybody's troubles.

Dr Sheila Lee: It was the end of World War II and all of us young doctors had been in the services ... we all were scrambling for practices to come to and we actually applied to fifty-two practices ... this is before the National Health Service, this is '46 ... and this one, it was old Dr. Duncan's ... and he would let us do just what we wanted. We were very idealistic and wanted to do our own X-rays, our own plasters and our own blood. Not all of these we managed to do but we did some of them. So it was here ... and once you do come to a practice and get to know the patients you don't very often move because that's the joy of it, seeing the different generations coming up you see.

But, first of all, I couldn't understand what they said. And they couldn't understand what I said. The accent and also some of the phrases, the phraseology. I mean, if they said, "I can't go to the ground." I hadn't a clue what that meant. It means, "I'm constipated." And then, if they came and asked to be examined and I said, "Yes, I'm afraid you're pregnant.", meaning they were about eighteen and not married. They'd say, "Oh dear and I didn't even enjoy it. He cot h'out of me." Well, I didn't know what cot h'out of me means but it means he raped me more or less.

... I was so appalled at the fact that women were at the mercy of men remembering to put condoms on that I was the first person in the town to get hold of a set of fitting rings and do Dutch Caps, which was the only method where a women felt she was in charge of her fertility ... This was about 1947/48.

I got absolutely fed up of people coming and saying, "I think I'm pregnant. Can you do something about it?" At first I thought they meant 'look after me', but I found they meant 'abort me'. Well, quite apart from the fact that it was illegal, I just wouldn't and I'd say, "Well I'm afraid you've got to go through with this. But never mind, by the time your labour comes you'll be in love with the idea of having a baby. But, when you come to me for your post-natal we'll have a talk and I'll fit you with something so that you don't have another one if you don't want it." And I suppose it gets round with word of mouth and some of them did ask me for it.

I got no opposition from patients but ... there was a Catholic priest here at St Wilfred's ... this was the time of the beginning of the pill, and there was a member of his church who was a nurse at Markfield. She'd got two teenaged children and she'd asked me if I'd put her on the pill. So I said, "Of course I will but I thought you people, Catholics you know, weren't meant to." I said, "I thought the Pope had encyclical that you shouldn't." And she said, "Well the Pope doesn't have to have my babies." I said OK and so I put her on the pill. And for some reason, this Catholic priest said to her, "Who is this dreadful women who's committed a cardinal sin by putting her on the pill?" Which was ridiculous because he knew who her doctor was. He knew me. And we'd met at death-beds and everything. But that was the only opposition.

The husbands wouldn't disagree. But, there was an expression around here called 'a beer baby' which meant that the husbands went out and got absolutely tight on a Friday night and then came back and I suppose nowadays you'd call it raping your wife. I mean, they just had sex. And they didn't wait to put a condom on. It wasn't that they disagreed with it. They were only too pleased to. But, I mean, they were nice enough men but they just had too much beer inside them and it had to be quick. So the woman had to be prepared.

For about the last thirty years, longer maybe, I can't think of one girl that I had to make arrangements for her to have it in a home for unmarried mothers. So there must have been a drop. In other words, I don't know about the figure ... but it meant that, well, every baby was a wanted baby. There used to be somewhere at Northampton you could send them if they were non-Catholics and there was a home called St Joseph's at Derby which would take the Catholic ones ... adoption was arranged from there.

I used to do, I think, Monday, Wednesday, Thursday and Friday, I did about an hour, an hour and a half ante-natal ... obstetrics and gynae' together. To do perhaps six patients in that time. But then, I mean, you did everything yourself. You did the weighing and the testing of urine and the counselling ...

When we started there was literally only one surgery and I used to just have a sort of hour in the afternoon, I think between four and five. My husband would do the morning surgeries and the evening surgeries. We had a room ... and we did our own dispensing, you see, before '48 before the National Health and the patients just used to come in and get their bottles from there. Well, that was all made into a very adequate smaller surgery and I used that.

Len Bramley: [Toilets — underground] were none existent! In fact later, nationalisation, they tried but they never made a success of it. But you could train yourself as you never wanted to go. I never used to go down there. If there's no toilet facilities, well, that's the only thing to do. You've got to train yourself.

Tony Turner: Well there were three blokes working together, making a new bottom at Number Six ... Two on them were, they'd be in their forties — all this out at night, boozing and the other one were a religious sort of a bloke, you know, didn't swear, didn't drink, didn't smoke nor nowt. They were all three working together ... Monday morning come, you know, after a good weekend, they always wanted to go toilet down the pit like, there ain't no toilets down the pit, you just had one where you could. This old bloke he says to them, "I don't know how you could do it. I've worked in the pit fifty year — I've never been to the toilet down the pit yet." I tell you, they come next day and give him some of those bommy mints — laxative, made him bad. Well he had to go out the pit, eventually. When he come back the next day he had to go to the toilet ... aye, they made him go, yeah.

If you worked in the pit bottom there were one but if you worked anywhere else, you just done it and buried it and that were it. Mind you, a lot of them didn't even bury it, you know, the dirty ones.

Dr Sheila Lee: A thing that absolutely horrified me ... and that's that there were literally no conveniences down there, and they're down there eight hours and when nature calls they just do it ... Somebody came along and they had a peptic ulcer and you probably know that one of the causes of a peptic ulcer is going too long without food, you see so that the gastric juices start biting into you. And I said, "Do you have regular meals?" "Oh, yes!" and then I said, "When?" and then I found there was this terrific gap and then this man, as I suppose a lot of them did, went home and had a tremendous meal, far too much. So I said, "Don't you call it snap? Why don't you take sandwiches or bread, cheese or an apple — why don't you take it down ?" He looked at me for a minute and he said, "Would you eat your lunch if you couldn't wash your hands after you'd been to the toilet?" And I said, "Is it like that?" And he said, "Well yes. There's nowhere, you just go in a corner and do it." I think it's terrible.

There's pneumoconiosis, the disease of lungs. There's a lot of that. And also we'd got to be very much aware that when a collier died — you used to warn them before, the man, and the woman — but when they died there would be a special certificate given and there'd be a post-mortem and the lungs would be sent up to Sheffield because then, if they proved pneumoconiosis, the wife would get an extra pension. There are still women around now that get that pension. Obviously you gently brought that subject up long before you thought they were going to die ... but you say it to the man first, that you would want your wife and family to be comfortable and this has to be proved and, therefore, to do that the pathologist has got to look at your lungs and so you won't mind that will you? — and I can't think of anybody that said no.

My husband always seemed to be in contact with ... the miners' representative and he used to ask for my husband's reports on different people, on different injuries that they'd had ... although it occurred in the pit, how much was due to actually the way that the pit worked and how much was due to the man being careless.

In 1948 ... Bill Horton, he was a deputy and a friend of my husband ... he said that it would be a good idea if we went down to see the environment in which many our patients spent most of their working lives. He invited me to go down too and I was surprised at this because I knew that there was a superstition that if a woman went down the pit it brought bad luck. But I was told that that didn't follow because I wasn't looked upon as a woman, I was looked upon as a doctor. So I didn't quite know how to take that, but anyway I went down and the usual thing, you're searched for matches or anything like that. Then you're given a pair of overalls and a helmet and you go down the lift shaft and then you seem to walk for miles. Then you realise you have to crawl on your hands and knees and then there were sorts of alleyways going out like little alcoves and there was the chipping sound and there were colliers on their knees hammering away. A lot of them would turn round and say, "Hello Doctor! Hello Doctor!" and I don't think my husband had any idea who they were and I certainly didn't, until perhaps within the next few weeks they came to the surgery and they'd say, "You didn't know me when I was in my pit black." ... And you saw these buggy things coming along and that was important because you saw how some of the injuries were when the buggies got out of control and squashed them ... It was interesting and I think both of us felt a greater respect for a collier after having been down.

Anon: The commonest that would be reasonably specific to mining would be the so called 'beat knee' which was produced by the fact that many miners would work on their knees. They would wear knee pads to protect them to a certain extent but bits of coal and dust would get between the pad and their skin and friction caused inflammation and consequently redness and swelling of the tissues on the front of the knee. This really was similar ... to 'house maid's knee' because in the earlier part of the century there were lots of house maids who scrubbed the floors and they were down on their knees in the same way. ... Similarly there was a so-called 'beat elbow' which was caused by repeated knocking of an elbow on some hard object, usually stone in the region where they were working ... the beat elbows were never so much a nuisance as the beat knee.

Because of the nature of the coal in Leicestershire ... the pneumoconiosis is produced by coal of harder consistency than that which exists locally. So in anthracite mines there would be much more of that particular disease.

The change in mining from the 1940s to the 1970s has meant that there were far fewer people suffering from bad backs. Partly because there were fewer miners working underground, the machines did so much of the work that had previously been done by men and partly because the miner in the 1970s was a more skilled worker than the miner in the 1940s. If you came out of the army in 1945 you were physically fit, you had a fortnight's so-called training and you were then working on the coal face earning your full pay. This wasn't the case in the 1970s where much more training was necessary.

At War

Margaret Sparrow: Well, I was seven years old when the war broke out ... it didn't have much effect on children. It was more of a game ... At school we really had to work hard because school work just went to one side because we were expected to do so much. We were always being told to 'do your bit'. We collected waste paper for salvage. We collected, during Summertime, rosehips. We collected foxglove leaves for making a drug. These were dried at the school on wire frames or strung along the hall ... we also collected foxglove seeds, that's digitalis ... we collected books — the book drive — you took ten books into school for salvage, you were made a private, you took twenty books into school, you became a sergeant. If you took fifty books you became a lieutenant or a captain. The more books you took, your badges came off and another badge went on. We did the school garden. We'd got school meals at that time and a lot of vegetables and fruit from the school garden was used in the kitchen.

We had a National Savings group. We raised quite a lot of money. And one of the highlights of our National Savings effort, we actually won a battleship ... we'd no idea what this thing was but it was colossal ... it was big enough for six or seven people to go up and walk around the deck. It was just a token thing that was brought into the village while you received your certificate, just for one day and stood outside the school ...

They came round with wheelbarrows, collecting saucepans — for the metal, I suppose.

Ken Bowley: If the air raid siren went, even if we were in bed, we had to be taken downstairs. Underneath the stairs was a pantry ... and the bottom shelf was a concrete slab and Mother used to make a long bed up for myself and my brother. We were pushed under there until the 'all clear' went. We used to think it was a bit silly ...we used to say, "If a bomb drops on the house, Mum, we shall still get it." And yet I can remember looking at pictures in the papers of bombed buildings and usually ... the staircase was still standing ... I never thought there was any danger in a rural community of getting bombed.

Ellis Walker: I remember the first bombs as fell ... there was four of them dropped ... that was 1940. What they called them at that time of day was 'screaming bombs'. When they came down, they screamed ... That's when things began to change, I should say for the better when the war started ... up to 1939 things were very bad in the district. Folk were beginning to get more liberal to one another. With their sons and daughters going in the forces and the Land Army, it seemed to bring the community closer together as they took notice of one another ... I was just in my twenties ...

What made me so bitter ... my father worked at South Leicester colliery[1930s]. He worked in the stall system ... my father worked with three of his brothers and they was accused of filling with a shovel instead of with a fork (that was to pick the larger coal out and leave the slack) and they were sacked. My dad was black-listed and that's what made me so bitter about these Glovers ... he couldn't get a job in the area ... him and his brothers were victimised ... I would never doff my hat to anybody and I've never called anybody 'Sir' ... When the war broke out, I was at South colliery ... it came to joining the Home Guard ... Mr Glover said, "Right. We've got to have fire watchers on the colliery surface." He nominated me to join the Home Guard ... I had to go. So when we gets there, all we'd got were broomsticks and pick handles ... Well, I always remember the first rifles coming, being issued for the Home Guard ... this Glover ... Dunkirk had took place ... I said to him, "Things are getting bloody bad, aren't they?" He says, "Yes." I says, "What are you going to do, Mr Glover? Are you going over to America? Are you going to be one of the first out of country and leave us all behind?" I says, "Before you go, now they've given me this

New Lount Home Guard on exercises

gun, the first time they give us a bullet (if Hitler gets here) the first bugger as is going to go, is you." That's how things really started to change. They started to think of you as human beings. They got frightened ... because I'd got the hatred about what they'd done to my father ...

Ken Bowley: The blokes who worked at the pit and were exempt from the forces, they had to do their bit on the 'home front'. The colliery had its own Fire Service Unit and the men were trained like part-time firemen, I suppose ... They also had to take their turn at fire watching. There was a very large pit bank, or spoil heap at Ellistown colliery — the old pit bank which had burned itself out — the top was flattened ... Right on the top of it was a fire watcher's hut. I can remember my father letting us stay up one night, when he was on duty and taking us up on top of the pit bank and we could actually see the bombers going over Coventry. We could see the fires and the searchlights and everything over Coventry. It was a mixture of horror to think that a town was being bombed and yet excitement ... as a ten year old, first of all being allowed to stay up and to be taken up the top of the pit bank and the excitement of seeing these bombers going over. Mixed emotions really.

Reg Thomas: Frank Porter had obviously seen service in the First World War. He was bald as a balchin and brown as a berry ... he was a general factotem. He came into his own in the colliery Home Guard ... He used to man the sentry box at the end of the colliery drive ... he'd got the only rifle ... When Mr Butterley came down in his lovely Canadian Buick ... Frankie Porter would jump out of his pillbox, stand right to attention, shoulder his rifle and give the most exaggerated salute ... he did it to nobody else ... he was the perfect Jonesy from 'Dad's Army'.

Frank Smith: A lot of our pitmen had to go in the forces because they were regulars. See, pitmen did this. They'd be in the Territorials or ex-regular army. Territorial Army was very big in Coalville and Whitwick ... used to march up and down. We used to laugh at them sometimes but they were the first to be called up in 1939. A friend of mine came from the artillery to work in the pits and they fetched him and we all got — I nearly said sloshed — but we got merry Sunday lunchtime and in the evening he were in uniform.

You know these sun-beds, it was something like that — in a ring — and you used to wear goggles and you had five minutes on the front and five minutes on the back and that was supposed to replace the sunlight we weren't getting because we were working from dark in the morning 'til dark at night.

I remember that at the outset of the war, 1939, I was earning two pounds, fifteen shillings and when the war finished I was earning about eight pounds, ten shillings. When I started work, it was one shilling and eleven pence a day[1925].

Ernie Harris: In the war years, things changed. I'd got married six months before. We had a new managing director who was a very helpful, forward looking man. He offered me a house to rent, to get married, at the colliery. When you were offered these properties, you paid a nominal rent but you were more or less regarded as being on call at all times. So when war came, that increased. I remember Sunday September 3rd when the surface engineer came to us and said, "War has been declared and we've got to provide an air raid shelter and black out all these winding engine houses so no light can be seen. And we've got to do a lot of that before we go home today." The managing director was there as well. He brought several of the miners, provided them with sandwiches and cigarettes and an air raid shelter was constructed before we went home that night. It might have been twenty feet long and perhaps nine feet wide and it was built of the arch girder work that they used to send in the pit — coated with zinc and then covered in dirt. Looking back, I don't think it would have been very efficient. Later on, they made much deeper ones in the old clay pit.

Each colliery had its own platoon of Home Guards and you had to do training for it. You had to go on duty on a rota system, perhaps for two hours over a twenty-four hour period. Then weekends — mock battles and all that sort of thing. In some cases you went for some training with the military. I remember going to Nottinghamshire to learn how to work, dismantle, fire, etc. a thing known as a Blacker Bombard. We had lectures on the Lewis gun — the colliery had a Lewis gun to fire at enemy aircraft. Each member trained with a Sten gun. We were called out on one occasion, early one morning. An enemy aircraft had been shot down and the crew had baled out and were somewhere in the countryside. But there was no action as far as we were concerned. That was the closest we came.

In my own case, I was called out during the night to go into the pit to start a pump that wasn't working or something like that, and then back to bed. We've been out as many as three times in one night. You see, in those days they didn't maintain a night shift of mechanics and electricians and so on, that all came after nationalisation. I often look back now and wonder how we had the energy to carry on.

Reg Thomas: In traditional mining systems, if you think about a map of a mine for the north, south, east and west. If you go north, you usually call the coalface on that side of the colliery — North Number One, North Number Two ... and you knew where they are. Somebody else coming to the coalmine would know, for instance, that it was the north. Now, Mr Butterley had his own way of doing things in those days and the underground maps of Desford read like a geography map. We'd got Malta, Tobruk, Abyssinia, Antwerp ... they also tell a historical story because they were all happening at that time ...normally it should have been called Middle Lount Number Four, perhaps, but he called it Tobruk ... We all knew them and the men knew them but anybody outside wouldn't know where on earth to start looking for them.

I also think about the office staff at Desford ... most of the office staff, the young men, went into the army and they all came back over time ... Bob Forsythe went in the navy. He got his leg blown off in Malta so he came back early. Nothing daunted Bob. By this time, he'd got a metal leg. I can see him now — we used to play cricket at lunchtime, the girls and the lads, and Bob always used to stick this metal leg down the wicket. He was never afraid of the bowling!

The Home Guard. It was a real 'Dad's Army'. I think they'd got one Canadian 303 rifle between them (I wasn't old enough to be it in.) And I recall when they went shooting down in the clay hole — target practice — I used to sneak off and go with them ... They had a Lewis gun ... and all the Home Guard lads ... my recollection is that only me, the office lad, hit the target with that Lewis gun. We had an exercise one night and I think Desford was fighting Bagworth colliery ... I was on the switchboard ... but they cut the telephone so I had to be a runner from Desford up the hill to Bagworth. I was taken prisoner by the Bagworth Home Guard. They took me into a room and gave me tea and coffee all night. I was deemed to be out of action by the referee.

Florrie Harris: When the war was on, we used to get together and have concerts. We would go to the Thornton Club and have a concert. The money would go to the soldiers and that, to help them. We had some very happy times, singing all sorts of songs, then. Singing was a great thing, really ... I remember two prisoners of war coming to one of the concerts. They really enjoyed this. I can't remember the name of the two boys now but they did visit with a Willett family in Bagworth. They were prisoners of war and they were allowed out ... When I had my first child, they made me a little toy which was wonderfully made. It was a wooden toy in the shape of a bat. They'd got like four little chickens on the top and they were attached to a string and if you shook the bat, these little chickens came down one by one as if they were pecking the corn ... wonderful craftsmen ... Italians.

89

Stan Moreton: I was called up in the RAF in 1940. They got to know that I'd worked at a mine and I was released to come out of the forces to work at the mine but I must go back to work at the mine I'd already worked at which I did and I stayed there for forty-seven years. I was on the surface, not underground and our hours were a shade longer than the underground men ... I spent nearly twenty-nine years in the boiler house, cleaning boilers out and getting them in condition to make steam to wind the coal out the pit ... cleaning them underneath and inside.

Leslie Roberts: Most of us wanted to go back to our old jobs. There wasn't much choice, really. I started back in 1947 with the magnificent sum of six pounds a week ... by the time my emergency tax and whatnot had been stopped, we'd got just over four pounds to live on ... I worked there [colliery office], I think for just over twelve months ... couldn't really settle so I went down to Snibston, got a job and worked with my dad. Worked with him [as a sawyer] just over three years, before he died.

I left there and went into the police force and did nearly three years on the force. I left there ... went back to the Coal Board in the wages office at Whitwick Road. Couldn't really settle there and went back on the police force ... and I stayed there for the rest of my working life.

Ernie Harris: We had them on the surface as they had to do some training before they were allowed underground. People, like myself, had a Bevin Boy with us to train him. I had one who, I think, was Austrian. He told me in broken English, he didn't understand everything. He didn't understand how there was a gate post but his letters also came through the post. It was confusing for him. There was another young chap who was a student of languages. I told him that by the time he left the mine he'd know another language that wasn't published in English literature. They were very helpful.

Two Bevin Boys were champion cyclists — Bill Duffy and Jack Pratt who was also an engineer who produced an invention to help support the roof. The Bevin Boys came from all walks of life. The man who eventually became secretary of the Baptist Union (Bernard Green), in his early days as a student, was sent as a Bevin Boy to South Leicester Colliery.

Bernard Green: May 1944 was spent at Cresswell Colliery, Derbyshire, on a brief training course. I was then sent to Coalville to work at the South Leicester Colliery at Ellistown. They were still the days of the private coal owners and South Leicester and Snibston Collieries belonged to the same company. Since there were no pit-head baths at South Leicester I was able to use the Snibston baths.

No accommodation was arranged for me, so I sought the help of the Rev. Percy Austin who was minister of the old London Road Baptist Church. He kindly arranged for me to stay with a Baptist Minister's widow, Mrs Vesty in Broomleys Road. This was a temporary arrangement and eventually I lodged with Mr and Mrs George Roberts in Bardon Road and later with their daughter and son-in-law, Hilda and Bob Hinds of Bakewell Street. I cannot speak too highly of their kindness and of the way they allowed me to become one of the family.

The old London Road Baptist Church was a very welcoming spiritual home. There were also many village and small town churches, of all denominations, in the area. These provided the opportunity to gain experience as a young lay preacher. Coleorton, Griffydam, Whitwick, Ellistown, Hugglescote, Bardon, Shepshed, Bagworth, Desford, Hathern, Measham, Moira, Melbourne, Swadlincote and Coalville all played their part in preparing me for ministry.

My first job at South Leicester Colliery was on the bank in a coal wagon, stacking large lumps of coal so that there would be no slack made in railway transit. Two of us were expected to stack about one and a half wagons per day! Can you imagine what my hands and back were like at first? I had come straight from an English public school in Wellingborough, Northants, and had never done any physical work! But there were good friends to be found there — Jo Armson was the bank foreman, an active member of Hugglescote Baptist Church, and the older man, Fred Davenport, who I think was a local Methodist. I also met and got to know quite well a Mr Rowell who was the miners' agent in the National Union of Miners, of which I was a member. My recollections are that he had a very difficult job. Before nationalisation came there was little or no collective bargaining and hard battles about wages, bonuses, working conditions, compensation for injury, etc. were fought. Mr Rowell was at the heart of these and often seemed to please neither the managers nor the men. After a month on the bank I went to work underground on Number One pit. George Stinchcombe of Central Road, Hugglescote was my working mate for most of the time. We were responsible for keeping the tubs moving in the pit bottom sidings. He was the clipper and Derek Billings and I had to make sure that he was kept supplied with tubs to send on their way to the various coalfaces and that the full tubs were marshalled as they arrived and kept available for those who loaded them onto the cage to go to the surface. Woe betide us if the traffic stopped in either direction! It was hard work, repetitive and monotonous but there was a natural and hearty comradeship among us all and having made up my mind that I must enter fully into the life and experience of mining, I gained much from it in the way of human relationships and understanding. It was excellent training for the Christian ministry.

Never having had any awareness of coal mining I found it fascinating to learn more and more about it. Occasionally I was told to go with a surveying group to help them. This took me to all sorts of underground workings, old and new, and to places where there had been falls of roof, etc. Packing and ripping, shot-firing and coal cutting, conveyor belts and loader ends soon became familiar matters, not because I did them but because other mates did them and these were the sort of things we talked about.

Pit accidents opened up a new insight into the cost of coal. To see the conditions in which, before modern automation, men had to work, especially in shallow and/or wet seam coalfaces, was a real eye-opener. I have ever since respected miners and am sad to see the decline of the coal industry in recent times. In some ways I believe they have been treated appallingly by the politicians.

Half-way through my time at South Leicester, nationalisation came. The paradise that was forecast and expected never came. Was it just a change of name to the National Coal Board while the bosses remained the same? Conditions only improved very gradually.

In my later time, the clerk to the under-manager, a man named Enoch Green from Broomleys, became ill and I became his assistant and then his substitute whenever necessary. This meant that I had to record those present and absent, deal with phone calls, complete the attendance and overtime records for the wages office etc. This opened up another world of knowledge but I found that it led to divided loyalties. I felt solidarity with the miners yet I was now working on the manager's side. At times it was not easy. Interestingly, one day the colliery manager, Mr Burdett, asked me if I would consider training for management in the industry! I appreciated his personal interest and encouragement but that was not my way forward. Eventually release from National Service came and I was able to enter a British University and Bristol Baptist College to train for the Baptist Ministry.

'From Coalpit to Pulpit' would make a good title for my adult life! But what a rich experience it has all been. I shall always be glad that mining was part of it. I learned much from it and made some lasting friendships. Insights into life and work, human temperaments and needs, etc. were of immense value. In some ways it made a man of me! I sincerely hope that it meant that I never lost the common touch.

N.C.B. trainees 1947

A number of vivid memories remain — walking from Coalville to Ellistown and back every day to be at work during the great blizzards of 1947, hurtling up and down the pit shaft in the cage each day and especially when the cages rocked and hit each other, getting used to eating snap mingled with coal dust; huge daily dinners in the pit canteen, topped with a pint bottle of milk; week after week during the winter months with little or no daylight because of being on day shift; and so on.

I thank God for those three and a half years, though I do not believe I could ever have settled to the job for life. Coalville has a warm place in my memory and I shall never forget the many people who accepted us Bevin Boys, foreigners as we were to the industry and made us feel so much part of the community.

Ray Allen: A shock in December 1944 — orders received to report to Cresswell Colliery as a member of Bevin's Army (I was hoping to be an air gunner). A shock because the nearest encounter to the bowels of the earth for me was the cave at Woodhouse Eaves. I went for training in underground mining and was sent to Whitwick which was a fairly modern colliery at the time.

At that time there was about twelve of us that used to catch the 9.00. p.m. Midland Red from Loughborough to Coalville. I was put on the night shift. This took a lot of getting used to after being a 'free spirit'. The work was hard and naturally dirty and often dangerous. Not all the natives were friendly, their own kin joining the armed forces to get out of the pits. It also took a while to get used to the local phrases — being greeted with words like Old Butty, Neffy, Cus, Fayther, and what did 'doss'na' mean? The pay wasn't all that great so after a while I went to work at Ellistown Colliery. Things started to look better — still night shift but I was put on contract work straight away and that meant more money. There were no showers at that time so we had to travel on the bus in our pit muck but we did get showers later and a good canteen and medical centre.

Looking back on those years I think they were some of the happiest. I worked with Scots, Irish, Welsh, Geordies, even a Pole and a Canadian. The one thing that stands out was that everyone helped each other. If there were breakdowns or hold-ups on the other shifts that made us late, everyone pitched in to help — lots of cussing, joking and laughter.

The Bevin Boys were not allowed to leave the mines until our demob number came, the same as the armed forces, in 1947. Oh! what things we were going to do and what jobs we were going to get. Alas, other people had the same wild dreams. I got a job that I enjoyed but the wages were no big deal and after struggling for three years to support my growing family, I went back to Ellistown. Then they brought automation into the mines, one machine and six men to do the work of twenty. At that time they needed miners in Australia and Canada, I chose Canada and never regretted it for one day.

Frank Smith: Very amusing, some of the Bevin Boys. A parson's son, he came, wore gloves. They wear gloves regularly now but he wore kid gloves, you know, and he was an artist, a marvellous lad. Some of the Bevin Boys, they came to escape the war, we knew that ... there weren't many made it. As soon as they could be released from the pit they left. There weren't many of them, if any, who made it to the coalface. Bevin Boys became a little bit of a joke. Some were conscientious objectors ... but this parson's son was an artist and when he got time, he used to draw on the side of the coal tubs, you know...draw faces, Hitler especially, and all that sort of stuff.

Reg Thomas: We had a Bevin Boy, his name was Ewart Booth. He was the son of a minister of the Methodist Church. At that time, and I've never thought differently since, I think that to be made a Bevin Boy was the most horrific experience a lad could have had. To go in the army was one thing, you know you're going in the army and you have a perception of the army, but to be forced to go and work at the coal face in a coalmine must be horrendous ... some took to it and some probably never did. We had one at Desford ... Ewart Booth particularly, and he'd come from a genteel background and, as I say, a minister's son ... Partly because he'd got a relatively good education and just coincidentally, we wanted help in the surveying office, he was allowed to be an underground linesman which is the underground element of the day to day surveying. You had the surveyor and his staff in the office and underground you had lads doing ... putting centre lines on to keep the roads straight. Ewart Booth did that for us. But for any other Bevin Boy who, against his will, was put to work in the coalface, it was criminal in my opinion.

We had a strange experience at Desford. One day, the manager rang me up. We had a lad called Arnold Pilenicks, he was a Latvian lad and the Russians had just recently overrun Latvia and his mother and family stayed put but he kept ahead of the Red Army all the way across Europe until eventually he fell into the Americans' hands. And by doing so he was able to come as a refugee to Britain. The manager said, "I've got a lad here, he can speak a bit of English, can you get him a job surveying?" and he became an underground linesman. He became very attached to my family because he'd got no family, and everyone loved Arnold ... but he developed TB and he had to be taken to Markfield Sanatorium ... the poor lad died. We felt very sad about that — took pictures of his grave and sent them to his mother. It was a sad, tragic thing particularly because he'd evaded the Russians right through the whole of Europe, sleeping rough, saw the Russian tanks behind him ... tragic.

Gwenda Taylor: They built the Nissen huts [at Ellistown] and all the concert room, dance hall, and there was also a big canteen where they all ate, and a laundry room where they could do their washing. Also, a smaller Nissen hut that was used as a little hospital base if they were sick. They came from Ireland, Wales, Kent ... more or less a lot from Ireland and Wales and they worked at Ellistown pit, South Leicester, and Bagworth. They were the three mines that those from Ellistown worked at ... some of them went home after a while. I think it was because they were homesick, you know. Some of them, after they'd been in Ellistown for quite some time, the people in Ellistown took them in their own homes because they got friendly with them. To go in someone's home, it was better than being in a campsite ... it was more homely and they got looked after better, so quite a few of them ended up in the villagers' homes.

Well, I was only young and, naturally ... they was all up there. Next thing we heard they was having a concert up there one night. You had to pay but everyone who wanted to, could go to the concert, so we all went up more or less to see what was going off. They were all young lads up there, so we went and got talking to them and after a bit they said they were going to see about having dances, you know, Saturday nights ... they'd got a bar in the concert place and they started having dances. Sometimes it was records, sometimes it was a little dance band. They'd probably have a dance one week, a concert another. And of course they all did little turns, I mean, the Welsh, they could sing ... and that's how we got to know them ... some of the girls went out with them for quite some time but I can't remember any of them actually marrying any of the Bevin Boys. It used to be the waltz and the foxtrot and then they started doing the jitterbug. The Yanks brought that in. They used to do the Lambeth Walk, Okey Cokey, anything that could get us all going. Coalville at that time had got quite a good drama group and they put on plays.

This dance hall and concert room was ever so big and then there was a library where they could sit quiet if they wanted to. Some of them came from quite educated backgrounds. Some of them were really scared stiff when they went down the pit because they'd never been in anything. Some of the Welsh boys, well they knew a bit about mining, but them from Kent ... The older miners, like my dad, used to take perhaps so many of them down because they were all between the age of eighteen onwards. They used to talk to them — encourage them. Some of them couldn't take to it at all.

Alastair Segerdal: I am the eldest son of Dr Alexander Segerdal, formerly of 54 Belvoir Road, Coalville. Forty five years ago, as a cadet in the Air Training Corps at Ashby de la Zouch Boys' Grammar School, I was all set to start my National Service in the Royal Air Force. By the time I had registered as a driver in the RAF, an old school friend, Philip Emmerson, told me about a scheme whereby young men could do their mandatory two year National Service as a coal miner. At that time, Philip's father was manager of Snibston Colliery.

Born and bred in the midst of a coal mining community, the idea of working down the mine was not that outlandish. I talked it over with my father and he arranged for me to meet the manager of Whitwick Colliery, Bill Hall. Mr Hall arranged a visit to the colliery for myself and two other boys. Such visits were not uncommon, both as a recruiting approach and a public relations exercise for visitors. Following nationalisation of the coal industry there was a nationwide campaign to breathe new life into the coalfields and present the industry as an up-and-coming viable area for careers in mining.

The idea of becoming a Bevin Boy was not without its advantages. I decided to work in a coalmine rather than lounge around in a post-war air force. There were also other incentives for me to become a Bevin Boy, one being a girl friend named Enid Hughes. Furthermore, on the visit to the coalface at Whitwick Colliery I was surprised at the number of miners I already knew. One of them, himself a Bevin Boy, told me, "It's not too bad at all, Al, here at Whitwick pit. Becoming a Bevin Boy like me is worth thinking about." After his two years' work as a coalminer he went on to become, of all things, a member of London's famous ballet troupe, the Ballet Rambert.

Like their counterparts in the armed forces, Bevin Boys came from all walks of life. But, unlike those in the armed forces, they made much higher wages. Bevin Boys were never a bunch of

Whitwick underground workshops 1958

second class coal miners. They did the same work as any other miner and they received the same pay. Quite a number of them stayed on after their two year stint and made careers in mining engineering and management.

In August 1946 I signed on as a Coalville Mining Optant, the official name of the Bevin Boy. In September of that year I was given an A 1 fitness grade and posted to Beighton Colliery in South Yorkshire, one of the training centres for Bevin Boys and other would-be miners. Beighton Colliery was specially adapted for this purpose, complete with lecture rooms and mining instructions, dormitories for the trainees, a gymnasium and coalface installations set aside for teaching purposes only.

Everything was run very much along military lines. At half past six each morning we were woken up by one of those sergeant major types. He even had a large baton-like stick and would bang it with all his might on some metal dustbins, bellowing at the top of his voice, "Six thirty boys! — six thirty boys!" For some reason, this early morning ritual stuck in my mind. In the two years that followed, this 'Six thirty' guy was one of the first things to joke about when you met new Bevin Boys fresh out of training at Beighton. Beighton was an interesting and instructive experience but I was glad to get back to Coalville at the end of this training period. My first two weeks at Whitwick Colliery were spent on the surface doing simple odd jobs. Most of this work consisted of moving stones from the coal as it travelled on moving belts towards the railway wagons in the shunting yards.

Bevin Boys wore the same clothing as any other miner — tough old working jackets and trousers. And, of course, a pair of steel-studded pit boots. Having extra warm clothing was a good idea because it was not as deep as some of the coalmines in the rest of the country and could be quite cold at times, especially for those not working at the coalface itself. Whitwick pit was also very well ventilated and there was always a steady stream of air moving throughout the whole underground system of roads.

Pit lamps were handed out to us from the pit bottom office and you either carried these lamps or hooked them onto your trouser belt. Face workers, deputies and senior persons in the mine always wore a much more sophisticated lamp fitted to their pit helmets. Apart from those at the coalface, there was always a slight tinge of snobbery attached to anyone with a helmet lamp! We then followed a deputy, Ernie, on a long walk along the road leading from the pit bottom to the loader. Further on from the loader were other roads which in turn branched off to the various coalfaces. They seemed to turn from about half a mile from the pit bottom to the loader area and were unlit for most of the way. They were wide enough to take two lanes of very narrow gauge tracks on which the coal tubs travelled. There was an 'up' line that carried the empty tubs to the loader and this ran parallel to a 'down' line that carried the tubs loaded with coal back to the pit bottom. These main roads were quite wide and high enough to walk along. They were permanent as long as the coal seam at their far end lasted. Like the coal seam, they often survived for several years.

As we approached the loader area, the road widened out a great deal to form what is best described as a large cavern which was about twenty feet in height. Unlike the roads, it was very well lit. Ernie introduced us to about five other fellows working there. I spent a great deal of my Bevin Boy period in this cavern-like space. It was here that the pit tubs ended their journey as empties and were turned around by hand under the loader. The loader was really nothing more than an enormous coal chute. In this position the tubs were then filled with coal from the chute and sent back on their journey along the rail tracks to the pit bottom. The coal came down the chute from a large opening which was the termination of a different kind of road, the one that eventually led to the coalface. This road was much narrower and it sustained a wide conveyor belt on which the coal was carried to the loader. These conveyor belts often ran for many, many yards. Quite often they would join another long conveyor belt rather like a road junction. The coal would empty off the coalface belt and onto the next conveyor belt. These particular roads were not too high and for most of the time you had to bend over to walk along them.

At the end of the day, miners from the coalface would sit on the moving belts and ride all the way to the loader area. Here they would trundle down some concrete steps next to the loading chute itself and walk the rest of their journey along the main road to the pit bottom. The loader area became a kind of social area for deputies and other officials who might be on their way to the coalface. They would stop and chat and drink tea in a little 'room' which was cut into the side of the wall. This was also where all of us who worked at the loader area went for our mid-morning break. Two of the Bevin Boys working at the loader area had the job of dealing with the tubs and I was the third one to help them in this work. We would often assist others on different jobs, of course, and they in turn were always willing to help us.

At various times I would also work in the roads themselves but 'work' is hardly the right work to use. You would sit for hours on end in those dark and lonely tunnels, keeping an eye on the tubs as they drifted by. If a tub jumped off the rails you had to stop the cable carrying the tubs. This was done by bringing together two overhead low voltage bare wires. You did it once to stop the cable and twice to start things moving again.

It was easy to get an empty tub back on the rails but a tub loaded with coal, especially when it jammed in the rails, was a different matter. You then had to try and handle it yourself and if this took too long someone at the loader, or the pit bottom, would notice the hold-up and make their way towards you. Many a time I would see their light in the distance — that distinct glow of a miner's lamp on his way to your section of the tunnel. Sometimes, it was better (and warmer!) to run like mad all the way back to the loader to get help. If the hold-up was really bad there was always a mad scramble to handle the problem because stopping the cable for any length of time halted the flow of coal tubs to the pit bottom. This in turn meant the loader had to stop and that meant the coal belts further up the line had to stop also. And, of course, it brought work at the coalface to a standstill.

At times like this, a man named Arthur Morgan would often appear. Arthur was in charge of overseeing the whole district and he would rush at top speed to wherever the hold-up was occurring. He was the clean-cut, outgoing, athletic type and could help you get a tub full of coal back on the rails within seconds. In an emergency he always seemed to appear out of the darkness, urging us all with his clear, resonant voice to, "Get things moving, lads! Come on — let's get things moving!"

At other times I was sent to work on the roads beyond the loader area, the roads containing the moving coal belts that came from the coal face. My work here kept me busy. When large lumps of coal fell off the belt, which was most of the time, you had to quickly haul them back on. I remember working at one of these belt jobs and it was almost knocking off time. The face workers would usually end their shift work some minutes earlier than the rest of us. That way they could be ahead of us at the pit bottom and not have to wait in a long queue for the ride up to the surface. During this time there was no longer any coal on the empty belts but we still kept them moving and the face workers would ride on them until they reached the loader. To this day I can still see the face workers bobbing along as the belt moved over its rollers. One of these face workers was a fellow by the name of Nap Ward. Nap was one of the more active members of the Whitwick branch of the NUM. He was a big, jolly fellow and somewhat surprised when I joined the Union. Yet, there was no closed shop at Whitwick pit and little pressure for anyone to join the NUM. As Nap bobbed along on the belt he shouted out to me, "Do you vote Labour, Al? Don't forget to vote Labour!"

The old assumption that working men and women voted for the Labour Party and that professional and middle class folks voted for the Conservative Party was very marked in those days. Mining areas were always noted for giving lots of votes to the Labour Party and Whitwick Colliery was no exception. There was a strong desire among all the miners to produce lots of coal and show its support for the Labour government as Britain struggled to get back on its feet. The miners would shout to one another, "Do it for Labour, lads!" and "We're working for Labour!"

Although the Leicestershire miners were politically on the left of politics they were always considered moderate in this respect. There was not the militancy seen in the north of England and the South Wales coalfields. Hence, a fellow named Pat Reilly who used to assist Raymond at the loader, was considered a bit of an oddity because he insisted on being an ardent communist! Although Pat was always shouting out about the wonders of Russia and Joseph Stalin, he was not a member of the Communist Party and never turned up at Union meetings on issues that might improve conditions at Whitwick pit.

To go back to that particular day when Nap Ward asked me if I voted Labour, well, here's what happened: The morning shift ended and I moved back to the loader area. On this occasion Nap hadn't rushed on ahead to be first in the pit bottom queue and both he and Pat Reilly were really slinging the insults at one another. Perhaps it would be more accurate to say they were half joking as each tried to outdo the other in insults! Soon we all joined in! "Long live Uncle Joe Stalin!" yelled Pat. "Stalin's no better than Hilter!" yelled Billy Brotherhood. "Go and live in Russia!" shouted Roland. "Pat, you're not a real communist," shouted Nap, "and why don't we ever see you at our Union meetings?" Then Pat would sing his favourite song to the tune of John Brown's Body: "Make Mr Churchill smoke a Woodbine every day when the Red Revolution starts!" It was rather an easy game to make fun of poor old Pat. Whenever you did so he always said you were "One of them bloody Tories!". On this particular day Nap told Pat that I had joined the NUM and Pat shouted back, "I don't believe you. He's a doctor's son. He's a bloody Tory!"

... another Leicester choice for us Bevin Boys was Banner's Milk Bar. It was the only place that served that new craze from America — the milk shake. But the big attraction at Banner's wasn't milk shakes. It was girls! The city of Leicester was renowned for its pretty girls and if they weren't at the Leicester Palais de Dance, they'd be at Banner's. Trips to Leicester were no problem as far as time was concerned because the day shift ended about half past two in the afternoon.

... I remember trudging along Belvoir Road in the early morning darkness through snow drifts that almost buried the lamp posts. I turned into Beresford Street and on towards the bridges that crossed over the railway lines from Snibston Colliery. The snow on the bridges was so deep it was impossible to know where the steps were supposed to be. I managed to plough through these drifts and reached London Road but there was no sign of any other footprints. Normally, at this time of the morning, you'd see several miners of their way to work. Nothing but silence. I was beginning to wonder if anyone would make it to work but somehow we did.

Britain's coal crisis was at its peak in the winter of 1947 but getting the coal out of the mines was only part of the problem. The big dilemma was how to move the coal once it reached the surface. Thousands upon thousands of coal wagons were being held up in almost impossible weather conditions and the barriers caused by the deep blankets of snow never seemed to end. Week after week, there was no break in the weather and week after week the miners at Whitwick struggled to keep things moving. To comprehend the miners' determination during that appalling winter is hard if you weren't there with them at the time. Working at Whitwick pit in the winter of '47 was an education in itself.

... Luck could be on your side if you followed up on the horse racing tips chalked on the front of the coal tubs. Day after day I would always see a steady stream of these tips but I never did find out who the tipster was. Maybe it was Nap Ward and maybe that's how he got his name! I believe the tips came from men at the surface since they would know the odds on a horse for that day's races. That way miners working below could place their bets to a surface worker via instructions on the coal tubs. Apart from racing tips and messages, now and then a series of otherwise meaningless numbers would be chalked on the front of the tubs. They made no sense at all unless you knew Roland, one of the other Bevin Boys. He belonged to a group of church bell ringers and his hobby involved working out new sequences for the group to follow when they pulled the bell ropes.

Another of the Bevin Boys I knew at Whitwick was a fellow named Peter. He and I would sometimes meet in the pithead canteen and tuck into the enormous lunches that were provided for hungry miners at the end of their day's work. It was still late lunch-time when the day shift ended. After our meal we would sit through endless cups of tea thinking up cartoons for the new National Coal Board magazine that had just started publication. The title of the magazine might had been 'Coal' but I'm not certain. Peter was a very good cartoonist and went on to become an artist when his National Service as a Bevin Boy ended. Peter had one or two cartoons accepted for publication in the Coal Board magazine and I too had one published. Because of the acute coal shortage in those days my cartoon was relevant to that particular period. I drew a picture of a typical Coalville street and in the middle of the street stood a little boy next to giant railway wagon crammed to the brim with coal. The boy's mother stood outside the door of their home and she was angry. In the caption she was saying to him, "I don't care where you found it. Take it back this instant!"

In the summer of 1948 my demob number became due and I rode from the pit bottom to the surface for the last time. I took my last shower in the pithead baths and I had my last meal in the miners' canteen. I drew my last pay packet from the colliery's old Victorian management office and strolled home in the August sunshine on this my last day as a Bevin Boy. And now, when I look back on those years, I see much more than just a bunch of coalminers at Whitwick pit. I see good men, kind men, hard working men and men with a special sense of duty, the likes of which we may never see again.

Leslie Roberts: I volunteered when I was eighteen. Most of the office went. You got a choice during the war of being a Bevin Boy ... I was going across the colliery yard one day and I saw them bring a lad out who'd been injured down the pit and I says, "Well, that's not for me. I'll take my chance in the army."

Jack Jones: We still had dockets and rationing of certain foods ... such things as bananas as were in very short supply as indeed, beer was. Hoskins — a Leicester brewer — were able to supply beer to a pub in Market Bosworth which brought people from far around and there was,

Vesting Day 1st January 1947

99

indeed, a ration on it ... two pints per man. These are things that many people today would not realise that in Britain we had rationing to that degree following the war.

Ronald Mayfield: Nationalisation was the finest thing God ever created. You can't tell these young ones because they haven't experienced it. They wouldn't understand what it was like.

Tony Turner: They weren't nationalised when I first started but in 1947 when they did nationalise, that's when they started altering ... improving things. That's when they started electrifying and that. I went back down the pit then. First of all I worked in the bottom to get acclimatised to being down the pit and went and did my face training ... had some laughs like and some bits of sorrow ...

Aubrey Peace: Vesting Day, when the pits became nationalised, I shall always remember it. We were going through a bad patch at the pit. Coal production-wise, we were well down. But second week after Vesting Day it seemed to instill a new spirit into us and we started breaking records. I think, myself, it's the finest thing that ever happened at pit, nationalisation. I mean, I've stood at the pit top when the men have gone down between five and half past five just for the sole reason — this is privatisation — just for the sole reason to get some wooden supports because they were cut back that much. Then when they started bringing in the steel arches, oh, it was a different pit. And I've often sat and thought, when we were private, when we were turning the shaft, why we didn't have more accidents.

We saw a vast transformation in the medical centre and the first aid to the pits. I remember the time when the deputy only used to take a small tin down with a couple of bandages and that ... But after a while we got the morphine come in and we'd got the canisters with our own blankets and stretchers. Vast improvement.

It was the finest thing that ever happened, nationalisation, but it was run wrong. Well, because when it come in it was run by Tory managers. That was the trouble. Coal owners, managers, they'd still run it. Well, they wouldn't run it for people, they wouldn't. They were running it for themselves.

Frank Smith: We expected roses round the door. I had the honour, along with the manager at Whitwick colliery, of hoisting the flag and putting the notice up — For the People by the People — etc. and it was a terribly bleak January 1st 1947. The men who worked at the pit thought there were going to be roses round the door and when they went to work on the Monday, it was still the same, nothing had altered.

But that gave us the chance — the National Coal Board brought in by the Labour government, I can assure you was the basis for the finest conciliation machinery ever produced in the world ... The difference was that the managers that had worked under private enterprise were still there. A lot of people thought that was wrong but ... a colliery manager has to have the ability and technical qualities that a miner didn't have. He had to have the ability to organise, the ability to plan. Well, we hadn't trained any men. The Labour Party hadn't trained anybody to take over the management of the pits and so we had to employ the old ones and they used to say that they were the same donkeys with different jerseys on. But, nationalisation was a good thing for the coal mining industry. It saved it. As you know, during the war, the coal owners, they were subsidised. There's no doubt about that but we produced the coal that made it profitable and at the end of the war the pits would have gone back to decadence and inefficiency and all sorts of things — but nationalisation saved it in 1947. There's no doubt about that.

Where it was all manual, pick and hammer, they started to introduce machinery, coal cutting machines producing three times the amount that a man would in less time. And, of course, there

VESTING DAY
January 1st 1947

MR. EBBY EDWARDS
Labour Relations

SIR ARTHUR STREET
Deputy-Chairman

LORD CITRINE
Man-power and Welfare

MR. T. E. B. YOUNG
Production

LORD HYNDLEY
Chairman

SIR CHARLES REID
Production

MR. L. H. H. LOWE
Finance

SIR CHARLES ELLIS
Science

MR. J. C. GRIDLEY
Marketing

THE NATIONAL COAL BOARD

A Message from the Prime Minister

To-day, January 1st, 1947, will be remembered as one of the great days in the industrial history of our country. The coal-mines now belong to the nation. This act offers great possibilities of social advance for the workers, and indeed for the whole nation.

If all alike—workers, National Coal Board and Government—shoulder their duties resolutely and use their rights wisely, these great advances will be assured. I send my best wishes to all engaged in this vital work.

C. R. Attlee

Cover of Vesting Day leaflet

was an influx into the pits after 1945 when they came back from the army, all the pitmen came back ... and nationalisation, as far as they were concerned, was a blessing. They could now talk on equal terms with the managers. You know, they'd still call them "sir" out of courtesy but you could talk to them on equal terms. I mean, they were our pits. It gave you a sense of participation and to some extent we did participate. We joined consultative committees which were set up, where the management and the workmen's representatives (right from the surface to the coal face) would sit together and talk about the plans for the pit for the next month or week. You'd got the plans on the desk and I've played some part in agreeing to this particular project or disagreeing with that. But in the main, it was just participating and that was half the battle. They [the management] resented it but they had to comply or else get out. I remember one especially pious individual ... he said to me prior to nationalisation, "I'll never work for a soulless National Coal Board. I couldn't possibly work for it." And he was a manager at a pit. The next thing we knew, under nationalisation, he'd got a job as an area surveyor agent. He weren't going to work but he did.

Now, a lot of people resented nationalisation but joined it because their managerial salaries were increased substantially. There had to be this difference — I recognised that, as a trade union representative — there had to be a difference for the responsibility of management because if anything went wrong the trade union bloke at the pit couldn't be held responsible, the manager

Nailstone Consultative Committee

was. Any calamity, the manager was the last chap. The buck stops here. So he had to have responsibility payments and one recognised that.

Managers had been selected under private enterprise because of their ability, from coalface workers, through to deputies, undermanagers and managers. That was the system in those days. Occasionally you'd get a university educated man who'd come in and spend a bit of time at the coalface and then become a manager or undermanager. But generally speaking they were up through the ranks.

Industrial relations was a big part of the success of nationalisation. It is in any industry ... working together and all that sort of stuff. You are talking to an area representative who was proud of the members of the Leicestershire Miners' Union. They were the best mine workers I've ever met in my life.

Ernie Harris: Nationalisation meant a lot of differences in procedures. For instance, there was much more paper work. Planned preventative maintenance came into being, often a lot controlled from headquarters at Coleorton Hall, through the colliery manager. More officials. To produce greater efficiency, I suppose. A lot more money was invested and there were people came into the industry who I don't think would have come into the industry if it was still private. It had great advantages but looking back — you can't condemn it because there were such beneficial developments — but, as a personal thing, in nationalisation you become one body, with privatisation you were a person. If you did what was right, you were noted, you got on by your merits and I think as nationalisation went on, a lot of that was swept away. Wages improved during the latter years I was at work, they improved a lot more after I left. The unions were taken more notice of, officials were regarded perhaps a little better than in the old days.

Reg Thomas: Just as we became nationalised, there'd been a lot of rivalry even in the private enterprise days between Desford and Whitwick ... when we were nationalised this continued. Mr Torrance became the General Manager, ... Mr Butterley became the Production Director. They still were together in a co-operative but competitive way. This was reflected down at the colliery level ... for instance Sam McKee, who became the manager of Desford, used to keep Desford Colliery producing coal (on a Saturday) and he'd have me continually ringing Coleorton Hall to see if Whitwick had stopped and how much coal they'd produced. And he wouldn't stop Desford until he knew we'd beat Whitwick ... that was also continued in football, but perhaps most important in First Aid. Whitwick was the absolute cat's whisker in First Aid competitions ... When we beat Whitwick at football it was an occasion to get drunk, if you were a drinker.

Elizabeth Allen: My father was in the Navy for fifty years ... whenever my father travelled during the world war the family had to go ... When he was finished ... we went to Deal in Kent and there he became the caretaker of a Wesleyan Church and that's where I started my life off in a shop — a drapery business.

I ended up marrying a Coalville miner. I was married at twenty-one, after courting for four years, to a Royal Marine. After eighteen months of married life and the birth of a little boy, my husband betrayed me. There was an illegitimate child and I had to leave. My home life became unbearable. I went to London to try to pick up the threads of my marriage and after I was about six months pregnant with my second son, he deserted me again ... I had to return to my parents in Deal. I went to work in a public house called 'The Providence' and I was there for two years, serving behind the bar. During that period I met William Allen, a miner at Bettshanger Colliery, who later became my husband. We started married life with two children but we had a very happy family life and we had seven children.

During the Second World War, my two eldest boys from my first marriage were sent to Wales. I'd already got two daughters and a little boy and expecting another one and my husband sent me to Coalville to live with ... his sister-in-law. Six weeks afterwards he got his discharge from Bettshanger and he came to Coalville and managed to get work at another pit ... he got his discharge on the grounds that he wanted to come to us. He went to Ellistown first and after a while went to Merry Lees and eventually to Snibston Colliery. He was a face worker.

Robert Stewart: I was in the Royal Air Force during the war, in the police section. I came back from abroad and I met the wife (who came from this area) in Montrose, Scotland. That's how I came down here, you see, went into the mines. I was in the mines before that.

At New Lount Colliery ... I did all jobs — coal filler, ripping machines, anything ... I joined in 1947. I found Leicestershire [accent] very odd — well, when I heard someone say, "He's bathing him." I thought he was bathing someone else but he was bathing himself. They'd say, "He's bathing him." Some did have difficulty with my accent because I speak very fast, Lanarkshire, Glaswegian, round that part of the world. I speak very fast.

It was a severe stroke I had. I had three small ones then I had a big one. I blame that on cigarette smoking, no doubt about it. When I finished at sixty down the mines, I was smoking fifteen — when I retired at sixty I went up to sixty a day. Self-inflicted. Well, one or two sneaked them when I first went there but I didn't. One or two did sneak them down. It wasn't permitted, it was against the rules and regulations, like, but it was done unofficial by some people. I think it's the dust, the environment. There's jobs in the fresh air that are every bit as hard but it's the environment down there. I used to dread it. I never liked it really. I used to dread the Monday coming. I stayed for the money, you see, I had a decent sized family, four children — it was wages.

Ron Gregson: It came to 1962, when the colliery [in Durham] was really coming to the closure and then the chaps used to come from different areas preaching the gospel. We had several meetings at the colliery at the time, in the Miners' Hall, because the colliery was closing and it was a crime because they'd never seen it before. It was a life industry, what we'd been brought up, and our father's had been brought up with. We didn't know what was happening, see. But we knew the colliery had to close because it was run at a loss for so long and these fellas came from Leicester and Derbyshire and Staffordshire and Nottingham, telling you how good the times were down other places and what you should do. So, we decided O.K. we've got to move. ... There was about six hundred men at Wingate [Durham] at the time and they gave you the option, you either got transferred to the Midlands or Wales or whatever or you stayed at your own colliery on salvage work. That was getting the rest of the stuff that was required. That would only be about a nine months' job and you knew you were out on your ear then ... I thought about it a lot and I says, "Well, we've got to move and if we move to Wheatley Hill [also in Durham] or wherever, those are going to close." ... So we moved to the Midlands.

I didn't actually pick Leicester because when the chaps first came, there was a chap came from Nottingham once and he give a good speech on Nottingham, so I says, "Oh, I'll have a bash at Nottingham." So I went and got details from them and I got a job at Rufford Colliery ... but it was only datal work, see ... just doing odd jobs, a set wage but I wanted piece work where I could make money, where you were paid on results, see.

Then, the following week, a chap from Leicester came, Tommy Cotterill ... and he offered me a piece job at Leicester, a contract job. So I contacted my local organisation in the North East and I said, "I'm sorry but I don't want to go to Rufford, I want to go to Leicester." So it was all sorted out because they did help you as much as they could at the time. And I came to Leicester ... I ended up in New Lount Colliery, that's where I first came to, in 1962, September. When we came in September 1962, they all told what prospects there were, wherever you were going and that and they said, "Oh, you'll get a house in a year. You'll get lodgings and this, that and the other."

O.K., I think the theory was good but they weren't quite right with the facts, see. So what I did, me and Bill White (a great friend, we went to school together), when we came down, there was twenty-nine of us came in the bus and we all came down determined to work but we were all split all over the place, see, and me and Bill were in lodgings on Bardon Road in Coalville ... We got settled down and we were on night shift at the time. We had to take night shift because that was the shift we were offered on the job we were offered. And we were on better money than we'd left Wingate for.

Well, comparing the money. When I left Wingate I was probably drawing about sixteen pounds and when I came down to the Midlands I was probably taking about twenty-six or thirty pounds home, so there was a vast difference, see. And we weren't working any harder ... we were making better money. You never know what you're going to earn — knew we'd been offered piece work but when you're offered piece work you've got to discuss things with the undermanager at the colliery about what you've got to do and what they're prepared to offer you. It's what you call bargaining. You made a bargain, see. You say, "Well, I can do this and that in a certain time." And that's what you do, see. In those days if someone could do the bargain quicker than you, he'd make a bargain to try and get more money than you. It wasn't as bad as a fight for survival but it was wits against wits.

Well, what happened ... they said, "Well, you will get caravans in a certain few weeks. You will get a house in a certain few weeks." So, what I did, we came down in the September and I had a motor bike at the time. I had an Albatross twin cylinder. I'd left it in Durham when we came down on the bus. Obviously, I couldn't bring it. So the first weekend I was down, the landlord of where I was lodging, he was a nice chap ... he says, "Well, I'll take you up North if you want to bring you bike back." ... So me and Bill went back and we came back on my motor bike ...

I said to myself, I'm going to try and find some information. Now, whatever those other chaps wanted to do that was up to them. But I says to myself, no, now I want my family down here, see. So, they did promise us these caravans at Ellistown, that's where they were ... so being a stranger in the area ... I jumped on my bike the first chance I had, the second week I was down ... and I found this site and there was no sign of anything. There was some old broken down army buildings ... so I says, now I'll find Coleorton Hall and I found the chap that was in charge ... and he said, "Well, the caravans, there's been of bit of a hitch and they won't be done for a while but we are going to start building houses." So I says, "Where you going to build houses?" He says, "Down a place called Thringstone." I says, "Whereabouts is that?" and he told us and he says, "We're just getting it all sorted out." I went down Thringstone and believe it or not, there was only fields, there was no sign of anything! There was just the fields. And I says, well, this is no good.

And in those days you never thought about telephones, so I just used to sit and write to the wife every night and she wrote back. I wrote and said: Well, I don't know what we're going to do. There's no signs of the caravans which they promised us, in three months I think it was. And I says, "The houses must be about two or three years yet." So she says, "What are we going to do?" So I says, "Aye, don't worry." Anyway, I was only down a few weeks and they hadn't made much progress. Obviously they were trying. There was one morning I came in from work ... and the Coalville Times came. Now, I got attached to the Coalville Times because it was the local paper, see, and I was just looking through it and I thought, ah! 'cottage to let' ... so I got on the motor bike ... I found this place up the forest and I got talking to the woman at the door and I said I was a transferred miner and that I was desperate for a place ... and she said, "Well, you must understand that it's a tied cottage." And I says, "I don't care what it is, I want my family down." So she says, "Well, you've got to do so many hours in the grounds and the wife's got to do a little bit in the house ..." She says, "I'll let you know."

That was the Friday morning ... On Sunday I went up again and I saw this Mrs White again ... and I says, "Well, I want to know. We're desperate to come." She says, "I'll let you know tomorrow." Monday, she didn't ring but I was up there again. I was determined and when I went up on the Monday she says, "You can have it." I says, "Great. We'll be down in a week."

I made all the arrangements and I got the family down in, I think it was, the December. I had two sons and a daughter and we came down ... The rest of the chaps that came with me, they were months before they got the caravans ... When they moved into caravans they were months and months before the houses were ready. So the prophesy didn't work out how they'd said, see. But I was in my house within nine weeks ... and we settled.

On and off, we lived there twenty years and I used to go in the grounds. It was wonderful in the grounds because they had about ten acres and I used to love it, you know. I used to go, when I had a weekend to spare, I used to go down cutting the grass ... in the Summer it was beautiful ... The only reason we left was because when I finished work I said, "Well, you know, I've worked at the pit forty-two years, I don't want to work for anyone else." So we decided to have our own place. So we bought this, see.

I probably sound like a broad Geordie now. I suppose I was a lot broader in those days because — well, when I first came down here when I went to Lount, there used to be a deputy ... Eric Fitchett and he was deputy in charge of the place where I was working and when I came down here I was put with two Leicester chaps to work — Johnny Dodds and Jack Somerton. ... In the next roadway there was four of my mates, Geordies all working together, see. Now, this Eric Fitchett — it's a rather strange story — he used to come in our district where we were, then he used to go where the Geordies were. We sat talking one days and he said, "Ron," he says, "I don't know, I can understand you but I can't understand them." He says, "They're all foreigners!" I says, "Well, I'm trying to make these people who I'm working with understand." A few days later one of the Geordies was off and I had to go with them and Eric comes in. He says, "You are a bloody foreigner, Ron." Simple as that!

Well, yes, you can understand anyone because the relationship in mining is second to none. You'll never get this anywhere else — mining is something that nothing else has got. The relationship's always there. You're always a miner and you'll always be, you know, close to each other. Understanding each other just comes natural.

What it was, see, when I was at Lount, you were working with a Russian, a Pole, a Scotch man, an Irish man and a Ukrainian. And so, I'm saying there's a common bond with miners, see. Why, it was during the war, because after the war, when a lot of Poles were in England — there was a lot in Scotland, actually they married Scottish girls, see — and there's quite a few of these Poles and these Czechs and that, they're good friends of mine and I've met them since I came down here ... and they were in this country, some as prisoners of war. We did have a chap at ... Lount. He was in charge of the belts and he was a German prisoner of war but he was a nice chap, he adapted to the way of life. He'd been working on the land, see, and then after the war they went to the pits. Johnny the Russian, Johnny Stanyard, he was ever such a strong chap, as strong as a bull ... and you talk about understanding people, Johnny never learnt English yet he lived in this country lots of years ... but he could make you understand, you know. Well, that's what we called him, Johnny Stanyard. There was one, I mean, you talk about names, there was one Pole used to work at Lount, Laddie was his name, Laddie, and nobody knew anything other. Even the manager used to call him Laddie and when they used to write his name down on the reports they always put Laddie because his name was probably unpronounceable.

And so when you're talking about understanding people, there was no problem. You had different terms for different tools, see. When you were talking about a shovel up North it was a 'shool' — "Give us that mel." That was a hammer, see ... if you wanted a pinchbar up North, it's a ringer down here — a crowbar. So you just picked these things up, see.

Tony Turner: [Durham Miners] they blended in the same, like. They shut them pits up there, they'd got to go somewhere, ain't they? There were a bit of a hue and cry, you know, at the time ... it all blowed over ... them Geordies, they're worse than the Irish for talking ... I never worked with a lot of them. When you did, you'd say summat, you know, you couldn't understand what they wanted — pass this or pass that ...

Margaret Kaiser: I met my husband ... through a friend that worked at the factory. She was going with this Polish chap and he had a friend that wanted to be introduced to a Scotch girl, so she took me. And that's how I met my husband. He was injured in Belgium and he was sent to Aberfeldy Hospital, a Polish hospital for the troops and that's how he came to be in Scotland. They were moved from there to a camp at Johnston near where I worked.

His mother said to him that the Germans were coming and she got a box of snap, put him on a train and said to get away, that the Germans were coming. He was only a young lad of fourteen. I don't know where he went from there. He never wanted to talk about it.

He was in the army — the resettlement army. ... Then, of course, he asked me to marry him and it was all arranged and then we came back to Ayrshire again. It was to another little mining village ... it was all miners. The first job that my husband had was ... at a saw mill. But when a family started coming along, the wages were very poor so he thought he would better himself and go into the mining where there was more money.

The mine where my husband was working was closing down because they weren't getting the output. So they were all given letters that they could either take redundancy or they could come to various parts down here and, of course, my husband chose Leicestershire. He'd been to see some other place near Mansfield and didn't much fancy it. He preferred this area, so that's how we came to be here. He came to Whitwick to start off with and then later he moved from there to Bagworth pit. I think they weren't getting the work they wanted at Whitwick so they went to Bagworth. Yes, I had a daughter and two sons. Well, my daughter was married before we came down here and one of my sons also worked at the pit with their dad ... and the youngest son, he was still at school.

The majority were from Cumnoch area though. There weren't very many from my area because there was only that one pit that was closing down. I think there were only three or four families from the same area.

It was awful [being uprooted]. It took me quite a few years to settle here but now I wouldn't go back. I'd say we were a bit better off [with wages] really. ... And there was a house available in this estate here for us. I was very lucky, being on the front, on Loughborough Road. I remember packing up, you know ... and getting it all clean and nice for the next person to come in. I used to be very house proud, everything had to be just so. And the same when I came down here, I could've cried, I thought, Oh, what a lot of work again, you know. But it was alright once we got everything all arranged to our liking. We travelled by coach. It was a long, tiring journey.

I found that I got on much better with the local people than I did with my own Scotch people. Well, I know they were from a different area and they thought different. I think they were a more aggressive people, the ones that came down from that area, Cumnoch. Not all of them but the majority were a bit aggressive. They seemed to mix in each other's homes at lot. Where I was from we were always used to keeping more or less to our own family. I was quite happy in my own home and with my family. That was my joy. I seemed to fit in better with the people around here than I did with the ones from Cumnoch area.

He [her husband] fitted in very well, right from the start. I didn't. It took me some time to get used to the place. But my husband, right away, he's the type of person that it wouldn't have mattered to him where he went, he'd fit in. People all liked him.

Peter Kane: I lived on what was commonly called the Scotch Estate, which was the housing estate built for the incoming miners from Scotland and the Durham area, built ... in the early sixties. And that basically gave the social complexion to the village. The estate, in a way, seemed to dominate the village because the old Thringstonians were basically from previous farming stock and very old mining families.

Oh, yes, there was always division. That's why the estate, which is officially named Woodside Estate, was called the Scotch Estate and ... set apart and because it's so compact on the one estate they did seem to dominate the village ... and I believe were resented by the old Thringstonians and it still goes on to this day, of course. But I believe there has been some mixture now and blending of the two cultures because as the young ones have been growing up they've married into local families and that, in a way, has helped to blend the village or more unify the village. Therefore, the division is not so readily perceivable but you scratch the surface and it's there.

Anon: When I think back, it must have affected him [her son] because he wanted to go back at a certain stage. There were two or three young lads on their way back to Scotland and they were caught at Derby. They ran away, yes. So they must have — although they weren't saying anything, inwardly they must have been finding it very difficult at that stage to fit in. Perhaps they just felt — well, for a start, speaking a bit different from the locals as they do and perhaps just being ousted from one part to another, it upsets them at that age. It must have upset them otherwise they wouldn't have done that, would they? Because they'd a good happy home life. At least my son had nothing to run away from. I think that it was an adventure maybe.

At Leisure

Eileen Smith: Father ... he was a miner, on the coal face ... and conductor of Snibston band. All his brothers and brothers-in-law were in the band and my brother was in the band and then my nephews have been in the band. Then it changed from Snibston Colliery to William Davis Band. He played the cornet but he also taught the young ones ... either in our living room or the front room. I think they used to have to join the band. I used to remember him teaching the youngsters and since I've been going to the Leisure Club with my husband, one or two have come up to me and said, "Your dad taught me to play the cornet and I used to come to your house."

He used to conduct the Anniversaries, at the different chapels. We used to call it 'sitting up'. They used to be on a platform and my dad used to conduct and one or two uncles used to do it at other chapels. They were mainly chapel people. But I can always remember, Dad used to smoke and, of course, drink — they used to drink a lot because of the dust, the coal dust from the colliery and they used to drink a lot, to get it out of their lungs really. When the sermon was preached he used to always go out, my dad did.

He used to conduct these Anniversaries where we used to 'sit up' and my mother used to join him then. My mother used to always wear hats, they used to do in the old days, and he was always proud of my mum. It used to be a whole day at these Anniversaries. That meant the afternoon service and the evening service, so we'd have to have tea and there'd be people who would have us over for tea. My dad wanted my mum there with him. Mainly miners, I think, would have us for tea — lovely spreads!

When they went to band contests — they lost some and won some — that was a nice outing. They used to go to The De Monfort Hall, Leicester, Belle Vue, Manchester and The Albert Hall, London, to play. They were a good band ... and to hear a brass band!

Wedding of Amy Lowe and Wilfred Beniston, with Snibston Band

109

They played at my dad's funeral. They all came, the band came to his funeral. And we have a photograph of my dad and mum outside Ebenezer Chapel, with the band, at their wedding.

When we were young, I don't think my mother took us along then. But, of course, my brother would go because he was in the band. He started at a very early age in the band, then he went into a jazz band. Well, I remember my dad playing merry England because it spoilt their playing. The older ones were in the band that long that they were old to me anyway — my dad's age. They kept on going until they died. They'd go on the Co-op Treats, leading the treats. Either Snibston or one of the others, maybe Ellistown band and that was a marvellous treat.

I think there were five of my father's brothers in the band. One was a trombonist. My Uncle George, I think he was on a big instrument, I can't remember what he played. My Uncle Ruben, he played trombone but his children didn't take it up. My Auntie Millie played the piano but not with the band, of course. In the early years it was men only, like in the pubs! I would have loved to have learnt. The one thing it did was spoil their teeth when they blew! Most of them had got false teeth because of the band playing.

I used to often clean my dad's brass buttons on his uniform. They used to have marvellous uniforms and a peaked cap, they were mainly in red and black, then green when it became William Davis Band. Many a time I used to clean the brass buttons and I used to hate the job because you couldn't get it on the uniform. They had what was called a 'slide' and it was metal and you slid all the buttons in and then polished them, especially if it was a contest. And we used to listen on the radio. There weren't many local, they used to travel.

Band practice was Tuesday and if they didn't turn up for the practice they'd have a real telling off. Christmas Day they used to parade in the street and play carols. They used to end up on Ashby Road. But then that finished abruptly because one Christmas Day they got frost bitten and, of course, their lips got frozen and they couldn't play. The men said, "We're not playing again." It used to be marvellous and we missed that immensely.

Leslie Roberts: Probably being in a mining community, brass bands, I really enjoyed them. So much so that in the late 1960s, when I was in the police force ... for three or four years, we went down to the brass band contest at The Albert Hall. And on this particular occasion Snibston Colliery was playing in the second section and they won it. We'd been to The Albert Hall to the main contest where all the big names were, like Blackdyke Mills ... Brighouse and Rastrick and all those. But Snibston, they won their section and it was a tradition after you'd listened to the contest, there was a concert at night and they used to give the results out of all the other competitions ... I think they announced it in reverse order, third, second and first but when they announced Snibston Colliery, the bloke that I was with ... as soon as they said Snibston Colliery — first, "Oh, you bugger!" he said. He was really thrilled ... But the Snibston Colliery band was a good band.

Reg Spencer: I remember the old Hugglescote Band. I think ... we used to call it the Bread and Cheese and Ale Band. I remember the band hut was down Castle Yard which was towards the Castle ... the pub ... his name was Locker that used to be the bandmaster, Mr Locker. Local people mostly [in the band] ... there'd be miners definitely. Well the only jobs there were, were the mines and the brickyard.

Harry Sheffield: There was one, it used to be called the Whitwick Silver Band, that was when I was young. I can remember them very well. At Coalville, there were two big bands there. The Coronation Band and what is now the William Davis Band. It was a big band and won a lot of prizes. We used to have miners' galas practically every year and parades and everything at Coalville.

Frank Smith: There was no Whitwick Colliery Band unfortunately. At Coalville and Ibstock — all pit men, mostly pit men naturally — but Whitwick Colliery never had a band. Mainly because our managers were football crazy and they'd got a good football team. And they can't do everything.

Bowls; cricket; football; the young ones attending football matches; pigeon racing; greyhound racing; walking; talking. They kept their own pigeons, in fact, there were several good lofts in Whitwick and they used to enter races. My dad's brother, he was a good pigeon fancier and his mate, they used to win prizes.

Used to play football too, miners. They always had a football team. My father was a good footballer. I've got photographs of him playing when he was seventeen. And I became a footballer, a goalkeeper. Miners were into everything. Whitwick Colliery, for example, became quite a well known team and they played in the Midland League. The miners always had a football team. They've got the Desford Colliery Football Club, the Bagworth Football Club.

We started the Whitwick Colliery Ace Cricket Club which was composed nearly all of miners and we became a good cricket team — before the war — because they ploughed the field up to grown corn, so it would be 1936 to 39. Longer than that perhaps. I was a fast bowler. We had some terrific men, Juddy Fearn and his brother, they were both fast bowlers. They were good colliers, because they were strong in the arm and they had to be fit to work underground, of course. They went on to play in higher leagues than what we played in. Generally speaking they were fitters and other chaps and not naturally coal face workers. In the district, during my time in office, we had a chap who played for Leicester County who was a fast bowler. Then we've got one who plays for Leicester County now.

Harry Bancroft: I've been in sport all my life, I played cricket with a team in Bagworth before I left school, in the Coalville League at that time. We weren't a very good team but it was a game. We did get a decent team eventually at Bagworth but I was playing with them before I left school.

I was very interested in sport, either cricket or football. I used to go as a scoring boy for the team when they went out but they'd never got a full team so I used to have to play. Well, then we started footballing. I got on with Bagworth, then I went to Coalville Swifts in the Central Alliance. Well, I was courting at that time of day and we were up for different long distance journeys. I was living at Battram. The wife was living at Desford. ... on Saturday nights I couldn't get home courting 'til about midnight. So I packed it in then. I played with Shepshed Albion in the Senior League. I had about six or seven years with them. I've got two Loughborough Cup medals for the Loughborough Cup and ... I've got a Coalville Cup medal for cricket and football. They used to fetch me every Saturday. Send a car to fetch me and off we should go. In fact, when I lived at Battram they came to Bagworth pit. I was in the pit. I came out in my black and the car rushed me home and got me washed and off I went.

I was a good footballer. I could've gone to Mansfield ... and Walsall. They came after me but ... what they offered to pay me wasn't as much as I was getting from work at the pit and I was getting from the Club that I was playing with. So I never bothered.

They've got their own grounds. Desford had a ground but Desford closed. Bagworth had got a ground. They play on that. I think there's football and cricket on their sports ground. There was a cricket team in Bagworth when I was a boy ... Bagworth was in the Coalville Cup final in 1921. Well then ... we left Bagworth and the interest went in the cricket club. Well, I played with Ellistown then, at cricket. We got in the cup final at 1926 when the strike was on and we won the cup, won the Coalville Cup, Ellistown did. They revived it once but it's gone again and the football's all gone in Bagworth. I think they started at the colliery a bit.

I'm all sport though. I go bowling now. All being well, I shall be up tonight for a bit of practice.

Philip Gill: The different faces ... we used to have them in numbers, other pits used to have them in names and they used to make teams up, football teams and play each other. And same with the cricket. I used to play cricket for Bagworth when they used to play different collieries because there used to be about seven or eight collieries around this area. We used to have cricket matches against them. I used to play football for Ellistown colliery. That's when I lived at Ellistown.

Harry Sheffield: I played cricket, football, tennis. Sometimes you didn't have the energy. There were days when you came home from the pit and you were that done in you couldn't finish your dinner. Your mum would put your dinner in front of you and you'd have a bit perhaps and your head would go down and you'd be asleep before you'd had a wash or anything.

Leslie Roberts: There was a bowls club at Snibston Colliery ... and they'd got the colliery cricket club and Aubrey Peace ... he was a wicket keeper. I can remember him being a wicket keeper.

Aubrey Peace: Round about 1950 ... the miners at that time, we'd got the country in our grip through the fuel crisis. At that time of day they used to ask us to work twelve voluntary Saturdays. That was six before Christmas and six after Christmas. I used to play football with Whitwick Colliery then — it was funny, as I worked at Snibston. And they used to go down the pit at five o'clock in the morning on a Saturday, fill ten ton of coal and go and pick up their shoes and that and go and play football.

I played with the cricket team twenty-five years at the pit. A wonderful twenty-five years with them. Round about 1948-49, now we used to travel on away matches, we used to have a pit lorry hosed down. On a Saturday morning, they used to hose it down. ... this lorry had been delivering coal all week, you know. They used to hose it down, drop a hut onto it, bolt it down and that's how we used to travel. They used to charge us sixpence long or short, see. Sixpence for your tea, that was a shilling. I only used to have a shilling pocket money so I was finished then. There was no idea of having a drink at night after the match.

We'd got schoolteachers and that in our cricket team. We'd got a damned good side as well, me duck. Though I say it myself, you were very fortunate to get in the team. You'd got to be above average ... we used to rush Tuesday morning when we used see them put the team sheet up, to see that you were on the team sheet.

Lena Gee: At the back of the pub, The Wagon and Horses, the football ground's behind there. They'd probably be down there on the Saturday afternoon watching a football match — Coalville Swifts, Whitwick Holy Cross, Coalville Town. That was their ground. You used to go down this big entrance, a long way. They'd all go down there and when they were coming back there were never no arguments and they were saying, "Well, best team won." or they'd say, "Well, they ought to have won." but there were never any arguments or swearing.

We were only kids. But my dad, if there were a penny being made anywhere he'd make it. He was a dealer, a real dealer. So we stood at the bottom of the yard because we lived at the side of The Queen's Head and it'd be, "Look after your bike?" All of them came to the football match on a bike. We used to take the bikes up the yard for tuppence! We used to think that were lovely but we had to give it to my mum. My dad said, "Give it to your mum it'll help to get the bread for tomorrow!"

Sheila Burns: My father [Dr Hamilton] was very keen on football ... he had a season ticket for many years for Leicester City and, in fact, was known to scout for them — look for players when he was up in Scotland. He used to go round all the little football matches in Scotland when he was on holiday. It was one of his great delights ... we became very friendly with a Dr Tommy Gibson, who became a G P in Mountsorrel and my father was alerted to him because Leicester City published that they were having a new player who was a medical student at Glasgow University and my father contacted him and they became bosom pals. This chap came down every ... Friday night to play football on Saturday and went back ready for university on Monday. Then when he qualified he came down as a G P to Leicester.

Carl Brown: I recall being told, as a lad, that Ibstock Colliery team played Leicester City in a Cup match and lost twenty-two — nil and the locals blamed the defeat on the fact that half the team had just done a shift.

Reg Spencer: As regards football, I used to go and watch what they used to call The Wesleyans. The field was where, I think, the Junior School is now at Hugglescote. It was next door to the recreation ground ... there was an old fella named 'Punch', all I know him as, is Punch and he was as deaf as a post and he used to shout like mad at the footballers. And, of course, the kids used to stand behind him and make all sorts of remarks. He couldn't hear, couldn't hear a thing. I always remember old Punch.

I used to play for Whitwick Holy Cross ... I had a short spell in the army and ... in charge of physical training was Joe Mercer, the footballer, Sergeant Major Mercer ... he used to get me quite a few games at football but that's as far as I ever got to going professional. I don't think I was that interested. It was a game I liked.

There were a lot of football teams ... even little villages. When I played for Whitwick we've been to Copt Oak and there's been only ... the two teams and two linesmen and the referee. There weren't any spectators!

Stan Moreton: Me and my pals from the pub, we used to go and see Leicester City ... when they were at home. I always took an interest in the referee — how smart he was in appearance and in his decisions. I was interested in soccer although I couldn't play. I thought to myself one day, I'd like to be a referee ... I wrote to Mr Williamson at Leicester ... he made an appointment to go to his house. He sat me an examination there ... papers in front of me, drawings ... well, he gave me my certificate there and then. He made it out, signed it ... I'd qualified as a referee. It was on a Tuesday, Bank Holiday — August — when we were on holiday from the pit. On the Saturday, end of that week, I'd got my first match. You got a small fee and threepence a mile, travelling on the coach, if you travelled on the coach. I nearly always cycled.

Leslie Roberts: The cycling club, Reynard Wheelers, had a mixed membership — quite a lot of miners, engineers, brickyard workers enjoyed the usual Sunday club runs to places of interest. They also entered time trials and track events in various parts of the county and at times further afield. Bill Roberts, a miner at Snibston was one of the better track riders and he won many trophies and prizes at sports events both locally and at Derby, Birmingham, Lichfield etc. He always enjoyed telling the story of winning two prizes at Birmingham — travelling with racing bike, kit and prizes by train to Leicestsr then having to ride to Coalville with his prizes, one of which was a large clock! Bill said he 'puffed a bit' when riding up the Groby hill.

The club was re-named the Coalville Wheelers shortly after the last war. Candy's cycle shop on Belvoir Road seemed to be a focal point for a chat, purchase of all our wants and repairs to our machines by Charlie Candy and Tom Allen. Some of the members of the club were Fred Candy, Cyril Robinson, Jim Powers, Bill Boot, Roy Brotherhood, Arnold Bates and David Pearson.

113

Bill Sharpe's gym class, Battram Council School 1930s

Edith Roberts: My dad ran a gym class held at Battram Council School. They did boxing and boys who wanted to join the police force went to get fit to build themselves up.

Reg Spencer: They used to have boxing at the billiard hall in Coalville, which ... during the war became a factory ... it was up Owen Street. We used to go to what is Hugglescote Working Men's Club, used to call it The Hawley Institute in those days and we used to play billiards. They had a 'dumb waiter' and you could shout down and ask for a drink .... and they'd send the drink up on the 'dumb waiter' and you'd put the money on.

Sim Woolley: There was a boxing club opened at Ibstock. It opened up at the back of the Whimsey pub in an old garage ... they converted this into a gymnasium and I joined this gymnasium and for about four years I was deeply involved in boxing ... from fourteen to when I was seventeen. In those days there were no amateur clubs in this area at all so it meant that if you wanted to box you'd either got to stay in your own village or box professionally. So I applied to the British Board of Boxing Control and got a boxing licence. I had twenty-six professional fights round and about Leicester, Nottingham, Derby ... I won all of them except one. The one I lost was at Loughborough when I got my nose broken.

For four rounds you'd get five shillings. For six rounds you'd get seven shillings and six pence. And if you went to Leicester you'd get twelve shillings and six pence for four rounds and fifteen shillings for six rounds, and eight rounds it was about one pound twenty-five pence, so you can see it was quite a profitable hobby.

I used to train, eventually, with Eric Jones, who was the fly-weight champion of the Midlands ... and I was with Eric Jones about three years and just to show how boxing is generally, in my opinion ... there's a huge racket goes off in boxing. At a certain stage I was supposed to be, or at least my manager was supposed to be, arranging a fight at Wellingborough so that I fought Eric Jones for the fly-weight championship of Leicestershire but it didn't seem quite right to me and my father didn't agree with it so it didn't happen. But probably that gives you an idea of the sort of things that used to happen. I was quite successful in boxing for those few years.

Frank Smith: A miner would gamble. He gambled with his life so he gambled with his money. Many a wage has been lost before he got home. Cards, horses. You're in the wrong area to talk about big gamblers. You've got to talk about Northumberland and Durham for the big gamblers. They gambled a lot.

Ron Gregson: There's always gambling, there always will be won't there? Men'll gamble on anything won't they? I've seen them playing pitch and toss with their wages in their pockets — they're chucking it in! And quoits and cards, all for money.

Harry Sheffield: Some gambled very bad, some didn't have a penny, some never did at all. Plenty I know of never dreamt of it. I know one chap was at work with us at Whitwick and he used to like a go on the horses. If his wife knew that he'd backed a horse she'd say, "You're not bringing it [his winnings] in here, you can throw it in the garden if you like but you're not bringing it in this house!" There used to be bookies runners all round this area, quite a few, you could give him a slip of paper, he'd take it to the bookmakers and then bring you your winnings next day. Joe Brotherhood and Harry Birchell were both big bookmakers, even the police bet with them but you weren't allowed to make bets in pubs.

Arthur Bale: There was the usual amount of gambling, I don't think there was anything done in excess. Leisure time? Well, when I first started we worked eight hours a day — seven in the morning 'til three in the afternoon and then later on the hours got cut down to seven so there was plenty of time for recreation and such like. There are quite a few working men's clubs knocking about where they used to spend the time of day. In later years there was a dog track in Coalville.

Leslie Roberts: Some of the miners were quite heavy drinkers. They used to earn very good money but most of it went on horse racing, beer and what not. And on occasions, very often, they would be found paralytic on the Ashby Road there, drunk. One spent that much money, that when he wanted to go out in an evening he had to borrow a neck tie. He didn't even possess one. But they were few and far between. Most of them were good workmen.

Gwenda Taylor: The men used to congregate at the top of the lane, probably half a dozen or eight of them and they'd sit there along the wall, what they call 'doing the colliers' squat' and they used to sit there with their newspapers, probably picking horses out but at the same time they'd be waiting ... to see which buzzer were going to blow, whether the top seam were working tomorrow or the bottom seam. If the top seam buzzer blowed and those men worked down that seam they'd be alright but if they weren't working tomorrow they'd get up and walk off, a bit disillusioned, you know — "I'm off again tomorrow." — that sort of feeling. Because eventually it come to the means test where they were on the dole that much they had to have money from the means test to help them out. That was before the war. But they used to sit at the top of that lane ... and there'd probably be one or two picking horses out ... but they didn't do it to squander a lot of money away because they couldn't afford it really.

They'd got a bookies in Ellistown but a lot of them used to go up to Coalville to place their bets. They'd got local people who took the bets in for them and then took them up Coalville, you know, and they'd probably pay them out. They'd collect the winnings for them and pay them out ... it was all done hush hush.

Aubrey Peace: I have a flutter on the horses, you know, and I'm very good with the form book ... that's my bit of leisure. And going for my holidays. Never smoked in my life.

Jim Eckersley: We did have a holiday, yeah. I always liked a little flutter on the horses. There was a chap at Whitwick called Jimmy Moore, everybody would know him from years ago and I went to work on the Friday afternoon and I called in and put five bob on the horses, twenty five pence. Saturday morning I went and I had fifty-four quid off him!

We'd never been to Yarmouth and we got up the Saturday morning and the weather forecast looked the best for the east coast. So off we went, with the four kids, to Yarmouth, in the old Morris Oxford. It was a fantastic week. There was this flat just off the front at Yarmouth. I had twenty pounds in my inside pocket, I think the wife had the rest. It was twenty-four quid for the flat, for the week, and I had the twenty pound in five pound notes, out of the winnings. So I said to the wife, "Have you got four pounds?" and he looked at me and the wife and the kids and he said "Oh forget the four quid." He thought I was skint. So I won the holiday for five bob on the nags and got four quid knocked off the price as well — which was quite a bit of money twenty-two years ago.

I've found that most of the miners, I would say, in this area are very thrifty. I liked a little flutter but that's as far as it went.

Reg Spencer: There was a lot of absenteeism in the pit. I worked with a fella that was a bit of a wag, well two of them ... they tended to have time off when they decided they wanted to go to the races. At this time the rest days had just started ... one would say to the other, "Where were you yesterday?" "Rest day." he says. His mate says, "You must have had your rest days up 'til about 1997!"

Horace Cross: Oh yes, there were bookmakers and betting. It was before the days of betting shops and ... at one time you hadn't got to have a licence. If you stood at Coalville dogs, you paid a pound for the lists of the runners and that was your fee toward the Government to make you a legal bookmaker just the same as anybody else.

The only way you could have a bet on horses in them days, legally, was by phoning in. And if you lived next door you were breaking the law if you went and took it to the house but you could phone and that were quite legal. That was the only legal way to have a bet in them days.

Jack Jones: Newbold Verdon was very much a pigeon racing village and Barlestone had some good pigeon trainers. A pigeon they had at Newbold Verdon was considered to be an absolute champion. It was entered in the King's Cup. The lads had quite large bets on it ... because it had been in training flights and achieved very low times and it was considered to be a champion. They waited expectantly for this pigeon to come in ... It was in well before its expected time and everyone was so excited because they'd virtually got the money in the bag ... but with the arm waving and the congregation waiting for the pigeon to come into the loft it didn't settle and come in. It just simply sat there a bit scared with all the commotion. I don't know exactly what happened to that pigeon but there was quite a lot of wrath, I think, that it hadn't achieved its object that particular day.

Gwenda Taylor: The bloke next door, Frank Hughes, he kept pigeons ... and he used to do racing. He used to have a bed in his shed when he'd be racing pigeons, to clock them in.

Jack Jones: There was obviously quite a lot of whippet racing and this had been traditional with miners ... it was a hobby and a sport. And, of course, particularly during the strikes and so forth it was a means of exercising and a means of taking away the boredom of the long days of not being at work. ... They raced them anywhere they could find a spot to race them. There was no actual whippet racing tracks ... possibly the Coalville dog racing track ... there may have been some whippet racing at some time.

Gambling has always been traditional with miners. In fact, the man at Desford, he was in the powder magazine ... and he used to take the bets and of course we had, during the '60s, the advent of transistor radios and they could listen to the commentaries in the powder magazine and some of them would hear the results of the race and nip down and endeavour to get the bet on the race that had passed its time and this chap ... he got caught a few times but he swiftly learnt to prevent this fiddling taking place. But there were some who had quite a happy time out of him.

I think in those days miners would bet on two flies going up a wall ... not all of them ... they were betting men. It think it could probably be put down to the hard lives that they lived and the harshness and very much the way of life — gambling against nature if you like in order to extract the coal from underground.

Anon: The lads at the village used to go rabbitting at night with long nets, taking rabbits, which they used to supplement their meals. And they'd sell them ... round the local people, a shilling a time. They called at people's doors selling these rabbits. It happened when I was a boy and I did it myself when I was sixteen, and during the war, the last war. We had long nets running across the burrows. ... They were in the fields feeding and somebody went round and drove them into the nets. Then the bloke who sat at the nets, he ran down the nets and killed them. They used to hang like flies in the net itself.

All the men used to do rabbit coursing. That is, they'd hold their dogs and somebody would go down the field with a rabbit and let it go and then they let the dogs chase after it and kill it. I used to have whippets myself. My whippets used to run on the courses, Ashby, Hinckley ... Shilton. Numerous races, I had a little dog won every race. 'Mick', he was red, reddy-brown. I had two at one time. The Hinckley manager used to fetch us on Sunday mornings to race. They used to take us down to Oxford and them places to what they called a 'flapping track'. ... That was the track that they used to run Sunday mornings.

Horace Cross: We used to have good hearty dinners. Rabbit in the stew pot with dumplings. I used to catch rabbits. My mother said to me once, "It's a pity you can't catch rabbits with four back legs." — with being a big family!

Mostly round Shenton Park and Sutton Ambion and Market Bosworth, mostly round there. We used to bike it, about ten mile. When the pits were doing nothing at all. When you couldn't get any money for food at all. Previous to the '26 strike and then during that, I was a stall man at Whitwick New Pit, handfilling coal. I should be about seventeen.

Myself, my brother Sydney and my brother Walter worked at pits. The girls worked in Leicester factories. We got by [during the strike]. We had a good old grocer ... and I used to call for the groceries and pay Fridays, on tick as they called it ... He was Mr Holmes — a store against the Victoria Hotel on Whitwick Road, Hermitage Road. He said, "You must keep coming for your order. It won't always be dark at six. The sun will still shine both sides of the hedges. And I know you good people will pay me when you get back to work." Which we did.

It were difficult. You'd got no coal. We used to go fetching trees, logs, anything. I used to go get a rabbit or two to put in the pot. Well, we'd go out at night, on a dark night. You'd know your land where you'd got to go, the fields, the sets they're called. Set up your nets with the wind blowing from the rabbits to you, or they would smell you or hear you — the least noise — with long ears. And chase round and drive them into the nets. Put them in your bag. Eighty yards long, our long nets. If you went ferretting you had a small purse net and put them over the holes and put the ferret in. As the rabbit bolted, the net would catch him, you see. I used to set snares for rabbits and hares and if I went a ride round on my motorbike ... We used to go and pick the hares up and if I hadn't got a bag ... on the pillion cushion, my wife would put them on her knee to bring it home. I had some good customers as used to look forward to me bringing them a rabbit every time I went. During the war when meat was rationed, it were a great thing. I used to charge three and six then. But you could have charged half a quid and have sold them all. I used to make a rota. The people who were my regular customers, I used to start at one end and go right round and round again. I wouldn't let anybody have two. It is poaching, but when your pits are doing nothing and you were doing two shifts, two and a half, three shifts a week ... You couldn't earn any money in them days. I mean it were nothing when you got it.

There were a lot of poachers at Ibstock and Thringstone. They were hot beds of poaching. They didn't used to get caught much. I got caught for trespassing on land in search of game. It was a farce because the pit was off and a gang of us walked through from Margaret Street up to Normanton Wood and round back toward Heather. And I'd got a whippet and it were running along the field ... and it caught a couple of partridges up and one had got a broken wing or something and she caught that. So we sat down and I plucked it. Well, we had a game of cards for ha'pennies and in the meantime the farmer had seen us and he fetched the policeman ... I says, "It's a partridge." He put it down in the evidence as a pheasant ... it would have got killed anyway as it had a deformity on its wing, you see. So they kept it for evidence. It cost us half a quid apiece. About seven of us. But they had to wait 'til we'd got the money!

I used to run my whippet at Coalville dog track. Her name was Queenie the Second. She was a good black and white bitch. Very good race dog for her size and very good at catching a wild rabbit.

Eileen Smith: They liked their drink and their cigarettes. They weren't expensive but they liked to drink every night. But it was their only pleasure really. There was only the radio, no television. My mother's father was a miner and he drank a lot. Now, he did get drunk!

Mick Richmond: There was a bond definitely. Maybe a Saturday night you'd have a get-together or once a month you'd go out for a meal together. Just for a laugh. I think it took the pressure off you. We used to go down to the Jolly Colliers on Thornborough Road. I don't know whether it was the name that attracted us or what. That's where we just seemed to meet whenever we were away from work.

Reg Spencer: The pub I usually used was The Greyhound and it was always known as Neddy Moore's. There was supposed to be attached to the ceiling a glass and this was supposed to have been the last drink the fellow had that was murdered on 'the bridges' in Coalville. It was fastened to the roof and tied with a bit of string. It hung there and they always told me that. I could go into Neddy Moore's ... and have a pint of mild, ten Woodbines and a box of matches and get change out of a shilling.

When I first went to Desford the wage was nineteen shillings and fivepence a shift, that was not quite a pound a shift ... of course, you could make overtime and if you wanted to have anything overtime was essential. The weekly wage was to live on and overtime was a little bit extra for anything you wanted.

It was quite common to see people drunk. There was old Joe Grew, who was well-known for it, trying to roll the white line up in Coalville one day! Then there was the one we used to call ... Jack O'Bill ... and this particular day I'd be coming home about half past one, two o'clock ... and outside of our bungalow there was a seat ... a bus shelter ... and it was raining and he lay on this seat, singing his head off. The pub was just below, The New Inn at Peggs Green, and he'd obviously just come out of there and got as far as the seat, singing his head off in the rain.

Lena Gee: Friday nights, all along the row, they'd all be waiting for their husbands. Because Friday were market day you see. The old fashioned market, with the Orange King and all that. As soon as their husbands had had their meal and they'd got their wages you see, off they went to the market. Going to the market were lovely in those days. And that was an event to the women down Ashby Road, perhaps the only time they'd be out of the house. They didn't bother about drink but sometimes we'd go from the market and my mother would say, "We'll go to The

Redhouse." (It's The Steam Packet now) and we'd sit in the kitchen, in with the tub and the mangle and things like that and she'd perhaps have a shandy. Because we were friends — we weren't actually in the pub.

There weren't many women went sitting in pubs. And men, the bar was their domain, there was never a woman in the bar. If there was, she were scarlet. If a man and woman were together, perhaps, husband would be in the bar and her in the best room, as they called it. Most women didn't even go in but used to send to the 'bob hole' as we called it, to fetch half a pint of ale, perhaps on a Saturday night.

Mind you, there was the odd ones that liked their beer but never any disturbances. The miners worked hard. They were happy, cheerful, friendly and all like one big happy family. And what did they have? What did they want? They were satisfied with a couple of pints of beer — we'll say a couple of pints! — sixpence a pint it was, for bitter. That, and a game of dominoes in the bar at the weekend would be all they asked for.

Jack Jones: The mining community in places round here ... Barlestone was very much a mining village ... Market Bosworth had some miners, probably about twenty of us in those days ... but in Barlestone, it was very much a mining scene. I well recall the Sunday lunchtime that the men would be sitting in a row outside the pub, waiting for the pub to open ... the landlord used to draw pints off and have them on the bar and people used to walk in and take the pint and pay for two when they went back for a refill. Such was the demand of the miners for a drink and the swiftness and the eagerness of the landlord to supply the beer through that method.

Aubrey Peace: If the day man didn't turn up you'd got to be prepared to go next morning. Because there's either got to be a banksman there or a winder there. It's a must. The only time I used to enjoy drink was a Saturday night, after I'd done the Saturday afternoon shift because I'd been relieved and I knew I was safe because the night man was there. I could have a drink with confidence then. The wife will tell you the same but when I was on day shift I was always in bed at ten o'clock because ... you'd got to go to work with a clear head especially when you'd got about two hundred and fifty men in your hands, driving the shaft.

Robert Stewart: I took singing lessons after the war but I lacked confidence. I went to Measham, to Mr Price at Measham, but I was having to have a few whiskies to let go, you know. I was as strong as Secombe, I had a very strong voice — tenor. Every pub in Ashby had sing-songs at that time and they were all full. And I would cheer the men up and sing a song down the mine.

Jim Eckersley: New Years' Day was public holiday in Lancashire, already declared a public holiday, yet down here it wasn't. Neither was Good Friday. But on New Years' Eve — you see I had to work New Years' Day — I went to bed New Years' Eve hoping to get some sleep. But well, as soon as midnight had gone they were banging on the doors and playing the bagpipes and shouting, "Come Out!" I had to get up and it were — if you can't beat 'em, join 'em — kind of thing. I finished up across the estate, and the undermanager at Whitwick pit (his name was Bond) he was at the very house that I went to on Thringstone estate. We were there 'til four o'clock in the morning. I didn't go into work and the day after when I went, the overman said to me, "Where were you, yesterday?" and I said I was with the manager. Presumably he didn't go to work either. And that was tradition brought down from Scotland!

Margaret Kaiser: We used to go dancing, to the clubs. We used to go to Coalville, that was the furthest we went, and Whitwick ... to Margaret Street Club .... and St Wilfred's. Then, of course, when this club down here was built we'd go there too. That's the Ranger's Club down the road. At the beginning it was more or less just the Scots and Durham people that had come down and then eventually, you know, it intermingled. In fact, I think there's more from around here go to the Ranger's Club than any from the estate really.

... there were the retired miners ... they had their own little tote and they had their outings to various places, day trips ... for the wives as well. And we had our little dances. The last Sunday of the month they would have a dance and every first Tuesday of the month they had ... a morning dance.

Then we had the domino tournament for the retired miners. Of course, my husband was, at the time, accused of having a double blank up his sleeve! Because he was always winning with the double blank and, of course, if anybody won with a double blank they'd say, "Ah! a Freddie Kaiser." Some would say he was the domino king, he was always winning. So naturally when he did pass away, they thought it would be a good idea to have a nice badge ... in commemoration of him, for the dominoes, which gets presented every year before Christmas when they've finished the domino tournaments.

Peter Smith: The object of the Leisure Club is to provide recreation, sport and leisure for its members. It was set up in the early 1980s when the run-down of the Leicestershire coalfield was progressing.

We meet every Wednesday ... at Margaret Street Club. It is one of the largest ... leisure clubs in England. We have five to six hundred members. The main functions of the Wednesday morning club are that there's a tote, which brings in around five hundred pounds a week in profit — it's a massive organisation ... they also run a weekly raffle which brings in around forty pounds profit and a bingo session ... That is where the money comes from, over five hundred per week ... over twenty thousand pounds per year, which is used for leisure purposes. One of the main functions is the summer outings ... from May to September ... there's a choice of two each month. Most months there's also a trip to one of the major horticultural shows in the country. It's been known in the past that as many as thirteen or fifteen coaches have gone on one of these outings.

Other activities include trips to race meetings — probably four race meetings per year. The winter activities include indoor bowls ... Christmas shopping trips ... and a Christmas dinner ... and indoor games at the Margaret Street Club.

I have thought, well where are the ladies? There are no lady members and I'm not aware that there were any but people who worked in the offices and the canteens obviously one would have thought were entitled if they so wished.

We don't too often speak about the coal industry. We generally meet to talk sport or everyday events. It's not a political group and we certainly don't discuss Union matters. But it's a happy group ... I go every Wednesday for an hour and I certainly would miss it if I didn't go, for the fellowship. There's a magnificent feeling these Wednesday mornings — comradeship.

Jim Eckersley: We used to go down to The Bull's Head at Thringstone. At the weekend they used to have the old piano going and everybody used to have a sing-song. They used to throw coins in the middle of the floor. If you were any good singing they used to throw quite a few in, you know. There was this fella, Alec Kilday, you couldn't tell a word he said, it was strong Scottish but when he started to sing a song it come out in perfect English.

We used to go up the Miners' Club but that was a big difference when we moved down here. The undermanager at work, Malcolm Smith, invited us to Margaret Street, so we got a baby-sitter. I think it was about two bob to go in then — ten pence. We went in but there were kids everywhere and we'd never encountered that before because where we were from they didn't allow children in the clubs at all. Eventually we took advantage of that and took our young children in on Christmas Eve. That was a big difference from Lancashire. Malcolm said, "Club life is family life." They had a kind of league of bands that did all the clubs in the area every Saturday night. They were quite good, in fact. There was always dancing.

120

I went to chapel to sing but I wasn't good enough really. The start was local talent contests. I enjoyed the competition. Then in 1975 I entered a national talent contest, Bass Charrington Brewery contest. The final was at Blackpool. I won the vocalist's section, which was a cheque for two hundred and fifty pounds plus a three month recording contract with Polydor. Unfortunately, I didn't have any new material to perform so nothing come of it. But we had a good time, we enjoyed it. Perhaps if I'd made it to stardom I'd have left the pits and would be back on the scrap heap. So it was better to have a secure job.

When I was singing in a club up north this chap said, "I thought what a great voice you'd got but when I looked I thought you looked like an old man.". See, and I was only twenty-six. So I bought a 'topper'. When we moved down here, with the children, and I had a big drop in wages, I had to make it up with a bit of pay from somewhere else. I went to the Boot and Shoe Club in Leicester which was a mecca for budding club artists and got a couple of bookings. They were Saturday night, Sunday lunch and Sunday night at the same club. One occasion, I'd been to Whitwick pit Sunday morning. I'd come out of the pit baths and stopped in a lay-by on the A50, putting my topper on with the rest of my hair still wet through underneath. About quarter of an hour later I'd be on stage in Leicester with coal dust still in my eyebrows!

Collecting tallies at the end of a shift, Desford 1967

Anon: If you go down to the local club which we do every now and then because the father-in-law, he's the committee man. He walks around with his chest out, his hands in his breeches — he ain't got the pit belt any more — and they do get very religious when the bingo starts. That is the one time everybody worships together in Greenhill ... there is silence then. You

121

can hear a pin drop. Even the babies have learnt to shut up for the bingo. I don't think the Pope would get as much respect as the bingo!

Fred Betteridge: In the 1920s up to nationalisation we didn't get any paid holidays, we'd get probably two days off at Christmas, one at Easter and one at Whit, not Good Fridays, we worked Good Friday. When it was nationalised we got a fortnight's paid holiday and paid holidays on the seasonal holidays.

Jack Adcock: There was one day's pit holiday on Whit Monday but no annual holiday. If you had holiday you lost part of your pay.

Sarah Whittaker: We would go to the seaside, perhaps once a year, for the day. That was through the colliery and, of course, then there were the stations all about and we'd get on at what they called Heather Station, Heather and Ibstock, and go to Blackpool for the day, or something like that. I never did go on a week's holiday.

Len Bramley: I can tell you when the mines round here had the first week's holiday. That was 1944 that was. Prior to that you had two days at Christmas, two days at Easter, two days at Whit and two days at August. In 1944 was the first week's holiday with pay that the miners ever had. I can't remember if we had the other days with pay or not but I do know we got paid for that week in 1944.

In 1952 we were going to get a fortnight's holiday but they were so short of coal they actually paid us the holiday money but they wanted us to work the second week. The first time the pits ever knocked off for a fortnight in this area was 1953, Coronation Year.

Aubrey Peace: I never had no leisure time, I was always at work. I've seen the pit every day of my life bar my holidays. I even went to work Christmas Eve, Christmas night, Christmas morning, Christmas afternoon. I'd got a very good wife ... she never used to argue. I had 33 years of it.

Harry Bancroft: We didn't go on holiday while we were courting because we couldn't afford it, we were a bit tight for money. There were no holidays when I was a child. It was very rare, it was only those people that had a bit of cash that could afford to go. You could go to Leicester. Once or twice we went to Skegness on the train, on a school trip.

Reg Spencer: I remember ... once going on holiday to Skegness with my parents. And this fellow, I think his name was Richardson, I think he did a coal-haulier's business but he came this particular Saturday morning with an old Model T Ford and he took us to Leicester Station ... I'd never been in a car before ...

Brenda Clark: No, we didn't go on holiday. There were three below me and my father's wage wasn't big. The first time I saw the sea, I was nearly twenty and I was most disappointed, I expected the sand to be like crystal brown sugar, I went to Skegness for the first time and I didn't like it. Very disappointed.

In The Union

Harry Sheffield: I was [in a trade union] but ... everything was kept secret about that. You paid the chap as were collecting ... there weren't many in. I soon joined. I should be sixteen, I should think. We used to give this chap — I think it was about sixpence, that was about once a month. The chap as used to be the union man, he didn't have to let anybody see it being passed between you. I hardly ever remember a meeting being called but I knew where the union headquarters was — the man's house. There was nothing else ... it was always kept as secret as possible because if they [the coal owners] knew about it, he'd be thrown out of his job. He was the collector, you see, and he was in contact with the national union, really, as far as we knew ... It was all secret 'til the strike [1926] practically.

We went to live at Ravenstone ... I got fairly active in local events ... did a bit of entertaining, one thing and another to help out with anything in the village. While I was there we joined the Labour Party, officially ... and it wasn't long before I was an official in the Labour Party. Mrs Sheffield, my wife, and myself, we were given the job of organising collectors and that. And we used to go around any areas we could and persuade people to join. It was three ha'pence a week then ... and we got as many as a hundred and seventy or a hundred and eighty people paying ... and we really boosted the Coalville party up from practically nothing as I might say ... It weren't very long before I became the secretary ... I carried on for quite a while as the secretary, then I was the treasurer and then became the chairman — I went through all the offices of the party. While I was there they nominated me for the Coalville Council, you see — 1951. And they put me against the Tories, and this area where I was put, they'd never won, the Labour, before. And they thought I hadn't a ghost of a chance and the man as I beat, he were flabbergasted when he come to the count because I beat him easily. Eighteen years [on the Council] altogether. I had one year off ... I was defeated one year by six votes. It was called the Coalville Urban District Council — eighteen members. I was working at the coalface but I was on so many different committees, the safety first committee, the rescue brigade, besides the Union business — I was secretary of the lodge so I didn't have many spare nights free, as you might say, besides my Council work. Mrs Sheffield, she was a County Councillor, she became a County Councillor a year after I became a Coalville Councillor ... so between us we didn't see much of each other.

Frank Smith: My dad was a knock 'em down socialist. He was a leader of strikers and (not that they struck) they wouldn't be dictated to like some of the owners wanted to ... they wouldn't be said to, "You'll go there, or else." ... I found records when I was in office of my dad and his dad paying three ha'pence a week ... I was thrilled to pieces when I found this document. It was beautifully hand written. Francis Smith, Arthur Smith ... three ha'pence a week paid in the union collection book.

My dad took me to the first lodge meeting immediately I worked with him in the stall — I was then an adult in his point of view ... so he took me to the first meeting, Victoria Hotel, outside Whitwick pit gates and I sat in the first meeting and the man that I admired most was the chairman — he was the checkweighman at the pit and his name was Arthur Hinds ... he got the room in order, he was strict and I admired him for that. I was of course paying trade union contributions of threepence a week and I decided, "I'm going to union meetings regularly." I went to every lodge meeting they held ... got interested until, perhaps two or three years later, I got elected as the treasurer to the lodge which meant that when the secretary collected the contributions on a Friday, he'd give them to me, I'd take them to the post office and bank them ... I was nineteen ... From treasurer, which is the lowest post, I became secretary ... and then your achievement is to become the delegate, which puts you on a seat on the miners' council. Having had two years on the miners' council — 1936 — I was elected delegate. They had a ballot for secretary, a ballot for treasurer and a ballot for delegate every year. I'd not been opposed as the treasurer, hadn't been opposed as the secretary and I wasn't opposed as the delegate ... that's when my life really started in Trade Unionism.

Politically I was becoming wise, well I thought I was anyway, and I used to involve myself in everything going that was political ... I joined the Labour Party, became active with meetings and all sorts of things and in 1939, because of the inactivity of the Labour Party around that time, because of the tragic conditions the workers were in, I joined the Communist Party. And in 1939, when war was declared and I was still delegate at the Whitwick colliery, I went to them and said, "Now's your time to strike." and I got some sympathy but not a great deal. Even so, while I said, "Now's the time to strike." — I went, did my stint all through the war. We worked solidly from 1939.

In 1939, the beginning of the year, we were on two and a half to three shifts per week ... when war was declared we immediately went to six shifts per week ... we used to do ten yard stints which was something like twelve, thirteen tons of coal because we rested next day, but when war was declared we continued those ten yard stints for six days and that was extremely difficult, nevertheless, we did it.

I kept pushing my political viewpoint to the council and to the delegates and it was bouncing on deafened ears. Extremely patriotic, miners, you know, generally speaking — I'm talking about my own area — and we'd got to win the war. The Daily Worker, which I used to sell surreptitiously, you know, tuppence a time from under my waistcoat, at the pit, came out that this was an imperialistic war, that imperialism was fighting National Socialism — socialist, Labour ... and in 1941 when they made a pact with Stalin and he marched into Finland, Estonia, Lithuania, it became a democratic war and I finished just like that with the Communist Party. I'd never seen anything so hypocritical and I finished with it, resigned, prompt there and then, and we continued with the war.

Jack Jones: I went underground and was allocated the position of tramming tubs from two men who were doing the ripping of roads — enlarging the roadways. One of them happened to be Frank Johnson who was the NUM delegate at the pit and a very strong character, and he invited me along to the union meeting at Newbold Verdon on the Saturday night ... it happened to be the AGM ... two of the members of the committee had not attended and I found myself being nominated and elected to the branch committee ... I'd worked at the colliery then for some three years. [1951]

Conditions of work, I felt, were deplorable, no amenities such as toilets, hand washing facilities. The difference in pay soon became clear to me having earned forty-five to fifty pounds per week on development work — that was driving the roadway into the coalface and opening out the coalface. When I was on the coalface, filling five and a half yards in length by six foot high, four foot three inches advance each day, that brought me the princely sum of twenty three or four shillings per day. And if, in fact, I didn't manage to get that coal filled off, I didn't even get that amount of pay. And so the difference in wages on one coalface and another coalface and on various grades of work was very hard indeed to adapt to ... the arguments on monies were very prevalent on Fridays when they had to go down and see the undermanager — probably wait until half past five or six o'clock, having finished your shift at half past two, in order to argue about the monies you felt you were entitled to and you'd probably get a little bit more money put in by the undermanager, and someone the following week would be down at his cabin on the bank because they found they were short of money and so there was very much a wheeler-dealer situation in those days.

There was a minimum wage which was somewhere about seventeen or eighteen shillings a day ... there was a fall back rate of twenty six shillings if you were engaged on work that couldn't be measured ... miners were very, very dissatisfied because of these differences ... and you didn't know what you were going to draw until you, in fact, picked up your wage packet. It was very difficult to explain to a wife, you know, that that was, in fact, the wage and you'd not been fiddling the wage packet. And so there was these areas, I felt, that the union at that time was very, very weak. The demands for coal were not great, the need for coal following the war seemed to be declining ... we were producing all the coal the nation apparently required ... and the miners were greatly exploited ... but not quite so much as they had been prior to nationalisation because, at least, we had a five day working week.

<table>
<tr><td>

AGENDA.

1—Minutes of last Council.
2—Next Council.
3—Letters from Clerks' Association.
4—Letters re Foundry Trades Dispute.
5—May Day Annual Holiday.
6—Letter from Secretary, Building Trades.
7—Safety Shot Firing Apparatus.
8—Affiliation with Coalville Trades Council.
9—Resolution from Ellistown No. 1.
10—Nationalization, by A. Emil Davies.
11—Middle Lount Tip. South Leicestershire.
12—Nailstone No. 2 Resolutions.
13—Wm. Sykes' application for Old Age Pay.
14—Application from Secretaries re Ballots.
15—Labour College, London.
16—Conference & Congress, London.
17—Bradford Corporation & Loans.
18—Application Old age Pay, John Priestnall.

</td><td>

 RULES

OF THE

Leicestershire

Miners' Association.

ESTABLISHED FEBRUARY 11th, 1887.

Registered under the Trade Union Acts, 1871 and 1876, on the 31st day of August, 1887.

Revised and received the sanction of Council January 26th, 1891.

Revised and received the sanction of Council February 2nd, 1907.

Revised and received the sanction of Council May 16th, 1919.

Revised and received the sanction of Council January 29th and April 30th, 1926.

Begin : be bold, and venture to be wise ;
He who defers this work from day to day
Does on a river's bank expecting stay,
Till the whole stream that stopped him shall be gone,
Which runs, and as it runs, for ever shall run on.

</td></tr>
</table>

Agenda of Miners' Council meeting, 1920 and cover of rule book, 1926

I continued as a member of the committee, no particular aspirations. I did stand for the position of vice-chairman of the branch and got defeated. The union continued to press claims for such things as transport costs, concessionary fuel. We had a long battle in Leicestershire as regards concessionary fuel, whereby the miners were required to give up part of their allocation to provide a pool whereby old miners and widows could have an allocation of coal. This eventually came about ... it was acclaimed by the local press as being very much a community affair and miners had again shown their sympathies, in setting up this coal pool. I continued as the branch committee man at Desford and then found myself in conflict with the hierarchy in that I moved a resolution on behalf of surface workers ... who at that time were getting somewhere about eight

0-6-0 saddle tank steam shunting locomotive, Whitwick 1950s

pounds a week, and there had been men at Desford getting quite large wages for enlarging roadways — back ripping — some of these men had been getting seventy, eighty pounds a week ... I argued that it was unfair for two men probably living next door to each other to go to the same place of work ... one got eighty pounds and one got eight pounds. Their wives had to go to the same shops, same market ... this hit the headlines ... the headlines I well recall ... 'There's gold in them there mines'. And of course they were talking about 'four thousand pound' miners. While there were some getting these monies for some of the time the majority were getting a great deal less than that. I was subjected to a lot of pressure to withdraw the statement — I said I had no wish to withdraw the truth.

I was, in fact, put in the backwoods of the pit so I was not involved with many of the men ... people knew I was telling the truth and I think most miners didn't consider the suppression that I was subjected to justified, and I think their sympathies lay in my direction. This was a new experience for me because I always felt that the unions were there to safeguard your interests but here I found that it was the union representatives that were doing the pressurising against me.

I'd been on night shift for some three years and attending various sub-committees in the pit. I did a lot of welfare work at the pit and I felt that after three years when I was getting out of my bed and going to the pit to attend meetings in the daytime, coming home and going back to bed and going to work at night, I felt that it was time I either progressed through the union or got out of the industry. So we were approaching the AGM, 1971, when I decided that I would go for the branch secretary job at the colliery and I would go for the vice-president's position in the area and I would go for the workmen's inspector's position. I was elected to the workmen's inspector's position and I went forward to a ballot for the other two positions. I was successful in being elected the branch secretary and then, because no-one of the rank and file had held the president and vice-president's position I felt that I needed to get myself known over the Coalville area. I was successful in the area for the vice-presidency.

The chap who'd held it for some thirteen years, Nap Ward ... I went to see Nap ... down at the Hugglescote Club and it was packed in there on the Saturday night and there were about ten or a dozen kiddies pushed their way through and they were pulling at my clothes. They were saying, "We hate Jack Jones," and, "Jack Jones is a bastard." You know, little kids, it was quite embarrassing, standing there waiting to get a drink, everyone looking at me and laughing, so I patted one of these ... a little ginger lad on the head and I said, "Do you like crisps?" and he said, "Yeah." "Do you like pop?" He said, "Yeah." "Jack Jones is a bastard," he said. So I ordered ten bottles of pop and packets of crisps, that stopped them pulling at my clothes. Nap came pushing his way through with his beaming face and he held his hand out and said, "You've out-flanked me brother. You'll do, you'll do." That was Nap ... he retired and they found him dead in his flat up in Greenhill, with his Woodbine burnt through his fingers. He'd been sorting out his horses to have a bet that day. I think Nap died quite happy, doing the things he wanted.

Ernie Harris: I belonged to a union — it was a separate union from the miners. It was known as the Shopmen, Winders and Boilermakers Union — more or less a union for tradesmen. The headquarters was in Stoke on Trent. The only advantage we got out of the union was when they were able to negotiate for an increase in pay or a reduction in hours. That was about all.

Jack Adcock: After the war in 1918, of course they wanted to reduce the wages and of course that's what caused the strike ... they ain't got the sale of coal because the war had finished ... well, of course they had their meetings ... "Are you going to accept these wages or strike?" You didn't want a cut in wages. They wanted to put the wages down... The head office for the Union was at Coalville. They had meetings and that there. The wages wasn't big enough, you know, for a man to live on, then. We know the living was different to what it is nowadays but they wanted to reduce the wages. They didn't strike for a bigger wage. The owners wanted to reduce the wages.

Harry Sheffield: There's a good many got the wrong impression about that, you see. [1926 strike] It wasn't a strike, actually. The coal owners said we'd either got to work another half hour a day or have a reduction in our wages, there were no choice ... and the Union, getting fairly strong then, wouldn't have anything to do with it. They said the wages were too low as they were. The men were working as much as ever they could so they refused it. So they closed the pits. Only people who would do as they told them could go down the pit. Very few did and they were called 'blacklegs' and caused a lot of trouble. Nobody would look at them or speak to them. They were shunned, there were only one or two as I knew.

Straight the way they started soup kitchens. I think they gave us, from the Union, they gave us two pounds, each man — I'm not sure single men got anything — I know the married people got two pounds for two weeks then all the money had gone. I was saving up to get married, been saving up and we'd almost decided to buy a house ... everything went, every penny of it went. Helped my mother out and all that sort of thing ... hadn't got tuppence hardly when the strike finished — six months. But it was a lovely Summer, sun shining and nobody wanted coal actually, much. So they used to go and clamber on the pit bank for bits of coal and that. Everybody did it, practically, as worked at the pits.

Get a bag of coal — you were well away for a few days, otherwise you were tramping about the roads and scrumping anything as you could. Soup kitchens were still going. They were in different parts of the town and they used to have concerts to raise money to pay for the bread and soup and stuff. Miners entertained at different places and all that sort of thing. It was a big community affair altogether. They had parades. The secretary of the Miners' Union came to Coalville three or four times. His name was Arthur James Cook. He were a marvellous speaker and he really got the men together. Always a big crowd where he went, three or four thousand. He came from Yorkshire — he were a Yorkshireman.

The beginning, see, calling this national strike, and the railwaymen and the dockers were going to support us straight away. Mr Churchhill said as he'd bring the army and the navy to take over all their jobs, so at the last minute they backed out and didn't come out with us. So the miners were left all on their own. Well, the miners were bitter about it, actually, but they didn't think as it was going to last long, you see, thought it would be over in a few weeks. Nobody expected it to last very long but, anyway, they prepared for a long siege. They got soup kitchens and they started organising different things — parades and concerts and collecting money — some were sent to Russia to collect money from them. Jack Smith who was a noted man round here, he hired a horse and caravan and even went to London and collected a lot of money for the miners of Leicestershire alone ... If you wanted anything the shopkeepers would let you have it on credit and there were a lot of people with big debts — some were never paid off, I'm sure. All the money went, I can assure you.

Frank Smith: The strike was in April, 1926 and I started work in December '25. So I worked from January to April and then they were on strike. And I came out with the remainder. But because my dad was such a loyal kind of individual, he wouldn't start work, my mother persuaded me to go to the brickyard and I worked three months at the brickyard. I weren't strike breaking, like, but I was taking money ... in those days, I got eighteen shillings a week which was a lot of money which helped out with the family. Then the coal ran out so the brickyard finished ... The 1926 strike, to me, was a long memory of blissful times — sunshine all the time, no rain, catching rabbits with your dad, you know, digging them out and using ferrets and dogs to catch them, playing cards for matches and all that sort of stuff. No money for booze or anything of that description, no drink ... but sitting around ... fantastic time. It was hard, my dad tried everything, he went, what we used to call 'outcropping' — he went digging holes near Lount Colliery to get coal out of the side of the holes where it's near the surface, rabbitting, they say rabbit's beautiful but not when you have it for breakfast, dinner and tea. It was rabbit, rabbit, rabbit. Of course we stole a potato or two from the monastery and apples ... because that lasted a long time you know.

I remember the finish of the strike. My dad, because he was a staunch trade-unionist and socialist, the strike lasted about twenty six weeks ... but they kept my dad out and I, for thirty-two weeks. Couldn't get a job anywhere. The managers phoned from pit to pit: "This man's a trouble maker ... good worker but a trouble maker." And we were out of work for thirty-two weeks. That made my dad more bitter than anything because he demanded his rights, a good living man, religious but demanded his rights ... he hated dictators. He was a very democratic individual but because he voiced his opinions and the deputies and the managers heard him and it got repeated ... he got a reputation for being a trouble maker. He wasn't a trouble maker, he just said what he believed in.

Reg Wood: I remember that, because my father and them they was all on strike and they decided to get what they call Federation coal. That was down ... Woodville, and there's some allotments and gardens on the right hand side of there and they sank shafts down, you know and got this coal. They went down, I should think, down about thirty or forty feet and there was a shallow seam of coal and they used to pull it up with a bike wheel and a bucket and a rope. Then there was a fella named Booth, a haulage contractor ... he used to buy this coal off them, off the miners as were sinking these. There were probably a dozen or so shafts sunk, you know, in these gardens as they were getting this coal, what they call Federation coal. And he used to come and bring a horse and cart and collect it up. Then the brewery lorries used to come from Burton on Trent and fetch it to use on the boilers, you see.

Arthur Bale: The wife had been and got a job at Corah's at Leicester. 1926 we had a six week strike in the coal pits and that's what made her go and get a job to eke out you see. But when it comes to 1929 we had a bit of a shock because she found out that she were expecting a second child so she had to leave. And she used to say "I wish I could get you my job. We should be alright." She was on power frame knitting ... All the rest were on hand flats, all the other girls, but the wife were on two power machines. And she said, "I've a good mind to ask the boss if he'd let you have this job." ... Anyhow, she came home one Tuesday and said, "I've got you this job. Do you think you can get off and come with me tomorrow?" I said "Well, I can get that alright." I said I knew this undermanager who wouldn't say no when I go and ask him for my liberty. So I went to see the undermanager and I told him and he said, "You go by all means and if you don't get on you can always come back." But anyhow, I were there for nearly thirty-eight years.

Eric Burton: When we was young and my father was on strike ... in the stream they saw this black substance ... and found out it was coal. They all got together and dug holes out. It was a yard thick seam of coal. We used to go up there as children with anything, prams, any old barrows, bring the coal down they used to dig out. We'd always got a good fire at home but very little food. Today that same site has been mined and millions of tons of coal has been got out on it, at the Altons on the opencast field.

Lena Gee: We used to go across there with two buckets, a bucket each because everybody were hard up ... when the strike were on especially. Nobody had got no coal, you see, because they weren't working. So we used to go mostly before we went to school, across into the pit yard which were only over the road and these elevated tubs were running along ... from the boiler house and we used to pick the cinders off, fill us buckets and take them back. But at weekends ... Sunday mornings you'd be up early. The older children and there were women, seldom men, on the slag heap picking coal up you, see. And they'd got a watchman, Mr Wood, and I'm sure he used to keep out the way while we got so much coal into our trucks! Then he used to come and say, "Come on, let's have you off here! You've no business on here!" I'm sure he used to stop out the road while we got a bit! They'd all got trucks. Nobody'd hardly got a real wheelbarrow. You know, trucks, prams, pushchairs and all the lot. And the truck we'd got were as big as that settee nearly and it had aeroplane wheels on it. Great big handles, you know, and we'd be struggling along with it. And that was every Sunday morning as that would be done and he used to chase us off.

It were called Number Three and I can't even remember headstocks there but it had been a mine. It must have been one of the very, very earliest. It was closed up ... But that Number Three pit, when the twenty-six week strike was on and we talked about getting the coal off the slag heap, do you know what the miners done? They went across here and you know how the gold-diggers staked their claim, they went across there and got their own coal out ... But they daren't leave it. They used to stop all night because if anybody else went they couldn't turn them off, you see ... so they watched it. And the women used to take them something to eat if the men had got to stop all night.

... regarding soup kitchens I am sorry I can't tell you who organised or financed it, I think it was only opened one day a week. But seeing that the Adult Hall was the venue of lots of meetings in those days it could have been, the Ladies Guild, the Chamber of Trade or even the Mothers Union. You see the people involved in these things were never miners. It comprised of shopkeepers and what we called the posh folks who lived on London Road, Coalville. It is possible the soup could have been prepared and cooked then taken to the hall for distribution. I just don't know. But I do know what I have already told you about the collecting of the soup is perfectly true.

I also remember the Beniston's Brass Band, the band that consisted of all the Beniston's sons and sons-in-law and they all lived at the top of Ashby Road. Teddy Beniston was the head of this band I don't know what kind of work he did, but while the twenty-six week strike was on Mrs Beniston, his wife, invited two children from all the neighbouring families to go to a party held, I remember, in a large glass sun house at the back of her residence. I was fourteen and still at school, so I was invited along with my sister Sarah. It was great, we all had jelly, custard, cakes, tinned fruit and real butter on our bread. We also received a bar of chocolate when we left. That in itself was a real treat in those days.

Llewellyn Griffith: I remember that general strike very well. I was in Leicester at that time. In fact I used to get half a crown a time for wheeling and fetching coal from the lorries in these little barrows and delivering to people who wanted the coal because there was a kind of rationing of coal in those days. I think I made half a crown a day. I used to get sixpence a barrow load. It was quite hard work really, it was good fun.

Harry Bancroft: We'd got a little bit saved — I've often talked about it — we were saving up to put a deposit for a house, it all had to go. But there were quite a lot that didn't get through very well. They had to go cap in hand, quite a few borrowed money off different people but there were a fellow up Coalville, a priest, Father Degen, he used to help them a lot. Mind you, we lived, oh yes.

Sim Woolley: I do remember an incident during the 1926 strike. I would be five or six then. At the school they provided meals, lunch meals, for the children whose parents were on strike. They told us one day we'd got to bring a mug to school because they were making suet puddings with jam in, so I went home and took a mug back the next day and I had my ration of pudding at lunchtime instead of going home because in those days, I think the miners were having a rough time as you can imagine. This went on for several weeks until one day someone came in the class and said, "He shouldn't be having his pudding because his father's still at work." Of course, my father was a deputy you see and was allowed to go in to make inspection in the mines for safety. One of the very few who were allowed in.

Ernie Harris: The strike that I remember first was in 1926 and that was in my last year at school, the Bagworth Council School. Children were asked to take their own spoon and basins and you would be fed on soup and broken biscuits at dinner time. The soup was brought from the Plough Inn. Men of the miners' union brought the soup and the children sat in the schoolyard in a large circle and soup was poured into the basin. The biscuits were a gift of the biscuit manufacturers in Wigston known as Dunmore's.

Florrie Harris: In the times of the 1926 strike, I would be ten then, those days were very hard. We used to have a soup kitchen at school ... I'll tell you this, I don't remember another soup tasting like that, it was delicious.

I've known the time when my dad went to do hay-making for a farmer just to get a few shillings. And he'd be there — I don't know whether I'm quite right — but it seemed to us as though he could have been there at eleven o'clock at night. Nice and light and hot ... it seemed very late to us. He'd be working very late, hay-making, thrashing the corn ... just for a few shillings. My dad used to know where the rabbit runs were and because we couldn't afford meat, he used to set a snare on a Saturday night and get a rabbit for us to have for Sunday lunch. Very nice. They were allowed to go and pick coal off the dirt bank. It wasn't good coal, of course ... we used to go and help my dad pick the coal.

130

Mum used to go to do the washing for the manager's wife. She had a family of three or four girls and two boys. I remember once when they offered my mum a dress and a hat and a pair of shoes that would fit me from one of their daughters instead of payment and I went to our Sunday School Anniversary dressed up in these and I thought I were the tops.

Eric Burton: As a child, it was very, very skimpish, lets say that because, as I say 1926 there was a miners' strike. We had very little money coming in. We used to have whatever we could afford. The old squire used to come round now and again. He used to bring us some rooks that he'd been shooting. Mother made a nice pie of them, they tasted like pigeon. They had to be cooked a little bit longer and the backbone took out. It was very strong meat but it was a meal. I've seen my father catching sparrows under a riddle ... and then make a sparrow pie. The tedious job of plucking them and cleaning them and put them in a pie. We were lucky if we had bread and jam for supper.

I can remember the time as they were on strike and they was on the picket line and they used to do 'tin-panning'. They'd have old tins, beating them for all the miners that were going into work ... the women would go out and help their husbands out on the picket line, the same as they did in this last one.

Anon: I think he [Mr Torrance] managed to preserve a good relationship with the workmen in Leicestershire ... in fact during the miners' strike, 1926 I can recall walking round Coalville with Dad. There would be many miners standing around. They'd usually be offered a day's wages after their first day's work if they went back to work — I don't think anybody took it up, on the grounds of loyalty to their colleagues — but there was no obvious ill-feeling between them as workmen and Dad, as manager, during that rather prolonged strike. The miners' strike in 1926, I recall lasted much longer than the national general strike which was only approximately five weeks' duration ...certainly I know from heresay that it was the custom of many landlords who went round on Fridays to collect the rent that in many cases on the first week of the strike they said, "Well, I sha'n't be round again until this strike is over." Because they realised that at that time they wouldn't have the money to pay.

PIECE RATES.	Basis		51·25 on Basis.		Total new wage		
	s.	d.	s.	d.	s.	d.	
Tonnage rates	3	6¼	1	9·91	5	4·66	
,, ,,	3	1½	1	7·22	4	8 72	
,, ,,	3	0	1	6·45	4	6·45	
,, ,,	2	9½	1	5·17	4	2·67	
,, ,,	2	9	1	4·91	4	1·91	
,, ,,	2	7½	1	4·14	3	11·64	
,, ,,	2	10½	1	5 68	4	4·18	
,, ,,	3	3	1	7·99	4	10·99	
Short Stalls :—							
(a) one fourth, less than ordinary length	2	4½	1	2·61	3	7·11	per yard
(b) one half, less than ordinary length	4	9	2	5·21	7	2·21	per yard
Building up wastes in Stalls	1	6		9·23	2	3·23	per yard
Loose side heading in Stalls	3	0	1	6·45	4	6·45	per yard
Emptying dirt		6		3 08		9·08	per tub
Setting out Stalls	25	9	13	2·36	38	11·36	
Opening out Stalls	21	5	10	11·71	32	4·71	
Putters	1	3		7·69	1	10 69	per score

All the above Rates are exclusive of Explosives and Safety Lamps.
Any person who may be receiving Wages above the Scale shall not be reduced.
It is important that every person should keep an account of his Wages for compensation purposes.

Jack Jones: Having become Vice-President, we then had the first national strike of the miners, since 1926, in 1972 and they called on me to be the strike officer for the area. No one knew exactly what they wanted to do but we recognised that we had to picket the power stations and bring the country to a halt with cutting off its power supplies. And I organised the pickets for Willington power station out on the Trent, also Raw Dykes in Leicester ... as well as pickets watching the stocks of coal and the opencast workings we had round here. So I became very much involved in that strike and was accepted very much as the leader of that strike in this area.

It wouldn't be fair not to mention that not all the Leicestershire miners resisted the strike.[1984] There were in fact a number of our members, both here and in South Derbyshire who called themselves the Dirty Thirty. There would be somewhere about twenty-three or twenty-four of them in total who, in fact, felt that their consciences couldn't allow them to go through picket lines or not to support the national union. Well, not all of them were fully genuine. Most of them, in fact, participated in the strike for the full twelve months. They made a great play on the fact that I was not leading the Leicestershire miners into the strike. I was subjected to quite a lot of abuse ... they had their headquarters given to them by the Leicester City Council, in Charles Street, where they operated and they were quite successful in raising quite large amounts of funds because they had a catchment area going down to Milton Keynes, Peterborough, Bedford, Nottinghamshire and so forth ... I saw them on many occasions in Leicester City with the buckets out collecting ... they had provision here for showing incoming pickets where to go to find accommodation for them, led by Bob McSporran ... although there were other ones very prominent, Malcolm Pinnegar and people like that.

They were able to travel around and were able to widen their experiences ... I have to say that some of these, who were in this number were, in fact, on the sick during that period of the strike. Most of them have taken redundancy since the strike ... they came back and they were treated ... there was no viciousness as regard their participation in the strike and the fact that there'd been abuse from the picket lines ... of course they picked me out as a member of the National Executive on many, many occasions to harrass me when I went to meetings in Sheffield ... a very difficult experience of going to Sheffield along with Ken Toon of the South Derbyshire area. We were subjected to violence and abuse going to the meetings, both in Sheffield and London ...

... it was very much like a country under military rule when one saw the hordes of buses coming up the motorway on a Sunday afternoon conveying police officers up from the Metropolitan and Worcester and all places to secure the position in Nottinghamshire against the violence of the picketing and so forth that was taking place and one must say that in their turn the police did return a lot of violence against the picketers ... very, very ugly scenes that we saw night after night on the television which didn't enhance the support that was necessary from the British people for sympathy for the miners, in fact, it went very much the other way. I think that was one of the differences between the seventy-two and seventy-four strikes where miners did get the sympathy of the press and the general public, under Joe Gormley in those two strikes ... the '84 strike will always go down as a strike of violence and it will always go down as a strike led by Scargill where there was no question of appeasement whatsoever by either side. It was very much a question of a fight to the death which unfortunately the national union is suffering from today as a result ...

Anon: After a few years at South Colliery in Ellistown, the conditions got bad. Every job you done was hard — three times as hard for less money because at the time we had a bonus system in. My brother who worked at Bagworth pit walking up and down faces this size, didn't even need a shower. We were grovelling about, working in conditions, say, lower than this table, in mud, covered in mud and so everything was harder. Because their conditions were easier, he was coming out with, sort of a hundred pounds a week bonus. We were lucky to see nine pound to ten pound a week bonus. That was the big gap, doing a harder job, doing a more dangerous job

132

Man-rider, South Leicester 1976

and that was what caused some of the strife, I think — well, what led up to the miners' strike. In my opinion, one of the things.

Peter Smith: Scargill endeavoured to steam roller a strike without the ballot and the men of Leicestershire and of Nottinghamshire stood against him. They would have struck had there been a ballot and the ballot had gone for strike but Scargill tried to circumvent what was necessary in order to call a strike and that was a national ballot and the men of Leicestershire and Nottinghamshire stood against it. It meant that there was picketing, in particular from Yorkshire — came down to the collieries of Nottinghamshire and Leicestershire and, of course, the workshops at Swadlincote. At times we were heavily picketted. Not always by National Coal Board employees. I can quote an incident at Rawdon Colliery where there was a coach load of teachers had come in order to picket. Nothing whatsoever to do with the teachers! But they were there. But I must say this, that the police did a wonderful job and we even had to bring in the Metropolitan Police from London in order to ensure that men were able to attend their place of work without provocation and without personal injury. Because at times it did get a bit rough ... and, of course, it was a year long strike. As a result of that strike certain collieries never opened again because you just can't leave a colliery like you can a factory and start up again after a year because of the water problems. The roofs sank, faces were lost and, of course, collieries were lost. And this was an absolute disaster for the coalmining industry. The men never got anything out of it.

133

At some places the Union wouldn't even allow the safety men in. You see, normally when there had been a strike the safety aspect was always looked upon as absolutely important because the men wanted a job to go back to when the strike was over. But in 1984 it got very nasty and at certain collieries they wouldn't allow them in. So the waters came in, the roof sank and it wasn't viable to reopen.

Mick Richmond: My granddad worked at Ibstock Colliery and my dad worked at Bagworth Colliery ... eventually I followed him into the pits. It just seemed the natural thing to do. I did everything, from general mining, went onto the coalface, drove the machines, everything, you know. I loved it, really did.

I've always been involved in the Unions, always. My dad was a shop steward up north ... it's been bred into me really. Reading back into history, as far as I'm concerned, it [the Union's] been weak. It's nothing compared with like Yorkshire or South Wales, or Scotland or Kent. Basically it's a lack of leadership. When you look at the leaders round here, in past history, there's been good 'uns but there's nobody to me been outstanding, you know. And I think if there had've been maybe, and I say maybe, the young lads might have done the right thing in '84.

Jack Jones actually discouraged the strike in '84 round here. I'd got one hundred men out at Bagworth on the morning of, I think it was, 18 March '84 and he talked them back down the pit. I knew about Cortonwood when it started and I said to Benny Pinnegar, the co-leader of the Thirty, as they called us, I said, "We're gonna be out." And he said, "Well, if it takes just me and you, we'll be out." When the Kent miners marched up to Bagworth that was it, that was the start of the strike for us. I think that was 15th of March when they arrived in Leicestershire, to a lot of abuse. I got a hundred in the canteen at Bagworth and Trevor Irons, who was the Union delegate, he went running down to Coalville to fetch Jack Jones and he said, "Mick Richmond's going beserk, he's got lads out on strike." And Jack Jones, like I say, he talked them back down the pit.

Eventually ... we had seven lads from Ellistown, three or four from Whitwick and I think there was only one from South Leicester and that was about it. I think it ended up with about forty coming out from Bagworth and then a few drifted back, you know, it was going to be hard so they couldn't do it. I can understand it now but at the time I couldn't understand. The Yorkshire lads used to call them woolly-backs because they were a load of sheep ... apparently it goes back, right back to God knows when.

Well, I came home and I told my wife what was going off. We lived in Coalville, smack in the middle of town and my wife's from Scotland and she says, "Well, none of your mates are striking, why are you?" I said, "Well, I can't cross a picket line." That's it, I couldn't do it. We had three weeks like it and then she said, "I can't stand this." And she went up home to Scotland and she had a week up there. She came back, she says, "What are you doing?". I says, "I'm still striking." And she said, "Well, I've seen it up there, the effect that it's having and I'm going to stand by you." And that was that.

Me and Benny Pinnegar, Malcolm Pinnegar ... we were talking about the strike and I said, "Look, if we're gonna be out like the rest of the country we've got to get organised." So we got the lads from Bagworth together and we formed a bit of a committee. Then we learnt about the lads at Ellistown and Whitwick and South and we called them all to a meeting. And that's how we got going really. Funnily enough, Bobby Girvan said we'd got to have a name. I said, "Well, The Leicestershire Striking Miners." That's what it was. Then somebody did an interview for Radio Leicester and they interviewed a working miner and he was asked what he thought and what the vast majority thought of us lot and he said, "Well, I just think they're a filthy, dirty thirty", and that was it. I thought that was a good name and that's what we were called.

There was a fella used to work for the Leicester Mercury ... it was totally biased against us. He used to print a lot of lies. It was unbelievable ... we actually did interviews with him and then you'd read it in the paper the next night and you used to think, well, I never said that, you know ... The press coverage, it was good, but it was totally biased.

... but we had to get involved and let people know because we were starving down here. We got no help from the Social at all and we had to let people know in other parts of the country that there were thirty people and families ... on strike. Eventually, people used to send letters with money in and we got by. Scargill, more or less, he didn't ignore us but he seemed oblivious to the situation down here. We wrote to every coalfield and every leader — McGahey, Heathfield ... we had twelve months on strike and it's the hardest work I've ever done in my life. Me and Benny Pinnegar must have done thousands of miles. I mean, all the lads had to work to survive. We had a collecting group in Northampton. They lived, spent their time in Northampton, came home at weekends to their families and then went back again on the Mondays. We were just collecting and raising funds all the time. It was hard.

We got that good at collecting ... we became such a high profile group that I know at Christmas '84 we actually sent a van load of toys and goods down to Methyr Tydfil because we just couldn't handle it ... and we sent about a million cans of beans up to ... Derbyshire. That was a private pit where the lads all got sacked.

[Did you get any help from family?]

I think some of the families that were on strike did but my family certainly never. My brother was very embarrassed by my stance, my younger brother. My mam doesn't like talking about it even now.I know there's some lads, you know, their brothers don't talk to them ... it's very sad but that's how it goes.

I spoke at a meeting in Leicester with some guys from NALGO and they more or less put me down. And it was supposed to be a meeting to back us lot. The nurses and people like that, they supported us and the support that we had in Leicester was brilliant, in the city, but not in Coalville. The lads at Mantle Lane, on British Rail, they were superb. They were without doubt brilliant, you know. They stopped the coal traffic and everything, just refused to work. That was weird because you'd got lads working, miners working and they'd got brothers on the railway that were supporting the thirty of us. It was ever so weird. I think they got about one or two through a day. They used to do twenty-six trains a day but they wouldn't signal trains and they wouldn't man them. We used to tell the lads, if morale was a bit low, I used to say, "Look, you can't have half a war. If Thatcher's going to declare war, we've got to fight back." And we did. We didn't hurt nobody. We just tried to stop the coal from getting to the power stations to prove our point.

The Coalville Times did some good coverage on us ... Radio Leicester did interviews ... yes, we tried to put our point across. It was on deaf ears every time.

[Did you get help from the NUM headquarters in Sheffield?]

Yes, they paid my phone bill and Benny Pinnegar's phone bill. They had to because they were astronomical, unbelievable. We had to keep in touch with everyone and they helped us with that. That's all they did help us with. Scargill came down to my house in Beresford Street. I offered to take him round the coalfield just to see what was happening and everything seemed a bit too much trouble for him and in the end my wife kicked him out of the house ... he said, "I'll phone you." And he never came again.

We went up to Sheffield three or four times. We did have meetings with Scargill and Heathfield and we kept telling them about the leadership round here. We demanded that the Executive of the NUM hear us and put our case over but they were just looking after each other. I've got very mixed feelings now about the strike. I mean, I'd never be a scab in my life, you know, I could never do that but things that have happened since the strike, I've become ... very suspicious of what's been going off in the mining industry because that's what we knew would happen.

Sometimes we had a mass picket. We'd have lads from Kent or South Wales or wherever. Anybody was welcome, you know, because we were too busy to picket really. We had to go out collecting food. But we always used to try to do something ... we'd put two lads up at Nailstone and you'd have about fifty coppers there watching the lads. We had numerous offers from groups all over the country to come down and create havoc and that and we had to say no because there were only a few of us on strike. It was alright them coming down and causing trouble and disruption but then they'd go away and we'd have to live with it.

[Was there any trouble on the picket line?]

Unfortunately, there was in Coalville, yes. A couple of times, I think. I think it was lads from North Derbyshire came down and they broke one or two windows in the town ... we got accused of sending for pickets ... but it was the other way round. We asked for them not to come. They used to come down and well they couldn't believe it, what we were doing, what we were going through, how we were managing.

It was unbelievable. I think the policing bill for the thirty of us was five and a half million pounds for the year. There was a large contingency of police up at Bardon ... and they used to live in marquees and they had feeding facilities, everything. It was unbelievable. And our phones were tapped. We did an experiment one night, me and Benny Pinnegar. I phoned him up and I said, "Right, there's going to be a mass picket tonight at Whitwick." I said, "The lads are coming down." I phoned him from outside the Leicester Hotel and within twenty minutes there were cops everywhere. There were hundreds of vans and buses and they were all at Whitwick pit. Now if our phones weren't tapped they wouldn't have been there but we knew it was, so ... Every now and again you could sit in the house quietly and your phone would click, it wouldn't ring, it would click ... I just knew something were going off, you know.

Leicester City Council, they gave us an office in Leicester so that we could co-ordinate the strike. My wife phoned up to the office, to the strike centre one day and she got through to Syston Police Station, straight through. And it was sergeant someone and she said, "Sorry?" and he said, "What number have you dialled?" and she told him and he said, "Hang on." and he put her through to our office. That's the gospel truth, that is, yes.

We never saw Leicestershire policemen when the mass pickets were on. I don't know why that was. Maybe they were riot police, I don't know. Probably specially trained. But the police presence round here was unbelievable. I'll never forget it. It was a police state round here ... the measures that they went to round here were unbelievable but that was nothing compared to like Nottinghamshire. You couldn't travel. I went to pick one of the lads up at Newbold Verdon, a village outside of Coalville, and I had to drive past Bagworth Colliery to get to his house. And I was followed there by two police cars to his house. And he was going to get in one of the police cars and he says, "Yours is a better car than Mick's." he says, "So can you take me back?" The copper never answered him and we drove back. Followed us right to my house in Coalville. And then they left us.

[What was it like at home — how did you manage?]

It was very, very hard. We got by on mashed potatoes, beans — millions of beans. It was unbelievable how many tins of beans people used to give us. We got by best we could. We had logs, we had to go sawing logs up to keep warm. There were one or two people in Coalville that supported us. You'd probably find a bag of coal on your doorstep one morning, or something.

Because we weren't deemed as 'on strike' we got nothing ... we told all the Executive this ... the miners from Yorkshire and Kent and South Wales they all got money every week to assist them. We said that we were getting nothing at all ... there was no resolution passed to help us. But indirectly we did get money from South Wales and Derbyshire ... they'd have a collection at the pit or whatever, you know ... they looked after us. In Coalville you'd see folk doing their shopping and ... the wives would see ex-friends, and I say ex-friends because there was a bad feeling at the time, they'd be shopping and our wives would have nothing at all. I think somebody donated thirty chickens to us for Christmas. It wasn't too bad. It was something we'd never experienced and I wouldn't like to experience it again.

Like I said, there were one or two supported us but in the main they thought we were just trouble-makers. They just couldn't understand why we were doing it. There was hassle, yes. One or two of our lads got involved in fights in the town, in Coalville ... I had some brave person throw a brick at my front door in Beresford Street ... Tyres were slashed on cars. Yes, there was hostility. There are still one or two miners who feel very bitter towards me and the lads who were active in the strike. And yet there's lads who were working and they're probably my best mates now, so it's weird. There's even lads in the UDM, the scab union as I call it, and I'm involved with them at rugby and they're friends of mine.

We went back exactly a year after the strike started. We went down to London and Scargill and McGahey and Heathfield came out and said that the strike was over. The scenes down there were unreal, unforgettable. We came back and me and Benny had a meeting with the manager at Bagworth, John Bond, and he laid certain terms and conditions down and we did and we respected him, he respected us. And basically we went back to work. There was a weird feeling, there was a lot of bad feeling. We asked that the lads work together initially ... for a settling in period and we asked him to made it clear that if there was any intimidation we'd come out again ... and then three of us got sentenced to solitary confinement as we called it over at Nailstone pit. They split us up from the group and we went over to Nailstone and funnily enough we enjoyed it. It was a punishment mainly because I was one of the leaders and they wanted me to suffer a bit over there and lose money. But it had the reverse effect really because we made more money over there. We did overtime. Then I came back to Bagworth and we did even better because we went on nights and you see you got more money on nights. So it back-fired on them really ... but I couldn't settle. I couldn't enjoy my work any more ... Bagworth Colliery was never the same after the strike. I don't know, maybe it caused too much hardship. Maybe it caused too much bitterness on both sides ... some lads left shortly after they returned to work.

We went back in '85 when the strike was called off and I left in March '88, so that would be what, about three years I stuck it. But I miss it now. I do miss it because is was a job I loved. I went into contract mining which was a mistake because you're treated like dogs ... contract firms do as they like, there's no code of conduct or anything. You work, you go home, you work, you go home and that's it ... it was July 90 when I got made redundant at Coventry and I've never worked since ... friends in London reckon I'm definitely on a black list and any major contracts or whatever ... I'm on their blacklist as a Communist Activist, that's what I've been told anyway, which is a load of garbage because I'm not. I just stuck up for my principles. Everybody's entitled to their opinion and I stuck up for my principles and I think that should be the end of it.

[Have there been long term financial repercussions?]

Sadly yes. We had to sell the house in Beresford Street, mainly because the mortgage arrears had mounted up. My car got repossessed in February this year [1991]. It has affected us twice now. I sold my house to pay the arrears off in '85 and then I got made redundant in '90 and now my house is being repossessed ...

Anon: You got the union split. Some of them went into the UDM, some of the thick idiots, sort of thing — and I've got to say that because once you split a union, the union's dead ... it caused a lot of animosity because blokes wouldn't talk to one another.

Miners with heading machine reaching a new face

In The End

Herbert Blake: The shortest shift I ever did was my last. I went and left home about ten minutes to ten at night and by a quarter to eleven, I was back home. See, you never worked your last shift. You just went, took your tally out, handed it back in, then came home — said cheerio to everybody and came home. It went back to the days when Ball was the manager, before nationalisation, actually. When anybody retired, he used to say, "They don't work on their last day. I couldn't bear to have a man killed on his last day at work."

Ron Gregson: Why, everything got easier as the years went on. Pits always got easier ... Anyone in my generation or the generation before, it was hard work. The last few years before I retired I was a senior official at Snibston colliery and I enjoyed my pit life because when you do something all your life, forty-two years, you get used to it. It just comes naturally, same as anyone else doing their work. But during my last few years I was a senior official and I suppose I earned that and I had a good wage ...

Jim Eckersley: The offer was attractive for a start — early retirement, nice pension, nice big lump of redundancy money and well, I'd been in [the pit] thirty-seven years. The pit was on its last ... well it was ready for finishing anyhow, so I took the offer and finished. From Whitwick a lot of them finished on those terms. It closed soon afterwards. I don't miss pit work, no, not one bit ... fresh air's much better than being down there, I'll tell you.

Barbara Birkin: Yes, it was sort of a forced redundancy because he was on strike and when he went back they more or less told him that he would have no safety cover. They made his life difficult. If he hadn't have took his redundancy he would have got the sack because they didn't like the striking miners. When he first took his redundancy he hoped to start his own business but, unfortunately, it wouldn't work out ... but basically, I just went to work and we were trying to get set up. It was very hard for him to get a job because all he knew was mining and plus he's in his forties which makes it more difficult to get a job. We managed. We cut back.

They haven't got no large employment now, have they? I can't see it changing much unless some big industry comes in to create employment. The mines have changed so the town's got to change and it hasn't changed fast enough. A big proportion of the male population have lost their jobs and they've had to come down in their standard of living so probably it takes a while to accept that your standard of living drops dramatically because, I mean, they were the best paid jobs in Coalville.

Anon: A miner that has been working at Bagworth has been on round about four hundred, four hundred and fifty pound a week. But now you've got to drop down to a lesser paid job which a lot of them can't do. I think if Bagworth Colliery had've been open for round about another twenty or thirty year, I'd have stopped down the pit for the rest of my life, even though I didn't like getting up at half past four in the morning.

Peter Kane: Well, the elderly ones — when I say that, I mean those fifty plus — were in a sense devastated. They realised that they were too old to do anything else and many of them just packed it in and took their redundancy money ... and it's remarkable, actually, that quite a number of them, especially over sixties, who retired or took redundancy, very few are content with what they're doing at present because they lost a lot in comradeship and the habit of getting up and going to work ... it seemed to take a piece of their life away which will never be recovered. And, of course, some of them, not an inconsiderable number, actually didn't last very long when they took redundancy at the age of sixty-two, sixty-three. They looked forward, possibly, to a long life but quite a few of them died within two or three years of leaving the pit — low morale, the destruction of their way of life ... in a sense, as I said, they packed it up and some, literally, gave up the ghost.

Aubrey Peace: I done forty-three years [1983] ... and I was ready, I was ready. When you've had thirty-three years on shifts, same as I had, coal turning, then up the winder — same as I tell you, every day bar my holidays — I was ready. And I worked seven shifts right up to finishing. I finished on the Sunday morning and I picked my hat up and I shall always remember it, I picked my bag off the wall and they said to me, "You won't settle down." I said, "You'll see whether I won't settle down or not." ...and I've enjoyed every day, since. Yes. I've enjoyed every day.

Tony Turner: At fifty-five ... I took early redundancy, like ... I do bits of jobs, garden, go around next door — do a bit of painting for her — lives on her own. There's two things I never regretted doing. One was leaving school and the other was leaving pit.

Eileen Smith: Marvellous, [pits closing] very happy about it. I'm glad they've kept the name of Coalville ... Well, it's treated me alright, me being a miner's daughter. But, I'm very glad they've closed because it was a nightmare when the men used to go down the pit. You never knew if they were going to come back and ... I was always pleased when I saw my dad come through the back door.

Presentation of chair to Snibston enginewright, Edward Thornley on his retirement. Manager, J.Emmerson, on the arm of the chair

POEMS

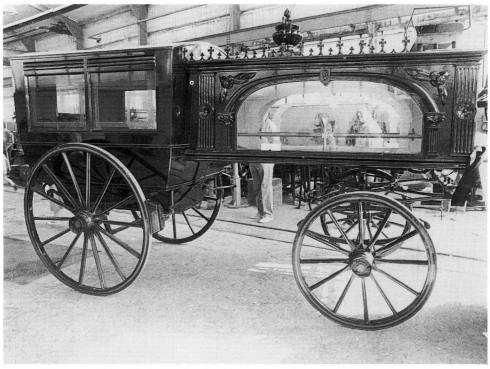

Hearse used for victims of Whitwick mining disaster 1898 (Coalville Times)

The Entombed Miners

by W. King

(Mr King was a workmate of the miners killed in the disaster. The following poem was printed and sold at 1d per copy to raise money for the relief fund for relatives of the dead miners.)

As the early morn was peeping

Over the forest so rare

Sad bitter news was leaping

From the mine into the air

The village wrapped in slumber

At rest from the world's care

Sleeping hours by number

Unconscious of the dawning scare

But soon the morning hastened
With life its day to wake
With sad sad news unchastened
The stoutest heart to quake

From lip to lip from ear to ear
This news was whispered round
Whitwick's pit's on fire, then with fear
They sought the mining ground

This fire is raging wild they cried
And the women sob and cry
Some husband, father or child
Is entombed from light and sky

Thirty-five are in the mine
To their rescue some boldly went
And battled hard day and night
To open their imprisonment

A mining hero, too, was found
His name was Charlie Clamp
Who went to warn his fellow men
An act of heroic stamp

Quickly his mission he fulfilled
Spurred on by his fading lamp
But O, alas, he now must sink
A victim to fiery damp

A hero, yes, we call him this
He highly deserves this name
He died whilst doing his duty
To his fellows beyond the flame

The rescue heroes worked and fought
As though for life and death
Although at times nearly fraught
By the deathly fiery breath

For three long days and dreary nights
They fought with might and main
In heading out a roadway
Past sulphur fire and flame

When at last the good news came
They have just finished the way
But the air and damp must battle
With their might for victor's sway

After twelve long hours of suspense
The rescuers, anxious long
Went with bold courageous hearts
And sturdy spirits strong

But alas, alas, for death's cold hand
And long since laid them low
And as they went along the road
They saw but death's dull glow

Our hero was the first they found
And next, O, pitiful sight
Seven men clasped as children
Each other with arms so tight

They were clasped together in life
They were clasped together in death
They were clasped together in strife
With the fire's sulphrous breath

May they be clasped together still
Not as they were clasped down here
But clasped where angels ever thrill
The eternal atmosphere

But now the poisonous damp
Made the men for life turn back
Leaving behind still twenty-six
Somewhere in death's dark track

With painful hearts they turn their steps
With the nine already found
And as they brought them up the shaft
There came a mournful sound

For now the rays of hope were gone
And death in all its power
Shattered the hopes of loved ones
Who had waited by the hour

In hopeless grief they led them home
Wives, sisters and mothers too
Where a little group is waiting
Father's return as they usually do

But how, how sad this touching sight
The mothers and children bereft
The staff upon which the home must lean
Is for ever for ever cleft

O wives with husbands by your side
Think of the husbandless ones
And fathers with your families
Think of the fatherless ones

O, men with hearts and feelings
With plenty by your side
Help, O help the helpless
All to whom this woe betides

Send forth your human sympathy
As brethren all should do
Do something to lighten the burden
Of those who must drink life's rue

O think of the stricken mother
The wife and the children too
Who have lost life's bread winner
O give them the sympathy due

Never never slight the miner
Though low his position be
He is life's heroic coiner
Help him with constant sympathy

Great helper of the helpless
Look down on this pitiful sight
Protect and preserve thy children
From this life's bitterest plight

Be the husband to the widow
The father to the fatherless child
And move us to live together
As one with love undefiled

Collier

by Joan Ball

There sits a man, enveloped in sunshine,

Natural warmth on a light, blissful day.

A freshening breeze brings joy to his being,

As he drinks with his eyes all there is to survey.

The soft leather sandals and panama hat,

Replacing the knobbed boots — the helmet —

As he carried a lamp, lighting the damp

And the bright beads of sweat on his back.

Hitched a rope round his girth, as he crawled to hack earth,

Black with the woodlands of some ancient tract.

Remembering the knock of the man with the pole,

Tapping on windows at four in the morning,

Informing the men that it's time for their shift.

With clattering heels on cobble-stoned roadways,

An army of boots on their way to the pit.

The clipperty-clop of well shod hoofs

'Neath shiny brown coats, passing by,

Bring tears of memory — a pony in harness —

Dragging its load in black, airless darkness,

Only to breathe Earth's clean air, taste sweet grass

When hauled up to graze on a six-monthly pass.

Blinded by light, but still within sight

Of a mountain of slack. Poor little hack.

Above in the trees the birds sing a roundelay

Deep down in time a yellow coat sang its wee heart away.

Destined to die if the air filled with methane,

Warning men to scramble to lifts,

Rising from tunnels like rabbits from burrows,

Until they are called again to their shifts.

Memories passed down from colliers of old
Scenes no artist can ever unfold —
The back-ache, the sores, the pain of a limb
Trapped by shoals of sharp slack
As loose timber poles slither and crack
And a corn callous hand vainly claws.
Now there are showers, no tubs of hot water
From bricked kitchen boilers — splashing and spilling
Onto soft hand-pegged hearths.
Heirs and their kin, blackened but fit,
With soft soled shoes on tarmac paths
Walk into parlours straight from the pit.

Shall we forget what has gone before,
Hauling the coal into deep cellar store,
Bucketing up to the stoves above
Bellowing flames as hot ashes fall,
Toasted bread on an old tin fork,
Small, eager hands pleading for more.

Maybe a glimpse of an old man's memory
Sifting his thoughts as he rests in the sun
Will be all that is left, a story just legendary,
Battles of hardship that had to be won.

Looking Back

by Lena Gee

If I could turn the clock back
I would turn it to the time
When I was a 'bottom-ender'
And I lived near Snibby mine

I would listen to the chuff chuff
That went on night and day
And wander round the engine house
Where I often used to play

I would walk up by the boiler house
To watch the wheels go round
Taking down and bringing up
The men from underground

I would watch them as they left the cage
Lights shining, faces black
All glad that they had done their stint
But tomorrow they'll be back

I would hear the hooter go again
Recall a cheerful shout
Break time lads, just pack it in
And get your snap tins out

Then leaving by the main gates
With tear drops in my eyes
I would turn once more to look around
And say my last good-byes

Snibby pit is silent now
Its working days are passed
Leaving many memories
The sort that last and last

The Ballad of the Leicestershire Striking Miners

by Tony French

In nineteen hundred and eighty four,
Thatcher and McGregor went to war,
They'd tangled with Scargill and others before,
But not with the Leicestershire miners,
The Leicestershire striking miners.

When the call came from Yorkshire, "Out, boys out."
Wales, Kent and Scotland gave a mighty shout
"Get your banners, your fingers and your workers out."
They were heard by the Leicestershire miners,
The Leicestershire striking miners.

Benny and Richo called a meeting and then
They hit the dirty thirty — oh so few men,
"You're the gallant men of the NUM."
Ray (Buckton) was talking of the Leicestershire miners,
The Leicestershire striking miners.

Where was Jack Jones? Where was uncle Len?
Where were the rest of the Leicestershire men?
When the deep mined coal movement was frozen,
By the stance of the Leicestershire miners,
The Leicestershire striking miners.

In Nottingham, Derby and Coalville town
Some miners took the shilling and they went underground,
They hurried past the pickets with their eyes cast down,
As they walked past the Leicestershire miners,
The Leicestershire striking miners.

In Coalville some miners were heard to say,
They'd had thirty pieces of silver in their pay,
Yes they'd all had an extra tenner a day,
Just to walk past the Leicestershire miners,
The Leicestershire striking miners.

Oh, the Iron Lady has a rock hard soul,
She'll crush who she can on the way to her goal,
But she hadn't met the ladies who are made of coal,
The wives of the Leicestershire miners,
The Leicestershire striking miners.

The strike went on but the end it came
To the working miners' eternal shame,
There is courage and pride attached to the name,
Yes the name of the Leicestershire miners,
The Leicestershire striking miners.

Nobody Need Know
by Bobby Girvan

Nobody need know we stood in your way,
Blocked your advance, turned you away,
Nobody need know your threats of violence,
Intimidation, well perhaps once,
Nobody need know we withheld your rights,
Provoked some aggro, maybe a few fights,
Nobody need know we stood like a wall,
Charged wildly on, made some of you fall,
Nobody need know we coshed a few heads,
Broke a few bones, filled hospital beds,
Nobody need know we smashed your face in,
Went for your ribs, kicked out at your shin,
Nobody need know we threatened your life,
Abused your sister, assaulted your wife,
'Cos that's what the media don't want to inform,
When we are police in uniform.

The Men

by Joyce Collins

I've had to go for an interview
About me redundancy.
It's earlier than expected
'Cos the pit is closing, you see.
We're having a farewell party
And we'll all pretend to be glad
But it's mixed with a bit of sadness
For all the good times we had.
There's Terry and Arthur, Roger and Pop
And names that just don't rhyme
But I know I'm going to miss me mates
Now I've done me time.
Me and me mates we laugh a lot
And lark about a bit.
I never thought I'd say this
But I'm going to miss the pit.
My plans are quite straight forward,
I'm going to enjoy me sen
That's what me missus tells me
But I'm sure I'll miss the men.
There's fishing, golf and swimming
And all that keep-fit stuff
And the missus is always complaining
That she doesn't get enough.
I might decide to stay in bed
Til eight or even ten
I know it all sounds lovely
But I'm going to miss the men.

Glossary

Advance —	Working the face away from the pit bottom.
Back ripping —	Enlarging the roadway by clearing the walls and roof.
Bank —	The area around the pit top or the winding gear.
Banksman —	Man responsible for organisation and safety at the pit top.
Belt —	Conveyor belt.
Bevin Boy —	Man conscripted into the mines in the 1940s, as an alternative to military service — named after Ernest Bevin.
Blacksmith —	Man working with metal, sometimes farrier for ponies.
Braking(tubs) —	Method by which tubs are stopped from moving.
Butty —	Sub-contractor who employed the miners in groups.
Cage —	Lift which travels up and down the shaft.
Catchprop —	Prop set prior to completion of timbering.
Chargeman —	Miner in charge of other face workers.
Checkweighman —	Man responsible for checking the weight of the coal.
Chock —	Roof support.
Chockman —	Man who moves the roof supports when advancing.
Danny —	Open sided truck for moving supplies.
Datal —	Being paid on a daily basis as opposed to piece work.
Deputy —	Official responsible for the safety of work areas.
Dirt —	Stone, dust, rock or worthless coal.
District —	An underground area.
Down cast —	Shaft through which fresh air enters mine.
Dowty —	Manufacturer's name for roof support.
Drift —	Incline from one area in the mine to another
Endless rope —	Continuously moving wire rope that tubs are clipped onto.
Face —	Coalface.
Filler —	Miner who loads coal into tubs.
Floor —	Bottom surface of roadway.
Gate —	Roadway leading to the face.
Getter —	Miner who works coal from the face.
Head —	Roadway towards a new face.
Headed out —	Describes new face ready to produce coal.
Header —	Miner who drives new roadways.

Holer —	Miner who undercuts coal.
Holing —	Undercutting coal manually.
Hostler —	Man responsible for care of pit ponies.
Limmer —	Pony's harness.
Longwall —	Method of working one long coalface.
Loose-all —	End of shift.
Maingate —	Gate leading away from the face, usually carrying coal.
Manhole —	Refuge hole cut into wall of roadway.
Moleskins —	Thick trousers worn by miners.
On-setter —	Man responsible for movement of cage from bottom of shaft.
Over cast —	Roadway crossing over another keeping air-flows separate.
Overman —	Senior official in charge of an underground district.
Packing —	Building roof supports in the waste after coal is removed.
Panning —	Moving conveyors up with the face as it advances.
Panzer —	Moving, metal conveyor which transfers coal from the face to the belt.
Pillar and stall —	Method of mining coal by leaving coal to support roof in between places from where coal has been extracted.
Pit bank —	The winding gear or the area around the pit top or the dirt heap.
Pit bottom —	Area around the bottom of the shaft.
Pit top —	Area around the top of the shaft.
Prop —	Roof support.
Putting —	Moving full tubs away from the filler.
Ramming —	Putting explosive charges into holes.
Ratcher —	Face worker.
Retreat —	Working coal away from the face as opposed to advancing.
Ripping —	Moving dirt as opposed to coal.
Roadway —	Underground passage.
Shaftsman —	Man who works on shaft maintenance.
Snap —	Food eaten at work.
Shot —	Explosive charge.
Stall —	Area of coal worked in between pillars or area where miners are employed.
Stallman —	Faceworker in charge of a stall.
Stint —	Length of face to be worked, period of work or any allotted task.
Sump —	The bottom of the shaft.
Supply gate —	Small roadway leading to the face.

Tally —	Small identification disc given to men going underground.
Trapping —	Opening and closing ventilation doors to allow passage of materials and ponies.
Tub —	Truck which carries coal.
Up cast —	Shaft through which exhaust air leaves mine.
Wall —	The face.
Waste —	Worked out area of a mine.
Winder man —	Man who controls machinery to raise and lower cage.

We gratefully acknowledge financial assistance from the following organisations:

Leicestershire County Council — Urban Policies Sub-committee.

North West Leicestershire District Council — Leisure Committee.

Coalville Publishing Company Ltd.

United Biscuits (UK) Ltd.

Barlestone Parish Council.

N.U.M. (Leicestershire)

Leicestershire Co-operative Society Ltd.

Coleorton Parish Council.

N.A.C.O.D.S. (Leicestershire Area)

G.M.B. (Midlands and East Coast Division)

Coalville and District Trades Council.

G.M.B. (Charnwood Branch, Leicestershire 2000)

Additional thanks go to the following who made subscriptions in advance:

Ray Allen, Calgary, Alberta, Canada.

Janice and Barry Bailey, Whitwick, Leics.

R Bainbridge, Coalville, Leics.

Denis Baker, Swannington, Leics.

Joan Ball, Leicester.

R G Beeston, G A Propery Services, Coalville, Leics.

R S Betteridge, Swadlincote, Derbys.

D Betts, Whitwick, Leics.

Barbara Birkin, Coalville, Leics.

C M Blow, Loughborough, Leics.

H T L Bonell, Ramsgate, Kent.

Alan H Booton, Quorn, Leics.

Denys W Boulton, Coalville, Leics.

Adrian John Brant, Morpeth, Northumberland.

Keith Brewin, Campbelltown, Australia.

Jean Broster, Ashby de la Zouch, Leics.

C Brown, Markfield, Leics.

Brian Buck, Coalville, Leics.

Anthony David Burbank, Loughborough, Leics.

K Burchell, Ashby de la Zouch, Leics.

D B Carter, Ashby de la Zouch, Leics.

Michael Cashmore, Donisthorpe, Leics.

J E Catlow, Broadstairs, Kent.

F B Chapman, Coalville, Leics.

Don Connolly, Leicester.

E G Cooper, Swannington, Leics.

Cllr. Adrian Cross, Thringstone, Leics.

J Driver, Hugglescote, Leics.

Joe Ennis, Rainham, Kent.

Norman Finch, Desford, Leics.

Debbie Fenn, Orpington, Kent.

Lena Gee, Whitwick, Leics.

J K Gibbins, Coalville, Leics.

Rev. Bernard Green, Abingdon, Oxon.

F Gregory, Bagworth, Leics.

Ron Gregson, Whitwick, Leics.

Pat and Ian Hamilton, Oakham, Rutland, Leics.

Robert Hanlon, Coalville, Leics.

Ernie and Florrie Harris, Whitwick, Leics.

Gerald Heathcote, Coalville, Leics.

Walter Heathcote, Coalville, Leics.

Margaret Hedges, Groby, Leics.

Hinckley and Bosworth A Team.

D R E Hines, Barwell, Leics.

Peter J Hubbard, Calgary, Alberta, Canada.

L J Jackson, Leicester.

G B Jefferson, Mansfield, Notts.

Jack Jones, Coalville, Leics.

R G Jones, Nuneaton, Warks.

Rod P Kemp, Hastings, East Sussex.

Kovacs and Son Engineers, Ellistown, Leics.

Roger Laidlaw, Wrexham, Clwyd.

J J Lee, Burbage, Leics.

Dr Sheila Lee, Coalville, Leics.

Leicester and County Co-operative Development Agency.

Leicestershire Libraries.

John Lincoln, Old Dalby, Leics.

Haseley McKinnell, Rochford, Essex.

J M McKinnon, Coalville, Leics.

Felix McTeague, Skegness, Lincs.

Peter Harry Maden, Loughborough, Leics.

Olive Middleton, Tockington, Bristol.

Professor D Muller, Claydon, Suffolk.

Rosemary Murphy, Long Eaton, Notts.

G R O'Hagan, Alfreton, Derbys.

Roy Palmer, Dymock, Gloucs.

H Parker, Ibstock, Leics.

David Parry, Letchworth, Herts.

Aubrey Peace, Whitwick, Leics.

Cllr. Steven Peace, Hugglescote, Leics.

Cllr. Alan Pearson, Packington, Leics.

Derrick Percival, Mountsorrel, Leics.

L Prime, Loughborough, Leics.

Val Pulford, Ravenstone, Leics.

Kay Richardson, Ashby de la Zouch, Leics.

Les and Edith Roberts, Great Glen, Leics.

John Rugman, Melton Mowbray, Leics.

Mark Sadler, Mountsorrel, Leics.

June and Barrie Scott, Whitwick, Leics.

Joe Shaw, Ashby de la Zouch, Leics.

Peter J Sivyer, Ryde, Isle of Wight.

George Slattery, Whitwick, Leics.

Michael E Smith, West Hallam, Derby.

Peter Smith, Coalville, Leics.

Peter Smith, Leics NUM, Coalville, Leics.

Snibston Discovery Park, Coalville, Leics.

Julian Socha, Penyffordd, Clwyd.

R Spencer, Ashby de la Zouch, Leics.

C Statham, Newbold Verdon, Leics.

Danny Statham, Ibstock, Leics.

Robert Stewart, Ashby de la Zouch, Leics.

David Taylor, Heather, Leics.

Harry Taylor, Barlestone, Leics.

Leslie Temple, Ellistown, Leics.

Reg Thomas, Llangollen, Clwyd.

G M Tovell, Hugglescote, Leics.

Judith Twigger, Hinckley, Leics.

Roy Walker, Buckingham

John Walton, Banbury, Oxon.

Stuart Warburton, Leicester.

Andy Warren, Ellistown, Leics.

G F West, Thringstone, Leics.

D A Woodward, Whitwick, Leics.

Victor Woodward, Whitwick, Leics.

Ian Wortley, Hugglescote, Leics.

R York, Coalville, Leics.

Gary Young, Rotherham, South Yorks.